THE VILLAGE CALLED GOAT HILL

Life in a Small Village on a Small Island

EVERSON JAMES PETERS

The Village Called Goat Hill
Life in a Small Village on a Small Island
All Rights Reserved.
Copyright © 2021 Everson James Peters
v2.0

The opinions expressed in this manuscript are solely the opinions of the author and do not represent the opinions or thoughts of the publisher. The author has represented and warranted full ownership and/or legal right to publish all the materials in this book.

This book may not be reproduced, transmitted, or stored in whole or in part by any means, including graphic, electronic, or mechanical without the express written consent of the publisher except in the case of brief quotations embodied in critical articles and reviews.

Outskirts Press, Inc.
http://www.outskirtspress.com

ISBN: 978-1-9772-4577-9

Cover Images © 2021 Everson Peters. All rights reserved - used with permission.

Outskirts Press and the "OP" logo are trademarks belonging to Outskirts Press, Inc.

PRINTED IN THE UNITED STATES OF AMERICA

DEDICATED TO:

My grandfathers, Joseph Neptune and Richard Ovid whom I never knew and my grandmothers: Bunah Alexis and Veronica Eva Peters who were the most loving grandmothers one could have but were recalled to their maker much too soon.

Acknowledgement:

This is the outcome of a project, which started during the summer of 2017 resulting from a discussion among some JCBs (Just Come Backs) at a famous rum shop in Hillsborough, Carriacou. These natives, who had migrated during the 1950s and 1960s, are referred to as "Just Come Backs". They shared their memories of life in the village while growing up. I found some of the stories fascinating.

There were no less than five drafts of this book, each reflecting the comments, suggestions and encouragement by a number of friends and colleagues. I am particularly grateful to Professor Gyan Shrivastava and his wife Tara who were the first to read the earliest chapters, could relate to some of the stories, and offered the initial encouragement. My friends, Dickie Goddard and Lennox Patrice and my cousin Albert Cox acted as my second line of critical and supportive feedback. My brother, Henry Raymond, who is a main character in the stories, helped in improving the accuracies of some stories. Veronica Marks, a friend and colleague from St. Vincent and the Grenadines agreed to be my main editor, gratis, and provided invaluable support throughout the project. There are others, who contributed significantly but prefer to remain anonymous. I am greatly indebted to all of them. I am also grateful to my wife, Cecilia and my sons Everson (Jr) and Dellon who have been waiting patiently for the completion.

Table of Contents

Preface		i
Dedication		iii
1	Introduction	1
2	The island and Goat Hill	5
	2.1 Introduction	5
	2.2 The different times	6
	2.3 The people	11
3	Growing up in Goat Hill and childhood memories	16
	The coming of the village school	16
	3.1 Keeping the surroundings clean	21
	3.2 Boys the Tenders of the livestock	23
	3.3 Collecting firewood	25
	3.4 Sugar apple season	27
	3.5 Getting the milk	28
	3.6 The staple meal: Corn for Coo-coo	32
	3.7 Green corn dumplings	35
	3.8 Roasted bakes	36
	3.9 Taking the animals to the pond	40
	3.10 Toting water	44
	3.11 Firewood day	48

4	Living with grandmothers	50
5	Festival times and Goat Hill's children	64
	5.1 Christmas	64
	5.2 Carnival	79
	5.3 When Easter came: Kite flying	95
	5.4 The Saraka and the Maroon	97
	5.5 The stone feast	107
	5.6 Regatta on Breeze Hill	112
6	The games that children played	116
	6.1 Boys and the vehicular toys	116
	6.2 Scooters	119
	6.3 The best pastime: Cricket	120
	6.4 Pitching marbles	123
	6.5 A game of stones	125
	6.6 Spinning tops	127
	6.7 Sailing toy boats and the making of the shipwright	129
	6.8 The making of complete individuals and the benefits of games	132
7	Socioeconomic activities in Goat Hill	134
	7.1 The economic base	134
	7.2 The Madevine's village shop and the Big Stone	137
8	Migration from Goat Hill	143
	8.1 Escaping the Great Drought	143
	8.2 A Goat Hill boy goes to England	147
	8.3 Max the lazy migrant	160
	8.4 Making it against all odds	164
	8.5 Filling the gaps left by the migrant husbands	167
	8.6 Migration and economic transformation of Goat Hill	169
9	The good, the bad and the indifferent of Goat Hill	172
	9.1 The Pervert	172
	9.2 The exploited	175
	9.3 The making of heroes and legends	176
	9.4 Diahee	179

9.5	The grandmothers	180
9.6	Nurse Cummings	180
9.7	The school master	181
9.8	The sea captains	182
9.9	Thompkin's Donkey	183
10	Tragedies in Goat Hill	185
10.1	A sea mine washed ashore	186
10.2	Fooled by the lull and the concrete house	190
10.3	Lost at sea	194
10.4	The burning of Maude's Kitchen	199
10.5	Ignoring the ancestral spirits	204
11	Development and curses	212
11.1	The contraband curse	213
11.2	The remittances curse	216
11.3	Consequences of the curses	216
11.4	Ancestral lands	219
12	From African socialism to tribal politics	221
12.1	Communal governance	221
12.2	Colonialism to revolution	223
12.3	Divisive politics	224
13	Caca Bawe for Caca Bawe	227
14	The new Goat Hill	236
14.1	Then and now	236
14.2	The future	241

Preface

GROWING UP IN the 1940s, 1950s and 1960s in Carriacou was not always easy for children. Nonetheless, there are memories of exciting times. There was a unique culture grounded in humility and discipline, and supported by elevated levels of determination. This resulted in many children doing well for themselves, their families and the island. When I tell my sons stories of my growing up experiences, they show excitement, occasionally. Perhaps, I have not relayed the stories well. With each passing generation, significant aspects of the way of life are forgotten. Often, the younger generation is not cognizant that each generation builds on the practices and lessons learnt from living during an earlier time.

In a world, inundated with all types of conflicts, notwithstanding the present enlightenment and obsession with modern conveniences driven by technological changes, there is a place for reflection on the past. We need to choose elements of our changing culture to strengthen to produce a more united island community. As Kayaks (natives of Carriacou), there are many aspects of our culture of which we should be proud and we should share them with the world by documenting them. It is noteworthy that some children of Kayak parentage, who have never visited Carriacou nonetheless know it well, through the stories told to them by their parents and grandparents. Ultimately, when these foreign-born children of Kayak heritage visit the island they are able to connect easily with places, people and activities. That is good!

The current generation reckons that life is better today than in the days of their great grandparents. This generation can boast about great strides in sanitation and health, communication, literacy, housing stock and inter-island travel. Grandparents look at today's children and argue for the days of old. Some of the older generation reminisce about the colonial days, and suggest, in their own way what they consider the decline of life in Carriacou. Who is correct? The world has changed and continues to change over passing generations. Carriacou has changed. Notwithstanding, there is a place for linking the past to the present. I give myself the challenge of making such a link.

I never considered myself a writer, but could not shy away from telling the stories as I remember them so that coming generations can connect to their ancestors. These stories are often reborn and rekindled during visits to the Corner Shop and other rum shops where the past becomes alive and every man gives his version of childhood history. A hundred versions of these stories are told and retold without the slightest hint of boredom because each version provides additional information and lessons for younger generations.

This is not a history book, although it includes some history. It is not a storybook although the book has some stories. It is not a socio-political conversation, although the life of Goat Hill would be incomplete without reference to social and political issues. It is none of these and all of these. It is like a 'sanouch', the once-popular Goat Hill dish that was comprised of all that was available around the house. The issues are so extensive that perhaps you can help me to determine how to classify this book. I trust you would help me by working out what it is.

Dedication

I dedicate this book to residents of Goat Hill, past and present in recognition of their hard work, strong family ties, preservation of culture and endurance under adversity. Specifically, to all the daughters and sons of Goat Hill whose childhood memories were limited to the experiences of parenting by grandparents, godparents, aunts and "nennens" either because their parents were forced to migrate to improve the lot of the extended families or because they never knew one or both parents for other reasons. I give especial recognition to the grandparents, godparents, aunts, "nennens" and particularly the grandmothers, who raised their children with unsurpassable dedication and commitment. I recognise the daughters neglected by their absentee fathers forced into marriage at the tender ages of fifteen and sixteen by their destitute mothers to avoid the disgrace of teenaged pregnancy and abandonment by no-good young men. I salute the exploited sons and daughters who had no one in their corner and those who became part of a life cycle of poverty. To the daughters and sons who still live in Goat Hill and who have been able to suppress the psychological scars that came from neglect and abandonment, I salute you for your determination and the success that you have enjoyed. Their testimonies give credibility to the greatness of Goat Hill. May the counsel from the experiences of life and the passage of time bring peace to your lives as you reflect on the good, the bad, and the indifferent experienced in Goat Hill.

Finally, I dedicate this book to my extended family including the Peters, Ovids, George, Francis and Derricks and in particular my parents, siblings, cousins and my childhood friends in the village. Although it appeared that we had little then, yet, we had a roofs over our heads, comfortable places to sleep and a fine extended family.

1

Introduction

A very long time ago, there were many small nameless islands in the southern Caribbean Sea, uninhabited and untouched. They emerged from the bottom of the sea when Mother Earth rumbled, just as the stomach of a man full with gas due to poor eating habits, and emptied the contents of her bowels. Some of the contents Mother Earth spurted out with fire and brimstone soon cooled in random layers, in the pristine water that cycled through the Caribbean Basin. Every few hundred years, Mother Earth re-experienced this stomach ailment and emptied her inside allowing the contents to fall in the same area. This caused a continuous raising of the seabed. Over time, the waves were unable to wash the deposits too far away from where they first landed. This was the genesis of the modern day volcanic Grenadines.

There were other islands in the Caribbean created differently. They also grew from the seabed. They were low-lying and composed of billions of shells and skeletons of marine animals accumulated on the ocean floor. Geologically, they were older than the volcanic islands, and although not many, they were the preferred resting place for many sea birds. In addition, there were the reefs. These grew and maintained their beautiful features under the turquoise green water. They too took their origins from the seabed, when free-swimming coral larvae attached themselves to submerged rocks deposited further from where Mother Earth had relieved her bowels of its hot undigested contents.

The hard surfaces that emerged along the edges of islands were the ideal spots for coral larvae, allowing them to grow at rates no more than one and a half metres per century. They ultimately burst through the surface as if they were white rows of opened cotton pods in a field where the surrounding blue water had replaced the green vegetation. Sometimes the white rows would come alive during the hurricane season, bellowing tunes that signalled the time for all living things to find a temporary hiding place. At other times, the white rows would disappear, in the calm waters during the dry season, for a short time, only to re-emerge more beautiful than before.

In the beginning, on these landforms there were no plants, no animals and no man or woman, just emptiness. It was God's creation, but there was no Adam or Eve. The new creations experienced annual cycles of dry and wet spells. Mysteriously, plants and animals inhabited the islands. The animals, some caught by the wind, and removed unwillingly from bigger islands were happy in their new homes as there was little competition for the resources available. Other animals came on logs as the floods rose from the inland drainage systems of the Amazon basin. In escaping the floods, these desperate animals landed on these uninhabited islands. They were now safe from the larger predators. These islands became their new homes, for eternity.

The wet spells were sufficient to maintain good tropical growth of indigenous trees: clammy cherry, marpou, Campeche, and gummier. The wild life, though few, flourished on the wild fruits. There were a few springs on the hills and the two or three seasonal rivers, where found, provided sufficient drinking water for the animals. For a long time, those animals were the only inhabitants. Many millenniums later, like some plants and animals before, people arrived in dugout canoes. They were explorers who arrived long before the Europeans. They settled where it was convenient and lived harmoniously with all that they found bringing life to the islands that had emerged from the bottom of the ocean.

The first human inhabitants were Cibony Indians who migrated from the Amazon area of South America, using Trinidad as a stepping-stone, around the time of the birth of Jesus Christ. These people were cave dwellers who survived by fishing, living off wild fruits and hunting indigenous animals. The second people, the **Tainos** (the Europeans called them the Arawaks) were also from South America. They came mainly from the northern bank of the Orinoco River in Venezuela. They pushed the Cibonys out. What happened to the Cibonys, thereafter, is hard to accurately determine.

When these early peoples, particularly the Tainos, arrived they observed that the islands, surrounded by bluish and greenish clear seas were rich in varying types of fish. Hence, the areas along the coast were ideal for fishing, particularly between the land and the reefs. They also ventured into the adjacent bushes to hunt iguanas and opossum, and to capture the occasional local doves that fed on the golden yellow fruits of the clammy cherry trees. The cultivation of cassava, corn (maize), squash, beans, peppers, sweet potatoes, yams and peanuts complemented the hunting and fishing. However, cassava, the main crop, was prepared for consumption by pounding the vegetable using stone tools, squeezing out the poisonous juice and then baking the dough-like paste into a flattened bread. They also made from the cassava what is equivalent to a modern day cereal product known as 'farina' or 'farine' in the islands.

In their small communities, the Tainos practiced polygamy and most men had two or three wives. The Chief was the biggest polygamist and often had many more, sometimes as many as thirty wives. After the first arrivals, there were many waves of Amazonian migrants to the islands. The Tainos were peaceful people. However, they often had to defend themselves from the Kalinago people (Caribs) which were the final wave of pre-Columbus people (aboriginals) to come to the islands. Ultimately, the Tainos were overpowered by the Kalinago people who had settled on an island which they named 'Kayryouacou' - meaning 'land surrounded by reefs'. It is on this island, which was later called Carriacou (pronounced Carr-ycoo), and is now part of the Grenadines that the unique village called Goat Hill was born.

The French were the first European settlers in Goat Hill (a village in 'Kayryouacou') around the 1740s. As the island of Carriacou where Goat Hill is located was small, the production was limited and the Europeans fought no great wars over it. Instead, they always linked Carriacou to Grenada, a larger island. Eventually, they ceded Carriacou along with Grenada, to the British in 1763 as part of the Treaty of Paris.

The Europeans brought slaves out of West Africa to replace the aboriginal peoples. They brought with them some plants like the tamarind, ockra (kingombo in the African Bantu language), and sesame (benne). They cultivated the lands of Carriacou with indigo, cotton, coffee and sugarcane. The French influence remains until today, manifesting itself in some surnames and in the names of villages. However, the British played the more significant role in the Grenadine islands and, as was expected, the influence is more noticeable. Nevertheless, the combination of the colonial influences and the culture of West Africa that dominated since the end of slavery remain interwoven in the lives of the people who stayed behind. It was out of this heritage that Goat Hill and many other villages emerged. Some of its people migrated, remitted earnings and sometimes returned which contributed to improving the standard of living. Each cycle of immigrants attempted to maintain a sense of history through a culture mixed with inputs from many lands.

2

THE ISLAND AND GOAT HILL

2.1 INTRODUCTION

The village of Goat Hill has always been prominent on the small island of Carriacou. Like all volcanic islands, Carriacou had rich soil that produced a variety of crops in abundance. During the eighteen hundreds, Grenada was famous for sugar production. This would be a surprise to many, that during the height of the sugar production, the total yields from Carriacou was more than that of the mainland Grenada which had an area of production five or six times that of Carriacou.

Goat Hill is a small village perched on a hillside overlooking the villages of Dover, Limlair, Meldrum, Belvedere, Eltham and Experiment. Windward and Doo-Doo are only a stone's throw away but are not visible from Goat Hill. A ridge running from St. Hillarie pond down to Experiment separates these two villages from Goat Hill. Above Goat Hill and to the south is Carriacou's highest peak, High North. During the first half of the twentieth century, Goat Hill was easily accessible by the main road (from Hillsborough to Windward) which formed the downhill boundary. A secondary road from Meldrum meandering its way uphill to the summit of High North was the southern boundary, while Experiment Estate formed the northern boundary.

If it were possible for a '*soucouyant*', that mysterious ruler of the night sky, to have followed the straight line drawn from a central location in the village, passing through the lone peak of Petite Martinique she would end up in Barbados. This would have enhanced the '*soucouyant's*' business by improving her trade in human blood during the night. However, this could not be, as the power of the soucouyant was only real in the bedtime stories used to keep children under control.

The village was strategically located for the fishermen who set their fish pots sometimes between the reefs and the shore. At other times, they set their fish pots further to the northeast of Petite St. Vincent or southeast of Petite Dominic. The fishermen used significant landmarks to aid in locating the position of the fish pots. They employed land-surveying techniques of lining up two landmarks on Goat Hill to form one straight line and similarly two other landmarks in any of the adjoining villages to form a second straight line. The intersection of any two lines facilitated the fishermen in finding the relative position of the fish pots at the bottom of the sea. Goat Hill provided two good landmarks. The first major landmark was a house with a unique roof, steep and with a steeple, designed to withstand the winds of any hurricane that passed its way. The house and its steeple were visible from almost all fishing grounds to the east of Goat Hill. Hurricanes were not as frequent to the island as they were in the northern islands from where news of much devastation reached Carriacou through the mail or from visitors. The second landmark was the evergreen marpoo tree at the top of High North surrounded by a variety of shorter trees that had all lost their leaves during the dry season.

2.2 THE DIFFERENT TIMES

The annual life cycle of Goat Hill began with the rainy season. Although it normally arrived in June, it was sometimes early, arriving by the middle of May or earlier. Occasionally, it arrived in July. Often, when it came in May people were 'fooled' as their early planting would be caught by a sudden resumption of the dry season causing all the young plants to wither away in a few days. The seemingly early start was usually only an occasional rainy day. Goat "Hillians" were not aware of the meteorological phenomena that created these variations but by looking at how abundantly the mango trees had produced or how much rain had fallen in January and February, they had a fair sense of the type of rainy season to expect.

The rainy season started with a tropical disturbance, announcing its arrival with thunder and lightning. The less risk-taking farmers would only plant when the first rains were accompanied by thunder and lightning. The clouds would move towards Goat Hill, passing over Petite Martinique, and making it disappear completely for a while. Then the winds would let the dark clouds drift over the reefs until they announced their arrival at Goat Hill with a light drizzle followed by heavy downpours. When the arrival was during the night, the raindrops on the metal sheets that covered the roofs would create sounds so soothing in melody that all who heard them would benefit from long deep and restful sleep.

Villagers knew when the season really came because everywhere 'rivers' would run. There were 'mini' streams on the side of the roads or in the natural gullies and watercourses where black volcanic boulders carpeted the V-shaped or U-shaped depressions. These would have been the path of permanent rivers had the island been larger and the rainfall heavier. In Goat Hill and the surroundings temporary streams existed during the rainy season. One day after the rains arrived new grass and weeds appeared everywhere. However, the trees on the hillsides needed a little time to produce new leaves with varying shades of green. Mango seeds discarded on the side of the road suddenly sprouted and just as quickly stray livestock, not yet captured by their owners, as was customary during the transition period from the dry to rainy season, ate them.

During the rainy season, Goat Hill provided a painter's dream as the different shades of green blended in the bright sunlight. The livestock tethered in the pastures appeared like brown and black blots on the tie-dyed green of a novice painter's canvas. There were black birds that avoided the stones and 'sling-shots' of boys hungry for roasted bony bird meat. There were sparrows, pigeons and doves of different species. The pigeons and doves never learnt and so ended up regularly into the traps set by boys as they grazed their cattle. There were grass snakes and tree snakes that were more afraid of people than people were afraid of them. These snakes were harmless. Then there were serpents that coiled high up in the mapou trees, resting all day before beginning their nocturnal search for food, only to return to the same spot after feeding. They seemed never to leave their resting place.

There were yellow butterflies, red butterflies, spotted butterflies and caterpillars of different sizes and colours. On the way to and from school, young children would jump after the butterflies, catching them with their bare hands and holding them captives overnight in small milk tins or glass bottles. The children were not as enthusiastic about capturing caterpillars but would poke them with sticks, and count the legs on each creature without recognising that they all had the same number.

There were the 'manicous' (opossums) lying in wait at nights so that they could raid the chicken coops and deprive poor families of their Sunday meat. The iguanas were difficult to see as they blended more subtly with the greenery everywhere. They were just as difficult to see during the dry season. The young girls loved this time of the year, as they would jump up and down the roadside, attempting to capture a butterfly to place in a bottle or under a calabash. They were short-lived pets, particularly for the girls. All these native animals lived in perfect harmony with each other as if to remind the village of the story about Noah, his ark and the big flood.

Sometimes during the rainy season, there were floods on the island. They could be more than a nuisance, sometimes deadly. For example, there was great grief when the raging waters of the September rains swept away the young Bartholomew girl. Goat Hill never flooded, as after a heavy rain, the water ran off quickly to be collected on the shores running from Windward to Bayleau. The runoff created a plume that stretched from the shore to sometimes as far as the reefs that protected the shore from the Atlantic waves which came from an easterly direction. The villagers believed that the sediments from the brown runoff were good for the sea grasses that populated the shores allowing small butterfish, doctor-fish and conch to flourish.

The dry season revealed another side to Goat Hill. The greenery had disappeared and trees without leaves and brown patched soil with large cracks in the shallow clay had replaced it. The hills shed all their garments to strike a naked pose, exposing the hiding places of the mischief- makers, both young and old. Looking up at Goat Hill from the distance, the large black volcanic stones stood out like black pigs foraging for whatever the earth would yield to them for food, only that these pigs did not move. The dry season was the time when water was scarce and villagers had to travel far for water. During a bad dry season or a drought, the search for water would take villagers to Criagston, Ningo-tree or even Beausejour which were two and three miles away. The livestock were all set free to fend for themselves as best as possible. At the peak of the dry season or drought, most of the animals would be 'skin and bones'.

At nights, Goat Hill was a quiet place except for the joyful sounds of children playing in the moonlight. In addition, the loud singing of drunken Gillah, as she cooked the late dinners for her children, would travel great distances to disturb the generally peaceful nights. The curse words would cut the night air as a sharpened knife going through a piece of cheese.

The one gas lamp at the doctor's house, which was located on a hill, about two miles away also illuminated the night. That lamp was the evening 'time-piece'. Nana would monitor that lamp for determining when to light the kerosene lamp that she owned. Some homes made their own crude lamps similar to a 'masantoe'. The downside was that the whole house was smoky and everything blackened. Soot was everywhere. The nostrils of the occupants resembled an inactive coal-pit and that was no laughing matter. Soot was everywhere. There were those who used candles instead. In the village, all lights were out by nine-thirty as the villagers retired early. If the lights remained longer, it was because some child was doing homework. However, this was not often encouraged as it was preferred that children should study in the natural light.

The nights also brought out the flambeau, French for torch or sometimes referred to as 'masantoe'. Masantoe is a corrupted translation of the French *'mettre eu feu'* or *'se metre en touche'*, meaning to candle. Perhaps the children did not get the patios pronunciation right. In any case, a flambeau or 'masantoe' was a crude lamp made from a glass bottle filled with kerosene and a wick made from cotton cloth or pieces of crocus bags. The user turned the 'masantoe" upside down regularly so that the wick could be fuelled to continue lighting. On a pitch-black night, when Henry's father went outside to urinate, he would report back that he saw a *'soucouyant'* or a witch moving from one village to the next to hunt his regular or perhaps a new victim. Henry's father really believed that what he saw was a *'soucouyant'*. However, it was only some innocent soul using a 'masantoe' to light his way home after a late night visit or on his way for an unexpected visit to the home of a single mother.

During the hurricane season, the villagers of Goat Hill could hear the roaring of the waves over the reefs. They sounded like a tsunami that the villagers knew little about. Nana would say, "You hear the bad weather? Children you cannot go to the beach tomorrow." Sometimes, by the next day, it was calm or the noise drowned out by the daily sounds produced as people went about their routine business. The reefs have always been a noticeable feature of the view from Goat Hill. This view later became the main feature on many post cards.

2.3 THE PEOPLE

In the beginning, Goat Hill was sparsely populated. The Indians that moved through the islands did not venture far enough from the coast to set up any communities inland. They were satisfied living close to the reefs where fishing was good. When the Europeans visited, they exploited the land and the Africans that they enslaved. The first true permanent settlers of Goat Hill were the freed slaves, their descendants and the free Africans who arrived after the abolition of slavery. They squatted on marginal lands, such as in Goat Hill. The original volcanic nutrients had either been leached from the lands, over time, or absorbed by export crops of indigo, sugar, cotton and limes.

There were four main families in the early days of Goat Hill. There was the Cox and Derrick lineage emanating from one Helen Cox. The legend said that she had a first set of children by one Mr Cox who was a free slave from Barbados. Mr. Cox most likely took his name from his master who was either English or Welsh. The story continued that Helen, exiled by Mr Cox, left some children in St. Vincent, and ended up in Carriacou where she got married to Mr. Derrick. He too would have been a free Negro with some property. They had two children together and bought a small estate from a Mr Dover thereby creating a village called Dover. Dover became an integral part of the life in the Greater Goat Hill.

Then there was the Francis-Delisle connection. This lineage was predominantly from the Igbo tribe in present day Nigeria. The history of this lineage is blurred but it is likely that there was a combination of freed slaves and free Africans. The original group went by the surnames of George and Ovid. The Ovids came from the eastern village of Mt. Pleasant while the George came from L'Esterre. However, the history of a practice of eating cats in the George lineage suggests that George may have originated from Martinique or Guadeloupe, where such practices existed. Over time, the Ovid lineage dominated. The Ovids came from Igbo land in Nigeria. How they came by the name is not clear as the name Ovid originates in the English-speaking world, from a Roman poet who lived during the reign of Augustus. Nevertheless, the name Ovid was important enough such that one of the classic Igbo songs that was popular during slavery praised Ovid for his skills in agriculture.

At the beginning of the twentieth century, Greater Goat Hill's population was around 300, with about forty individual houses. The village was eligible for consideration as an autonomous village. There were green corn mills, dry corn mills, a village shop and a small spiritual Baptist church. During the 1930s, the lone 'school-house' was relocated from its original location at Experiment to its new location in Dover. The 'school-house' provided accommodation for the school, community centre, emergency shelter and the place for services for Anglican Church worshippers once a month. The Catholics went to church in Windward. There were no Pentecostals nor Evangelists, as these Christian denominations did not reach the village in these times.

There were two carpenters, Decca and Abe, who had the reputation for producing high workmanship when sober. The men of the village who mostly wore khaki and dungaree trousers could depend on the lone tailor whose shop was never without apprentices especially during the school holiday. Nearly all the housewives were seamstresses and sewed their families' clothes. However, there was an ace seamstress and she designed and produced the wedding dresses that were required at New Year or at Easter when most weddings took place. Everyone was a farmer, young or old. In each household, parents and children all had their roles in planting and harvesting the corn, peas, cotton, or limes.

There were sailors and fishermen who depended on the boat owners from Windward for employment with little or no pay. Two of the sailors had not travelled beyond Grenada, but they boasted continuously about their experiences in the bright lights, the food and the women of the big cities. There were medicine women who prescribed different bushes for different ailments and gave specific instructions on the dosages and the method of preparation. Queen was one of the medicine women. She functioned as the village veterinary specialist, although no one knew from where she got her training. Her success was limited. However, the butcher who performed castrations on two-month old piglets provided support. There were teachers who started their careers after obtaining the School Leaving Certificate. Teachers were highly valued for their multiple roles. There were 'grave-diggers' whose payment was food and rum. 'Gravediggers' were special as they were believed to have connections with the dead due to their frequent handling of coffins. Over time, they graduated to be *Obeah-men* and feared by the superstitious villagers. The best of them was a one-legged *Obeah-man*, who provided services for clients as far away as St. Vincent. These clients had great confidence in the power derived from that form of 'voodooism'. There were masons too who did not get enough work to improve their skills.

Serious players of the Big Drum were absent from the village. However, the villagers danced the Quadrille to the music of accomplished violinists, tambourine and the iron triangle players. Other occasions brought out banjo players, guitarists, quatro players, and many shak-shak or maracas players. From this wide variety of musicians, Goat Hill developed a reputation of having one of the best musical bands on the island. The bands performed at weddings and dances at the school.

Cricket was the main sport in the village. All the young men played cricket but the village did not have enough of good cricketers so it collaborated with Limlair and Belvedere to create the island's championship team.

There was no radio station to give the obituaries as is done today. Goat Hill depended on the town crier who on his donkey would go from village to village, late at night or early in the morning, making the announcement in Patois:

> "Aye people, **Sa qetan parlez, lert** – *(Ceux qui l'entendent les autres)* who hear tell the others. John Brown in Goat Hill dead. He go be buried at 4 O'clock tomorrow, come one come all".

That was the invitation to go to a funeral. Goat Hill had one person who, without formally selected to do so, represented the village at all funerals.

In those days, there were no hecklers at political meetings. They did not exist. Mother England did not set Goat Hill free, yet. Papa Sylvester, Mama Sylvester and Mr. Patterson could scout for their support to go to the Assembly in peace. There was not much support since most of the people did not own property and hence could not vote.

There were homosexuals and lesbians though not many. They hid in the closet but the whole village knew who they were. Although it was taboo to talk about that topic, the villagers were generally more sympathetic to the lesbians since men were supposed to be macho. When the sexual orientation became too obvious, the individuals would migrate to another village or to one of the nearby islands. Goat Hill had its share of incest and sexual abuse: an old man allegedly fondled an under-aged girl; a father raped his own daughter. Cases of incest and sexual abuse were the best-kept secrets in the village. However, you could expect whisperings of the allegations at some time and at some place from one of the 'macos' in the village. In the meantime, the victims went through life suffering inside, sometimes abused repeatedly.

The village 'macos' or Peeping Toms and gossip-mongers provided stress relief and sometimes were responsible for the breakup of families. They could tell about what went on at nights. They would crawl on their bellies to position themselves directly under the place where husbands and wives were having their chats before retiring or perhaps were in a passionate embrace, expressing themselves with the appropriate language for the occasion. A village 'maco' could report every detail, using his expansive imagination to add dramatic flair the story.

Some men who had travelled abroad looking for work returned with a range of experiences from cutting cane in Cuba, Honduras and Costa Rica. Others who laboured on the Panama Canal or carried pipes and dug trenches in the Oil fields of Maracaibo, fought in the World Wars or contributed to the construction of the Lago oil refinery industry in Aruba also made their impact in the development of the village. They told many told stories of their sojourns, particularly those who were too old to make another trip. Others waited in hope for a call that would signal the opportunity to make the journey for another time. The young men who had many dreams of making it big so that they could build a mansion in Goat Hill looked for the opportunity from a godfather to pay the fare to get to these far-off places. Perhaps, selling a few cattle could help to pay for the trip but few had cattle in the right quantity. While the men waited to migrate, they played cards and dominoes to consume their idleness. They gambled using five pennies and farthings as the stake. When evening came, they hustled home to look for the food that they did not provide.

3

GROWING UP IN GOAT HILL AND CHILDHOOD MEMORIES

THE COMING OF THE VILLAGE SCHOOL

Schooling in Goat Hill had experienced great strides since the first family settled there. The first schools were privately operated with emphasis was on reading, writing and arithmetic. Learning was mostly by rote. The stories and poetry found in the Royal Readers described life in Mother England and although children could not appreciate the weather or food to which the stories and poetry referred, they forcibly memorised these under the threat of corporal punishment. Nonetheless, many of the early students swore on their dying beds that the lessons learnt promoted and maintained high moral values and integrity in the society. Children did their writing on slates, imported from England. As most children could not afford to buy the imported slate, the pieces of discarded roof slates that covered the estate houses were perfect substitutes. They were cleaned using saliva or bits of lily stock, only available during the rainy season.

In those early days, a successful school graduate would be able to sign his name, do additions and subtractions involving three digit numbers and read the ruler. The last skill was critical to become a good carpenter or a seamstress. The curriculum, handed down by the colonial masters, ensured continued servitude to white people or the black ones who had replaced them.

The Belvedere School, located then about one and a half miles from Goat Hill, might have been one of the earliest schools attended by a few children of Goat Hill. The principal, Mr Cox, and his teachers performed their duties out of the love for their jobs, as regular payments required by the parents were late and often unpaid. In many cases, delinquent parents would remove their children without paying any outstanding fees. Then a school came to Experiment. This school was closer to Goat Hill and took only a few minutes for children to walk from their homes to get there. They did not wear uniforms; instead, they wore clothes made from flour bags. Boys up to the age of thirteen and fourteen wore a simple shirt that reached their knees. They wore no sliders because only adult men wore sliders, and their private parts were visible when they sat on the wooden benches. The time for boys to leave school was indicative when their private parts showed definite signs of manhood. Girls were more modestly dressed. Above the age of ten years, they wore four strings slide bloomers made from an imported linen material or from the empty bags, usually of cotton material, which held one hundred pounds of flour. Many boys got their nicknames such as Talisman, and Canadian Best because the brand of flour was prominent on the backs of their flour bag shirts.

The Experiment School lasted about two decades. In 1925, the most important landmark in Goat Hill, the Dover Model School, replaced the Experiment School. The school's campus, which included a well-put-together headmaster's residence, ensured top class living conditions for its occupant. The resident headmaster's life saw further enhancement by regular gifts from parents. These gifts were according to the parents' means and included meat, fish, eggs, and whatever they produced by farming. Sometimes they did chores for the headmaster's household.

With the opening of the Dover Model School, education became more available and there was an increase in the school population as the number of teachers and classes tripled. The new school also provided a place for public functions such as dances, weddings, public meetings and, served too, as a hurricane shelter. The importance of the school in the aftermath of disasters grew appreciably after Hurricane Janet, when it became home for numerous homeless families.

The first set of headmasters came from Grenada and included Mr. Modeste, Mr. M Z Mark, and Mr. Toussaint who served between two locally bred headmasters. Later a number of local principals emerged, including the Braithwaite brothers: Nicholas and Godwin, Ruby Compton, the first female principal on the island, Mr Sam Fleary and Mr. Bascombe. The local principals of Dover rose to national prominence, later becoming Education Officers; Chief Education Officer; and Lecturers at the national Teachers' College, when commissioned; Cabinet Secretary; and, Prime Minister. Over time, sons of the island managed the school including sons and daughters of Goat Hill, and in the last two generations, Goat Hill and the surrounding villages produced all the personnel for the school.

The presence of the new school did not automatically change the majority's perception on the importance of education. In many quarters, emphasis was still on having many children to help with household labour, particularly for crop and livestock production. As a result, for many years when crop production was at its peak absenteeism was rampant. Nonetheless, many parents and children made good use of school and the Dover Model School has been able to provide a good enough education to enable them to change their financial fortunes and to help lift their families and the village as a whole out of poverty.

Given all the chores that children of Goat Hill carried out during the day, it was surprising that nearly all of them attended school on a regular basis. In any case, many of the children's past times and home chores intertwined. School was perhaps the most important institution among the three for instilling discipline and values to children. The other two were the home and church, in that order. In a few cases, the church was of no importance because those parents did not go to church or encourage their children to go to church. For those people, their only encounters with church were their christening and funeral, both of which they could not appreciate.

It was at the Dover Model School that those generations of children, particularly those of 1940 to the 1960s, enjoyed growing up. Their lives were not unique. They built on the experiences of those who went before them and, at the same time, they passed on some of their experiences to those who followed. They blended their daily lives of play and school while contributing to each home through a variety of chores. The solid foundation that they received at school enabled many of them to rise to prominence in their various fields of life. In addition, it brought a new sense of pride, purpose and lasting memories for which the games children played created the oneness of people.

In the early days, the island's economy depended more on monocrop agriculture and less on remittances. Today, there is a reversal as remittances far out strip agriculture. During the period when men first migrated to Aruba and England, the village was without electricity or television. Water was a premium particularly in the dry season. It was a time when families were large, as there was no scientifically organised family planning. In any case, the justification was similar to other parts of the world where the family's wealth was measured by the number of animals owned. Hence, it was common to hear parents say that *"Me children is me wealth"*. Parents needed children to help and contribute to the life of the household, and particularly in lighting up the lives of their parents during the evenings. Nevertheless, growing up in an island village in those earlier times left lasting memories and taught many lessons that influenced many generations.

In those times, there was one commonality among the people – financial and material poverty. Back then, poverty had a different meaning from how we use the word today, because a peasant's worldview seldom included looking through the window and blaming those on the outside for his situation. People accepted their situation with the ethos "must always do my best". You learnt that you were going to face hard times, difficult decisions and possibly even failure at some point. There were going to be many bumps but those should not stop the progress. You learnt to find ways to manoeuver around obstacles and continue to push forward, never looking back.

The extended family structure was a common feature in the village and there were very few nuclear families. The Ovid's extended family was typical and comprised of a grandmother, grand aunts, mother, father and nine children, five boys and four girls, ranging in ages from five to seventeen. The gap between births of successive children was small and it was not strange for a woman to have two natural births in one calendar year.

A typical day in the Ovid household began with the whole family summoned to the living room for morning prayers. For those who slept on the floor, it meant being disturbed from a sweet early morning sleep. Before the praying began, the children would head outside to find a comfortable place at the edge of the garden to relieve their bladders, particularly if the night pail was unused during the night. Someone would have to empty the night soil into the pit 'latrine' as indoor toilets were not common. Pit latrines were commonplace although not everyone had one. The Government provided, for a small fee, a concrete platform and a concrete bowl, something that mimicked modern day toilet bowls with a wooden seat and cover.

During the morning prayers, one or two of the younger ones would fall asleep again, but usually they were not disturbed. After prayers, the calabash of sour-milk, which was removed from its 'safe keeping' on the lone shelf in the kitchen, was a treat to the children. Sour-milk was 'left-over' milk from the previous morning's collection, which they placed in a safe and cool spot overnight. The milk, after remaining in that position for a day, curdled leaving the fat or cream floating at the top. This fermentation process was due to the lactic acid bacteria inherent in dairy products. They skimmed the fat from the calabash and what remained was sour-milk. It was an equivalent of yogurt. Ultimately, they used the fat to make butter. Homemade butter was also a treat for the family on special occasions.

Every morning, the women removed the skimmed fat from the sour milk and placed it in a bottle until it was full. Then, as a pastime for the children during the evenings, they shook the bottle, agitating the contents, separating whatever water was present from the creamy constituent. The creamy milk constituent, which was essentially fat, had a yellowish golden colour from which homemade butter took its colour. That was part of Samuel's daily cycle. It often begun and ended with the cow. However, for Samuel as well as many of his friends, the day was much more than this and included many memorable activities.

3.1 Keeping the surroundings clean

After prayers, one of the first chores of the day was the sweeping of the yard. Generally, the small girls and boys of five or six managed that task. However, the age could be a low as three. For example, one morning George sent Roxanne, the baby of the family, on an errand to a neighbour's house. When it appeared that she was taking too long to return, George looked across the road and up the hill and, to his surprise, there was Roxanne with a broom, sweeping the neighbour's yard. The neighbour shouted across "We have work for all ages". Sweeping the yard began with finding the broom. When a new broom was required, one of the older girls would find the broom trees in the pasture or on the side of the road and break branches. With practice, they knew the right lengths and number of branches that could make a good broom.

When the girls were too young, the mother or a brother would have that task. The broom plant or shrub was hardy with oval shaped rough leaves. It stood out among the other shrubs as it looked as though a coat of grey paint was dabbed over smooth green leaves. The broom plants grew to a height of about three feet and were plentiful as all beasts avoided them. The homemade broom was good for sweeping the earthen yards, particularly for getting small bits of sticks and dried chicken pooh from between the stones, which seemed to serve no useful purpose during the dry season. The chickens were the main litterers in the yard. Since the chickens roamed freely, eating whatever was available including human waste in the bushes, they left their droppings everywhere, especially in the cleanly swept yard or on the steps to the house.

With continuous sweeping of the yard, what was effectively taking place was soil erosion. At the end of the task, the sweeper collected the accumulated soil with a piece of galvanised sheet used as a spade, and threw it in the bushes. The villages did not know then, about the concepts of land degradation or soil erosion, and they were unintentionally helping nature to degrade that part of the environment - the yard, all in the name of keeping the place clean.

When it rained too heavily overnight, there was no sweeping. However, if it rained lightly sweeping took place. The sweeper would avoid what mud there was by standing on the stones to sweep around and between them. Stones, placed in the yards, provided protection from the mud, when it rained. In addition to the sweeper, others in the house used the stones to move from the main house to the detached kitchen or to the outhouse or pit latrine.

During the rainy season when the corn and peas were halfway to maturity, then the collected soil from sweeping the yard would make a swashing noise when it made contact with the leaves at different heights. As the sweeper was only about five or six years old, this meant that, the collected soil and other rubbish would often land away from the intended destination. The families were poor but children learnt an early lesson that lasted for life. That is, they must have pride in their place of abode, by keeping it clean. Consequently, the importance of keeping their surroundings clean became a habit.

3.2 BOYS THE TENDERS OF THE LIVESTOCK

Now the boys had slightly different tasks, and as Samuel had many younger sisters, he was exempt from yard sweeping. Samuel, like the other boys, got up early, usually before the sun rose. They must tend the animals - cattle, donkey, sheep and goats. The elder boys tended the larger animals while the younger boys had responsibility for the sheep and goats. If as a boy you were lucky to belong to a family who owned sufficient lands close to home, then tending the animals was not too difficult. However, as lands for pastures were not well distributed among households, boys had to travel perhaps a mile or two to get to government owned lands or other large tracks of privately owned lands whose owners were overseas.

Samuel had to travel a good distance to reach his animals. One day on his way, he met Pupa who was returning home after an early morning visit to one of his relatives. On seeing Pupa, Samuel shouted "Good morning Cousin Pupa". Pupa did not reply. Samuel repeated his greetings four times before Pupa responded with *"Good morning! Good morning! Good morning me foot! Good morning could put food on the table?"* before continuing on his way. Only few adults behaved like this. Samuel took this negative response in stride as he knew if he did not greet Cousin Pupa, a report would be made to his mother who would first give him a good talking down before administering one or two lashes with the tamarind rod.

An overnight or early morning rain did not delay the trip to the pasture. As there were no raincoats or umbrellas available, the next best cover was used – a crocus bag. Crocus bags, made from sisal fibre, were used to export cotton and limes from the smaller islands, and nutmeg and cocoa from Grenada. Crocus bags had many other uses, including providing for a comfortable sleep on the wooden floor. The livestock farmer used the crocus bag as a substitute for the raincoat, by tucking the bottom of the bag such that it created a hooded coat without sleeves. For a small boy of seven or eight, the bag covered him well, reaching somewhere between his ankles and his knees. The crocus bag raincoat provided unpleasant challenges for a boy like Samuel, of eight or nine. When soaked from the rain, it collected about one or two litres of water and felt like an overweight modern day school bag. Another challenge was that it gave little or no protection when one was travelling against the wind. Since there was no way to pull the sides of the bag together, in a short time the front part of a boy's clothes would be wet, adding a few more pounds that he must carry. It did not matter how wet and heavy his crocus bag was, he did not remove it, as it was much more comfortable to carry it about the body than to take the cold rain drops directly on a scantily clothed body so early in the morning.

Once the boys got to the location of their animals, they could be faced with a number of scenarios. For example, on one occasion, Samuel recalled his experience. First, the overnight rains on the backs of the sheep and goats, exposed to the elements, had caused one of the animals to suffer from severe cramps. The poor animal may have died soon after the rains began because by the time Samuel reached the pasture, rigour mortis had already set in as the legs and head were as rigid as a concrete post. The other animals fared better, as they were able to find some cover from trees within the reach of their ropes. Samuel cried and cried. He was afraid that he would be blamed. This might have been the case in many other households, but the Ovid family was very understanding and knew that the children could not be culpable for acts of God. That was a major household loss. As the family did not eat strangled animals, Samuel dumped the dead sheep in the nearby bushes where stray dogs would feast. Burying the animal was not an option, as Samuel alone could not dig the required hole. In any case, this location was far from any home or the main road hence, no complaints would be forthcoming from passers-by about foul smells. Had the same incident happened to a family in the Ravine, they would have skinned the animal and salted the meat for use over the next few months. What poverty can do!

3.3 Collecting firewood

On his way back, notwithstanding the loss of his favourite sheep, Samuel still had the presence of mind to collect some firewood for the kitchen fire. He had noticed that the wood heap was low and the next wood day was Saturday, two days away. Samuel got two pieces of Campeche and three pieces of Cutlet. Campeche firewood, when well dried, produced the strongest and longest active fire and was a premium for the household cooks. The Campeche wood also came in handy in the rainy season when it was difficult to get bundles of wood for the oven. Two pieces of Campeche could heat up the oven in little or no time

On the other hand, Cutlet firewood, when well dried, was easy to handle, as it was easier to split and chop into small pieces to put under the pot. Cutlet firewood produced a light blue gentle smoke that circulated throughout the small, detached wattle and dab kitchen with limited windows. The smoke remained temporarily confined before escaping through the spaces available in the walls of the building. There was no chimney for the smoke to rise, otherwise.

For Samuel's mother, it was better to cook outdoors when using Dog wood, Clammy Cherry wood or Cottonwood as the smoke produced by these woods was usually unbearable. If she used these woods in the indoor fireside, for example, when it was raining, she had to leave the kitchen area every eight minutes or so. Those regular visits outside allowed her to get some fresh air and her eyes to recover temporarily, thereby minimising the tears that flowed almost continuously during her cooking chores. The only other time that she had shed more tears was when her mother had died when she was fourteen.

Although it was interesting to understand how women coped with the different types of firewood, minimising the negative impacts, the full story must include the process of starting the fire. Samuel's home was usually the first to light a fire in the morning. Other households would spy on Samuel's home to see when the smoke came through the many available openings. Although a box of matches was only two cents, not all homes could afford this. Samuel's friends came to his home to get some fire, which they would carry on a piece of metal sheet or a pan cup or whatever else was available. It was like one smoker getting a light from another who had an active cigarette. In this way, Samuel's home served as the village's lighter.

At times, it was fun to start a fire but on some occasions, it was a serious hassle. It all depended on the wood that was available. There was one main challenge with Campeche wood; it was difficult to start a fire. One needed to start the fire with small twigs from other trees and a good complement of paper and cardboard. If it were a wet and cold morning, some kerosene would be required. Kerosene was a premium commodity and was used sparingly. In cases where the family had kerosene available, one had to be careful when using the kerosene as one could use most of it without getting the fire lit. Kerosene was not a cheap commodity for the villagers.

Sometimes there was luck for one person and a loss for another during firewood collection time. In an area about the middle of Breeze Hill where the big locust trees grew was a favourite place for village boys to hide green pieces of wood to allow them to dry over time. It was Samuel's lucky day as he contemplated how fast he might be able to collect enough wood to make a bundle. Although there was no template for sizing the bundle, the boy's mother could estimate whether the size of the bundle of wood was appropriate for him by just comparing it to his size. There was no science involved. It was all intuitive. That worked most of the time.

On this lucky day, Samuel found some half dried wood, cut into three feet lengths, well hidden under a cluster of bushes close to the big locust tree. That was about fifteen metres away from the main track, which everybody used to and from the pastures. As it was not locust season, the person who left the wood there to dry over the previous month must have felt reassured that the wood was safe. There could have been no expectation that someone would have gone there. The only possibility was that one would have passed through these entangled shrubs and vines, which concealed the wood. It may have been that someone had been searching for an escaped sheep or goat, which might have been trapped in the area. Samuel did not feel guilty for taking the wood, as on many previous occasions he had not benefited from his efforts of hiding green branches to dry away from prying eyes. This common practice of cutting green branches and hiding them to dry reduced the efforts of children finding wood when it was required on a rainy day and provided more play time when there was a direct request for producing a proper bundle of wood.

3.4 Sugar apple season

The sudden loss of his sheep caused Samuel to forget one of his daily routines during this season of sugar apples. At that time of the year, sugar apples were plentiful. The sugar apple plot, which was a common resource, was located in the boundary of government lands called the Forest Reserve and lands that belonged to the Mc Intoshes. No one seemed to know where the Mc Intoshes lived or whether they were still alive. However, this was not a matter for a sugar apple hunter, who wanted to ensure that he was the first on site particularly in the early mornings or late evenings when harvesting took place. Typically, the first persons to reach the plot would survey the trees and locate the biggest and smoothest looking sugar apples. This indicated that the sugar apple was at the highest state of maturity and had the potential to be sweet, but more importantly, it guaranteed that it would be ripe enough for eating within a day. To facilitate this, Samuel would dig a small hole in the ground about six inches deep, enough to hold one layer of sugar apples. He would line it with some grass or leaves taken from some distance away. The dozen or so sugar apples were placed inside then, covered with more grass or leaves. To further camouflage the site, Samuel would place one or two branches with prickles on top of the site. It was also very important to choose the site properly; away from the paths of friends. Of course, that did not always work well as a friend or a neighbour from another village could find the site accidentally and make good of the hidden treasure. Usually, on occasions like this, his only worry would be that by evening the sugar apples might be over-ripe. He did not like over-ripe sugar apples, as he could not control the juices that would fall on his clothes and advertise for all to see that he had recently had a sugar apple feast. He was a private person.

Family members treated sugar apples differently. Clare, Samuel's younger sister, by eleven months, loved sugar apples. This was her favourite fruit. There were two sugar apple trees in the garden close to the house. Anytime Claire got one or two mature sugar apples, she would hide them under the wooden house, between the wooden beam and the floor and would visit her hidden fruits twenty times for the day. Each time, she would feel the fruits to see how the ripening was progressing. She would imagine that it would be soft the next time. That was fifteen minutes later. Clare would touch the fruits so often that only the outer area of the fruits became soft, leaving the inner portion as firm as a newly picked fruit. This often brought disappointment to her as on occasions when she believed that a fruit was ripe and ready she opened it and found that the inside was too hard to eat. Claire would wrap the remainder with paper and return it to the hiding place to continue the ripening-process. This did not prevent the regular visits for testing whether it was really, ready. In fact, the visits became even more regular after the first testing.

3.5 Getting the milk

While Samuel was struggling to pull the dry branches for the firewood, he happily discovered his older brother Henry had already finished milking the two cows that had given birth earlier in the year. Each cow gave about one and a half gallons of milk. Henry's preparation for a morning's milking began the afternoon before. This was one of his favourite times of the day. During Art class at school, he often painted the scene of dusk as the sun disappeared behind High North and below the horizon that was visible. He often imagined that the scene would be better from the neighbouring villages like Bogles and Upper Belvedere near to the Patterson's plantation house. As the sun disappeared, it often left images of a range of colours from orange to deep red. Such images would attract modern day smart cell phone photographers to take instant photos or short videos to show to their foreign friends how great life was in the tropical islands. It was around this time that Henry would gather the cows and calves and take them about a half a mile away from the milking spot. One by one, he then separated each calf from its mother by making all sorts of noises while chasing the confused calf to make distance between mother and calf. Then in the darkness of evening, he would hurriedly take the cow away in the opposite direction. Meanwhile, he must double check that the calf was chased far enough. When a calf was determined not to be separated from the mother, it would dodge Henry by running in circles or, when the cow did not want to leave its young, it might refuse to make the quick dash back to the milking spot. In such cases, Henry would become so angry that in order to establish his superiority he would administer some blows to the calf, which he considered in order. That usually worked.

With cow and calf separated, Henry felt comfortable and free to carry on with what fourteen-year-old boys did in the absence of electricity, radio, television or cinema. It did not matter what mischief or pleasure he was involved in, he must rise early in the morning to head to the milking spot, collect the cow and return to find the calf. This was usually not too difficult, as both cow and calf would respond to each other's calls in the early morning. Henry was not always successful at separating cow and calf overnight. Sometimes the distance was not sufficient. At other times, the calf heard the cow's call. With the right wind, speed and direction, the sound can travel between the separated cow and calf. On a moonlit night, the calf can also find its mother. That was, however, rare. When that happened, Henry would be disappointed on reaching the milking spot as the cow's teats would be empty and the calf well fed.

As Henry contemplated his milking assignment that morning, he remembered with some trepidation what had happened to him twice in the preceding two weeks. During the previous two weeks, when he had finished milking and was about to lift the bucket, the cow, as if angry with him for separating her from her three-month-old calf took action. She had raised her left leg like a football striker taking a penalty to the goal, and with a perfect backward swing, which connected the bucket perfectly centre and had it flying to the top corner of the imaginary netless goal. As the bucket returned to settle on the patch of cactus, known as '*rachet*', all the milk had fallen to the ground. The milk, as if wanting to divorce itself from the bucket, cascaded out, only hampered briefly by the heavy sea breeze that was typical of that time of day.

Today, Henry must be methodical. First, he must secure the cow to a sturdy branch located about one foot above the neck of the animal. For this, he used the cow's chain, which was connect to a rope around the neck as a collar used on a dog. The twelve-foot chain, extended by a piece of rope, was used normally to tether the animal providing a fifteen feet radius of freedom to graze on whatever grass or shrub that was available. As he was securing the animal, he kept saying to himself and the cow, which perhaps had some understanding of why this extraordinary security was needed, "Not today, not today". He pulled the chain and rope over the second branch on his milking tree, then as if pretending to commit an execution by hanging, pulled the chain so that the head of the cow was pointing towards the heavens. The cow had little room to manoeuvre its head. It was forced to keep it in that restricted position until the milking was completed.

Henry had another major task to perform before milking the cow and he was well prepared. He had brought with him some extra rope, which he used to tie the cow's kicking back leg close to the hoof and using the full length of the rope, pulled the leg backwards and secured it to a guava tree. The tree was positioned well, and Henry wondered whether some blackbird had dropped the seeds there, after lunching on ripe fruits up in the bushes. Perhaps the birds used that spot as their toilet. Whatever its origin, it was a perfect tree for Henry when milking his cow.

Henry then washed the cow's teats with water that he had brought in the milk bucket. He was not as methodical with the washing as he was with the earlier restraining. After splashing the remaining water on the front and back parts of the udders, he sat on a stone that seemed to be a comfortable seat, albeit, only for a short moment as the rough edges of his temporary seat pricked his bottom. He paid no attention to the seat, as he must be efficient in his milking. He was simultaneously contemplating the other major chore that he had to complete before school. He pulled each teat until it was dry, yet his bucket was only half-full. There was always a strategy to get more milk from the cow. Henry moved away from the cow and allowed the calf to take over.

The calf began sucking one then another of the teats. As they were dry, the calf signalled to the mother that it was now doing the milking. At first, that seemed not to be working and the calf began to use its head to butt the udder as if to loosen whatever milk was in those internal milk pouches. The story in the village was that when the calf began to nurse, in these circumstances, it triggered something in the cow's system to allow the best milk to come. The cow tricked Henry by allowing him to take second grade milk. Perhaps it was natural for the cow to respond differently between the pull on its teats from Henry's fingers and that of its calf's mouth. The milk that came to the calf was creamier, the type that Henry would pull straight from the teats to his mouth. He had to get his timing right. If he returned to milking before the good stuff came, he would not get the amount to meet the desired level in the milk bucket. Henry looked at the untouched teat for a sign to act. As the teat stiffened, an indication that the mother had now sent down the good stuff, Henry pulled the calf away. He first drew some of the second milk, as it was called, straight into his mouth. It tasted good. He sat on his stone seat and repeated the process of pulling at the teats until very little milk came. They were dry once more. He moved his milk bucket to a safe spot and then began the process of releasing the cow. Henry untied the rope from the guava tree, then from the kicking leg. He then released the head of the cow. This major task was completed. The only thing left was for him to find a location to tie his cow for the day's feeding. As it was the rainy season, this was not too difficult since grass was plentiful. Henry then took his milk home.

At home, his mother filled three empty rum bottles kept particularly for this purpose. The two neighbours' children collected two of the bottles of milk. While Henry's cow gave milk, these families would each get a bottle of milk. Although they had cows, they were in calf and it would be another six or seven months before they could get their own milk. In any case, by the time that the neighbours' cows had started producing milk, the yield from Henry's cow would have reduced significantly, and would ultimately stop, given the calf's demand. Then it would be the neighbours' turn to send milk to Henry's family. No money changed hands. There was great understanding between neighbours and families.

3.6 THE STAPLE MEAL: CORN FOR COO-COO

Corn was the staple of Goat Hill. No one could avoid it although some were frustrated with its excessive use. One person who often lamented about corn was Puppa G. He would recite as if in poetry:

> *"Corn, you have to plant it.*
> *Sweat to weed it,*
> *Sweat to break it,*
> *Sweat to grind it,*
> *Sweat over the pot to cook the wangoo (other name for coo-coo),*
> *Sweat to eat it, and then*
> *Sweat to shit it out."*

All of these were true. Corn and its application had this effect.

Henry's next major task, before school, was the grinding the corn for that night's dinner. His family did not own a mill. In fact, there were only five mills in the village to service forty or fifty homes. Only the "Big Shots" had a mill. There were a few differentiating characteristics between the 'Big Shots' and the other villagers. Owning a concrete cistern and corn mills were perhaps two of the most obvious features of "Big Shots." The cost of a corn mill was not exorbitant, but the excessive competition for cash made having a corn mill less of a priority for the adults. The children thought differently as they all wished that they had a corn mill at home. Perhaps they wanted to be "Big Shots."

When Henry collected the five pounds of corn seeds, which were stored in a drum after the last harvest, he contemplated how to deal with the corn that was in the funnel of his neighbour's mill. The mill was made from a tempered steel drum about nine inches in length and six inches in diameter. The inner solid cylinder rotated on the outer drum to produce the crushing effect. Both drum and cylinder were shaped like cut out cones so that they fitted like male and female. The inner cylinder was formed with shafts on both ends and were connected to metal handles by a nut. By turning the handles, the rotating drum on the inside squeezed the corn seeds against the outer drum crushing them into small pieces. The clearance between the inside and outside drums was controlled by wrapping a small cord around one of the shafts on which the two metal handles were attached. The wrapped cord pulled the inner barrel so that the distance between the inner and outer drums became smaller. To obtain a fine corn meal the cord was wrapped to its fullest.

The metal handles were only about three quarters of an inch in thickness and about six inches in length. The constant turning of the mill handles would often cause corns and blisters in the palm of the hands. When the hands begin to hurt from the grinding, a common solution would be to use an old kitchen towel or other piece of cloth that was available to wrap around the metal handles. That provided some protection to the palms but was not convenient, as it would cause the grinder to lose control of the handles, by the hands continuously slipping away. It reduced the speed of grinding. When that happened, it was usually a good time to get some help. It was time for one person per handle. Grinding corn with two persons required great coordination and some youthful skills. Timing was important. If the timing was not right, then there was a jerky effect and one became aware of this from the sound of the mill. That was not good as it could damage the mill by breaking the barrel or the shafts that connected the handles.

On the day that Henry went to the neighbour's mill, he became angry when he saw that the funnel was full of corn seeds. He must first grind these seeds before he began to grind his corn. The first grind was the hardest. Henry would be lucky if he were not asked to give the second grind. He prayed that Miss Maude had stock piled enough corn flour in her lard pan otherwise; it would be additional grinding for him. For example, one Monday morning Miss Maude's corn flour supply was very low because her mill had not been used for a few days. She kept peeping behind the slightly drawn curtain, ensuring that no one could see her and was relieved to see Henry with the five-pound butter pan approaching. He prayed that it would be easy sailing that day. However, that was not to be, as Miss Maude wanted corn flour for breakfast and lunch that day. Henry did the usual. He completed his two rounds of grinding of Miss Maude's corn and as he was about to begin grinding his own he was informed that he needed a third round for Miss Maude. She generally did not mind doing the third grind herself as this was the easiest grind. However, on that day she was not in the mood. Henry was displeased.

Henry had no choice but to grind the seeds but he slackened the cord so that the grind resulted in most of the seeds breaking in half. They called this cracking the corn. That was done when corn was needed to feed the chickens in the early mornings. Cracking was easy as it required little effort and it took little time to have the funnel empty. Miss Maude saw what Henry did, but felt sorry for him as it was getting late. Further, Henry had given her a pint of milk three weeks before without his mother's knowledge. Keeping corn in some form in the funnel at all times was the sure way to have the next neighbour who came asking for a favour to pay for that favour. By grinding what was in the mill, the neighbour would have provided unpaid labour, which, in a way, was giving the owner a return on the investment for purchasing the mill.

3.7 Green corn dumplings

Grinding of dry corn was much more difficult than grinding green corn. In August and September sometimes a little earlier or a little later, one of the favourite foods was green corn dumplings. Green corn seeds were converted into a fresh smooth moist paste, by using a traditional green corn mill. The mill was also used for grinding coffee, cocoa and other spices. It was single hand cranked and easier to use than the dry corn mill.

The mill was clamped to a table's top with at least a two-inch overhang or it was bolted to the working surface for more semi-permanent installation that lasted throughout the green corn season. The solid cast iron body was not painted. The detachable grain hopper was about five to six inches in diameter. An oversized crank arm and large wooden handle allowed maximum advantage using one or both hands. The metal grinding plates were adjusted for controlling coarseness and the amount of effort required to turn the crank arm.

Freshly processed green corn retained the natural oils, flavour and nutrients and was much more nutritious than that which is purchased from modern supermarkets and health-food stores. Samuel and the whole family loved green corn dumplings. The dumplings were made by adding a small portion of wheat flour and a little salt to the mixture before kneading and rolling the dough until it was smooth and consistent enough to be formed into round, oval and flat dumplings.

Like the dry corn mill, not many homes in the village had a green corn mill. That did not stop the making of green corn dumplings or green corn porridge in most homes. Sometimes Samuel's mother did not want to disturb the neighbour for the use of her green corn mill. At other times, the mill was otherwise in use. On those occasions, she used the stone mortar and wooden pestle made from Campeche wood (The stone mortar belonged to her family dating back to the period after the emancipation of black slaves on the island.). She would throw in a handful of the green corn seeds in the mortar and pound it until it was soft and smooth. She repeated this process until the bowl of corn was completely processed. There was however, one disadvantage of these processes. When neither mill nor mortar and pestle was available, some house-wives would innovate, using a grater to turn the green seeds on the corn's cob into a rough paste. There was no consistency of the flour from these methods. Sometimes, when eating the dumplings, Samuel or his siblings would find whole seeds that they must chew before swallowing. Of course, that was not always possible and the whole seeds could be seen in the faeces under the calabash tree where Samuel's younger sister had relieved her bowels.

3.8 Roasted bakes

When Henry returned home, tired from grinding his and Ms Maude's corn, there was just enough time to drink the cup of fresh milk, spiced-up with a bit of cinnamon and some Santa Maria leaves, and to gobble down three freshly roasted bakes with a bit of scantly spread margarine from the two ounces purchased the evening before. He was lucky that there was enough money to purchase that much. On most occasions, only an ounce was bought. Most villagers ate roasted bakes without any butter or margarine. Only on special occasions were fried bakes entertained and when that happened, it was like Christmas. Fried bakes were for the "Big Shots". Now making roasted bakes was an art and children knew the houses where tasty roast bakes could be found. Samuel's mother made 'fairly good' roasted bakes. She used baking powder to get her dough to rise, but some homes used baking soda. When baking soda or baking powder was not available, women used ashes from the fireside. To use ashes, they put two or three tablespoons of ashes in a half cup of hot water, stirred it for a few minutes, then strained it using a piece of cotton cloth. The ashes produced a hybrid between leavened and unleavened bread. Cooking with wood ash may have been an African tradition. However, natives of the Americas were known to use wood ash in their cooking. Native American Indians made flat bread with corn meal, and used a very early type of leaven made from wood ash. The early colonists in the Americas used a similar method, which perhaps was the origin of its use in Goat Hill. Ashes were used also in the cooking of "bhaggie" or callaloo from okra leaves, okra pods or the indigenous spinach.

To roast bakes, a fire was lit in the inside fireside (fireside within the detached kitchen) which was a set up of three stones on the elevated counter with the wood placed between the triangular openings formed by the stones. Samuel's mother would place the broad iron pot on the stones, making sure that it was well settled. She then rolled a piece of dough made from wheat flour, salt water and a little margarine or homemade butter if available, flattened it so that she got a flat circular or oval shaped bake and placed it into the hot pot. She was always very careful that her hands did not touch the pot since she could get a severe burn. Each adult and child had his quota (a specific number determined by the combination of size and age) of bakes for breakfast. With her computer type brain, Samuel's mother was never short of bakes since she would often make three or four extras for one of the neighbour's children who sometimes had nothing for breakfast except a cup of bush tea.

Once Samuel's mother was through with placing the bakes in the pot, it was time to cover it. The bottom or top piece of a forty-five-gallon oil drum was the preferred pot cover. If a drum cover was not available, piece of galvanise was a good substitute. Samuel's mother would then start a fire for the top, by using a fire stick from below with some pieces of wood that were cut or broken for that purpose. Fire was then placed on the cover so that there was fire below and fire on top. Samuel's mother inspected the bakes from time to time to ensure that they did not burn. Inspection entailed lifting the pot cover high enough, holding it with a piece of cloth. Sometimes the cloth was wetted to prevent it from catching fire as she peeped to get a good view of the bakes. From time to time, the fire was regulated so that the bakes did not burn or become brown too quickly. If that happened, chances were that the inside of the bake would be raw.

Sometimes, to avoid the smoke that circulated through the kitchen, Samuel's mother would make the bakes outside. The outside fireside, which was permanently placed, was very convenient as the wind would blow the smoke away, allowing Samuel's mother to be free from running eyes and nose as she almost always experienced while cooking on the inside fireside. The inside fireside, on the other hand, was not the preferred option as the cook had to endure the smoke which hung around for a while before exiting through the single entrance or the gaps in the sides of the kitchen. The inside fireside was useful when it rained, particularly, when the cooking or baking was incomplete before the rains began. After long use of the inside fireside, the interior of the structure would be blackened with soot and soil the clothes of those who ventured within. For most, it did not matter much, as the clothes worn in the kitchen were not one's best and, in any case, there was no food as appetizing as food cooked on wood fire.

Now that Henry had had his breakfast, he must hurriedly prepare for school. As there were no bathrooms, he must stand on the heap of stones at the back of the kitchen and have his wash. When there was a good shower of rain overnight, Henry could afford to use a half bucket of water (about two gallons) for his wash. He washed face, then hands and feet using an old sponge that he found at his grandmother's home. He then rubbed vigorously under his arms. He looked around to make sure that no one was passing by on the road that went along on the leeward side of the house. Believing that it was safe, he pulled his pants down to his knees, and then gave a quick wipe in the groin area. Henry was only able to keep his pants on during the wash because his mother was not around. If she were around, he would have to wash standing naked on the stones. That was the practice for all children up to the age of thirteen or fourteen

Bathing in the yard

Henry was lucky that it was not the dry season. In the dry season, the water quota for washing for school was only a few cups. Of course, in the rainy season, especially if the rain was falling during the morning, one could have a proper shower by standing on the stones and allowing nature to do the rest.

Rationing of water for self-washing was not as meagre at the beginning of a school term or the weekly or bi-weekly scrubbing. Children had to stand on the stone and using a full bucket of water, the mother in the case of the early teenagers, and the older siblings in the case of the younger ones would give a good scrubbing. The lacrosse or the rolls of dirt that had accumulated since the last scrubbing would roll off the body. A 'Cacabeke' bush, which was good for all things, was used in place of soap. It was difficult to see the real colour of the residual water in the bucket when the washing was complete.

Once, Samuel's mother scrubbed him on the heap of stones in preparation for the new school term in full view of his friends. He was very uncomfortable. They had come to wait on him so that they could all head downhill to the schoolhouse like the Goat Hill posse. The heap of stones served another important purpose. It was used on a Saturday for bleaching the white clothes. Samuel was trying to hide his private parts with his small hands causing his friends to laugh. The boys laughed out loudly while the girls only giggled. Samuel's mother administered two slaps to his backside and said to him, "You think you is man because you have 'pwell' (pubic hairs). These slaps, which brought more laughter, settled the matter. Samuel surrendered to his mother's rough hands and allowed the wash to be completed. Once that was done, he was okay. Samuel remembered that during the previous school term, one of his schoolmates had made fun of him during a Monday morning body inspection. Then, when his friend opened his mouth for inspection by the teacher, she reported to the class that she saw a few grains of rice stuck between the teeth. She asked the student, "When last did you eat rice?" He replied, "Last week Miss". This resulted in a lesson on how to make your own toothbrush from black sage wood; and to substitute ashes for toothpaste. The teacher also explained how good the pigeon peas leaves were for keeping the teeth clean. Samuel had made his black sage toothbrush on his way from tending his sheep. He only now needed to get to the fireside. Using his fingers, he administered some wood ash to his teeth and with his wooden toothbrush, he spread the ash on as many of his teeth as the time would allow him.

3.9 Taking the animals to the pond

School lasted for six hours, from nine in the morning to three-thirty in the afternoon, with a lunch break of one hour from noon to one p.m. After school, like morning time, was full of excitement with chores distributed over the two-hour period before sundown. Boys were good at time management. For example, Henry would not go home immediately after school. He would use his roller and head to the pasture where he had left his cattle. With his three exercise books, his Student's Companion and the Royal Reader Book 6 in one hand and controlling his roller with the other, he sped on his way to the pasture. The roller was the metal band on a forty-five gallons drum in which imported cooking oil was sold. The best rollers however, were the rims of bicycles minus the spokes and tires. Without knowing it, the roller was instrumental in making Henry the athlete that he was. He had represented his school at the last three Annual School Games during the dry season, usually sometime around Easter. Henry, on reaching the cattle, would free them as well as the donkey that his father insisted on keeping as the family's primary means of transport. Henry would leave his roller hidden, such that nobody else could find it. In any case, if it were found, it would be easy to claim as he had marked it with what looked like Chinese lettering. Everyone knew Henry's roller by the special markings.

As he headed to Big Pond, the cattle and their calves ran in single file, their long chains leaving a trail in the tracks, and producing a musical sound once they crossed the bitumen road. The animals needed no guidance. They got used to the regular evening trips to Big Pond. If dogs could be trained, so could cattle. Henry could claim success as a trainer, but this was accidental and involuntary.

Henry was warned against riding his donkey with the chain loose as those on the cattle. He did not understand the need for wrapping the chain on the donkey around its neck. One day as he was racing downhill on his donkey, while trying to keep up with the cattle, he fell off. He was hurled through the air and he landed on some snake bush. One of his legs was entangled in the loose chain. He was dragged for about thirty metres on the road and sometimes in the earthen drain along the road but he was lucky. The donkey stopped only when it encountered a herd of cattle crossing the road in the opposite direction. The cattle were moving slowly as they had just finished drinking water in the pond and were full. It could have been much worse for him if the donkey had bolted into one of the gardens adjoining the road to the pond. He was not hospitalised but had to remain without pants for a few days while the badly bruised skin on his arms, legs and butt healed.

For some time, Henry could not carry out any of his regular tasks. He missed his friends and was miserable while he remained in bed. Notwithstanding being exempt from his regular chores, he preferred mobility. His father took over the task of watering his animals and was not pleased since he had accused Henry many times before of being careless. In this case, he felt that Henry should have wrapped the chain around the donkey's neck before getting on its back.

After three weeks, Henry was fit and ready to resume his regular tasks. He raced after his cattle to Big Pond. His cattle waded into the pond until water was up to their necks before they began to drink. While drinking they would often relieve themselves of both liquid and solid wastes. The donkeys did not venture into the pond. They avoided getting their hooves wet and would stand on the edge of the water, straining their necks to drink as much as possible to keep them until the next day. Henry could tell when his cows had had enough to drink by looking at their bellies expanding outwards. When all their ribs became invisible and they looked like they were in calf, Henry knew that they had reached their limits. Once the animals were finished drinking, Henry would begin a slow march back to the pastures to tether them for the night. However, first he would have to hide the calf so that he could get milk the next morning.

Sometimes an animal was unable to return to shore after having its fill of water. This was the case usually in the dry season. The bottom of the pond became softer towards the centre and the depth of mud on its bed increased exponentially towards the centre. Occasionally, an animal could encounter difficulty while trying to find a good spot for drinking as it could find its legs sinking until its belly was resting on the mud. When this happened, the animal had to be assisted in getting out. Boys would hold on to the chain and rope, and like if participating in a tug-of-war against the animal, pull until the animal was free. There were times when it was not that simple. The animal, if it resisted could find itself sinking deeper. At such times, someone had to enter the water and use additional ropes and additional men on shore to increase the force on the animal. Sometimes one or two more adults would have to venture into the water to assist the animal by trying to lift it off its sunken moorings. It could get even worse and the animal was left in that position overnight. On the next day, with the overnight plans, additional manpower and ropes, the tug-of-war would resume. If the animal survived the night, there would be success as it became easier to pull the half-dead animal that was unable to offer much resistance.

When grass in the pasture was scarce or when the animals needed to be fattened for sale or when more milk was required, boys like Henry were responsible for grazing the cattle on the sides of the road. This was done before they were given water. As if programmed, they would slowly eat the grass and shrubs that grew on the side of the road. That task could take as long as two or three hours and longer on weekends. When they reached the pond, their bellies would be halfway out. Water then filled the empty spaces left in their stomachs. While grazing the animals, boys would play many games: marbles, racing with their rollers and cricket with homemade wooden or recomposed melted plastic balls. The more studious boys would use this time to do homework or study for the School Leaving Examination, if they were attending the Dover Model School (a primary school) or for O'Levels if they were lucky to be at the recently opened Bishop's College. The animals were good live models for boys to practise their knowledge of the anatomy of the animals. Sometimes, fights broke out among the boys for different reasons.

Occasionally, there could be some misfortune for a boy who was not vigilant in ensuring that the animals remained on the side of the road. This was the case with Scope one Thursday afternoon. He was friendly with the twins from a neighbouring village. They were his own age. He had gotten hold of the twins' bicycle and had made the round through Meldrum, Belvedere, Windward and back to Big Pond. The twins had shown their entrepreneurial skills by giving other boys the opportunity to learn to ride. In return, the boys undertook chores on behalf of the twins. They took the twins' cattle to the pond, grazed them on the side of the road and tethered them in the morning or afternoon, or cut grass for the cattle during the dry season.

Scope had provided his service to the twins and decided to make the best use of the bicycle. His long ride infuriated the twins, as they had to wait a long time for his return. It was during this time that Scope's cattle, which were left unattended, entered Margaret's garden and damaged the lush looking corn plot. Scope was in serious trouble as his grandmother would be responsible for compensating for the damage. Neither Scope's grandmother nor Margaret was satisfied with the appraisal provided by the agricultural officer. One thought the compensation was too small while the other felt it was too large. The animosity that resulted from this incident was short-lived. As the good "flogging" that Scope received seemed to satisfy the victim. Everything went back to normal at the end of the corn season, when Scope's grandmother offered Margaret two crocus bags of corn, which was considered more than the estimated losses.

3.10 Toting water

While Henry was taking his cows to Big Pond for water, the girls had to collect water from the government communal cisterns for household uses. Water was collected either in the morning from six to seven-thirty or in the afternoon between four and six. During the rainy season, only homes without a cistern or inadequate storage due to large families, collected water from the communal cisterns frequently. The older girls and sometimes boys had to tote the water in a bucket or typically a pitch oil tin on the head. To protect the head from bruising due to the friction between the bottom of the water container and the head, a piece of rag would be wrapped into a circular cushion, which was about six to eight inches in diameter. This cushion was referred to as a "carta", and the size depended on the size of the head, correlated to the age of the person.

A pitch oil tin held about four gallons of water, a lard or butter pan held a little less. An empty "klim" (milk) container came in handy for toting water by the smaller children between three and five years old. When walking, the person carrying the water must be able to balance the bucket on the head using one or both hands to keep it steady. Some people were so good at balancing that there was no need to hold on to the sides of the containers. They could walk for miles with the bucket of water on their heads while swinging both hands freely only occasionally placing their hands temporarily if they missed a step. To maximize how much water was carried, the buckets or containers would be filled to the brim. However, while walking, some water would spill over the rim of the container. To avoid losses, two or three branches were placed in the container with the water. Generally, the branches were taken from the rain-bush which was one of the few evergreen found on the island or from plum trees which were preferred. They were thought to be safe. The branches dampened the wave action of the surface in the bucket.

Another method used for avoiding losses from leaky buckets which was not always effective but used where the opportunity arose, was to caulk the holes with whatever was available. It was useful when the hole was not at or near to the bottom of the bucket. Dried soil would be made into a putty, by mixing it with small amounts of water. The mud putty was placed on the outside of the bucket so that the whole was covered. If the distance that the water was carried were not too far, the mud although softened would still be in place at the end of the journey.

Henry's youngest sister used the mud putty once. She did get the putty mix right. As she walked with the bucket on her head up the hill, the water slowly escaped through the hole producing a brown solution as the soil was suspended in the clean water. There was a constant dripping of the brown water on Linda's hair, face and blouse. Just before Linda got home, the brown solution thickened and began drying out. So thick was the muddy water on her face and blouse, she could have been mistaken for a "jab jab" if it were carnival Monday morning.

Filling the buckets took time. The rate at which the water was discharged from the pipe, which was connected to the cistern, about a foot from the bottom, depended on how much water was in the cistern. The flow rate was higher in the rainy season than the dry season for the obvious reason that by the time the dry season came along the storage was depleted significantly.

To get water from the communal cistern, households paid one dollar for three months' access. If the home was central to two or three cisterns, there was an advantage by paying for each cistern. That home could get water from all cisterns. Goat Hill homes were in a half-mile reach of three cisterns: one at the local school, one at Top Meldrum and another at bottom Meldrum. When water became scarce, for example during a severe drought, households were restricted to one cistern and two or three buckets (equivalent to six to eight gallons) three times per week. As Henry's home was not too far from the school cistern and as the family was large, there was an understanding among the villagers that his household could get a little extra, but it was not much more than the average.

In extreme dry seasons, water from the communal cisterns was supplemented by water from the pond and the dug-wells. Stories were told of water from the ponds being used for drinking purposes. It was not safe, but it was the only water source available. Some of the elders told stories of the water experiences in the earlier part of the century. The pond water was taken while the animals were drinking and persons were not perturbed even when the animals relieved their liquid and solid wastes in the water.

Later in the century, water availability improved and pond water was used mostly for livestock and a few household activities. At home, the pond water was used for scrubbing the wooden floors. If the sediments, that gave the water its brown colour, were allowed to settle to the bottom of the container, the water could then be used for washing coloured clothes. In extreme circumstances of water shortage, it was used for cooking.

Fetching water from the wells usually needed the presence of an adult. Henry and his sister Josephine were often responsible for overseeing the younger children fetching water from the wells located close to the sea. That water came from a thin lens of freshwater that floated on top of the seawater. During high tide, the seawater pushed the freshwater upwards allowing the level of water in the well to rise. That was the easiest time to collect water, as there was sufficient for all who threw their buckets down into the well. Old knocked-up buckets were used as a new one was soon disfigured from the constant banging.

To obtain a bucket with maximum water in it required the skill of pulling up slowly while at the same time ensuring that it did not touch the walls of the well. The most frustrating thing for Josephine was the constant bursting of the rope that was used to pull up the bucket. Josephine's rope seemed to be the oldest and knotted from constant joining. She was careful, most of the time, to allow the bucket to collect only about one and a half gallons of water before pulling. Whenever she was in a hurry, she would allow as much water as possible to enter the bucket before pulling it up. Alas! Her rope was not strong enough and it would arrive without bucket. To retrieve her bucket, Josephine would have to search for someone else's rope and attach a hook made from a piece of discarded metal wire. With luck, she could find a hook that had been discarded after a previous effort of retrieving a lost bucket.

The best fun associated with fetching water from the well was when high tide coincided with moonlight. Henry was always retelling the experience of when his grandmother, Nana, woke them from their beds to trek to the well in the early morning. Her clock was the fore day morning crow of the village cocks. On one occasion, his grandmother miscalculated. It was not the fore-day morning crow but the first crow at about 11p.m. Henry, his four siblings, his seven cousins and four neighbours journeyed to Backra well about three quarters of a mile away. Backra well was located in the village of the Scottish descendants. In fact, the word Backra was associated with white people.

Usually, two trips were made before day light. On that particular occasion, Nana marshalled the troops and by daylight, six trips were made. Everyone was tired and sleepy. Nana had miscalculated by the cock's crowing and the moonlight. Nonetheless, the drums were filled with water so a trip was not necessary the following day. That was the first time that the children were allowed to stay away from school without being sick – the standard excuse.

3.11 Firewood day

We already know that occasionally Samuel, on his way home, would carry some firewood to reduce his efforts later. Every home had a firewood day, which was either Saturday or Sunday, depending on the observed Sabbath. In the Ovid family, firewood day was Saturday. Firewood day began with the children doing all the morning chores: sweeping the yard, toting water, seeing about the animals and milking the cows. Samuel's mother would assemble all the wood carriers from the extended family. That would be a contingent of about ten to fifteen. There were four mothers from three households, all connected through marriage or by blood. Then there would be the children, mostly boys. Sometimes one or two tomboys were included.

In preparation for the field trip, the cutlasses or machetes were sharpened. That was done on a piece of grinding stone. Henry would take about five minutes to sharpen a cutlass. He was fast at this. Cutlasses came in different shapes and sizes, usually resulting from wear and tear over a couple of years. The cutlasses were sharpened on a communal grinding stone, which was a piece of special limestone, imported from England. The circular stone looked like a flywheel mounted on a wooden horse by a wooden shaft connected to an extended handle. When the handle was turned, the stone spun in its vertical position. The objective was to get the stone to rotate as fast and as long as possible. One person turned the stone, starting slowly until it gained momentum, while one or two others would each be sharpening cutlasses simultaneously, by allowing the blades of the cutlass to rest on the rotating outer surface of the stone. To improve the efficiency of sharpening, some water was poured regularly onto the rotating surface. That happened long before sharpening files and electrical emery stones were available.

Once all the preparation was completed, the firewood bunch would head up to the hills above Goat Hill. Persons with good memories would recall where a partly dried tree was seen one or two weeks before. Often a tree looked dry but after testing it by chipping a small piece off the bark, it was recognised that the tree was green and full of life. There were a few trees like these, which were best at their deception during the dry season.

The adults on the team would determine a good area to explore for the presence of dry wood. Once an area was identified, the wood carriers were dispatched, in pairs, in as many directions as would allow for the making of temporary tracks. On such days, Henry would reach into the thick shrubs and bushes first and, once chopping was heard, it was known that he had found the treasure, a dry tree standing or fallen or a branch that reflected some injury or disease to the tree in the recent past. When Henry had completed his chopping, he would then pull the wood out to a clear spot usually on the earthen and grassed road that connected Goat Hill to the peak of the hills above. Then soon thereafter, all would return to the spot with what had been collected. At that stage, the quantity of wood was assessed to see how many bundles could be made. It was a bundle per person. If the quota were not reached, then the group would progress higher up the hill to find a new location. That process was repeated until it was judged that there was enough to provide an appropriate bundle for each. The size of the bundles depended on the age, sex and size of the individual.

Collecting firewood could last for eight hours from 9 am to 5 p.m. When dry firewood was scarce, the day trip could last until the sun was beginning to disappear. Sometimes, the quota was not reached by that time. On such occasions, the bundles were smaller than the normal size. Each bundle was carried on the head. Similar to the head cushion for toting buckets of water, one was needed to carry the wood. However, the more common cushion was made from branches that had good leaves and which could be formed into a green pad that looked like a wreath used to decorate graves after burials.

4

Living with grandmothers

Almost all Goat Hill's children remember their early life with their grandparents, particularly their grandmothers. Grandmothers played an important role in the upbringing of children. Grandmothers were often good storytellers and were largely the first storytellers. Like the black birds that protected their chicks in their nests from the flying and climbing predators, grandmothers protected their grandchildren with similar zeal from child bullies or from the corporal punishment of the children's parents. Often they were rescuers for their grandchildren who may have been in a place of depravation. Stories of grandmothers as providers of special treats or going hungry to ensure that the little ones did not go to bed hungry have been told many times. Finally, in most families, grandmothers were the counsellors, teachers, nurses, financial controllers, peacemakers and social workers.

Henry and his cousins enjoyed spending time with their grandmother, Bunah. She would sit on a stone in the yard with her own grandchildren, plus others from the next neighbourhood to perform her various duties.

There were Anansi stories. Anansi was one of the most popular of the animal tricksters in the mythology of West Africa. He was the spider-god, half-man and half-spider who outsmarted all the other animals in the forest. Often, the children did not readily get the moral of the story of the creature who used his wit and cunning to get an advantage over animals who were bigger and stronger than he was. He was often selfish and even cruel, although sometimes he would help other creatures, but only when it suited his own purposes.

There were also stories about the "Lajablesse", the pretty-faced woman, with one cow foot and one human foot, who tricked many simple-minded men. The "Soucuyant", the old man or woman, who could fly, and would transform into balls of fire, shedding his or her skin before entering its victims' houses. It was alleged that the "Soucuyant" could pass through any small opening, even when all the windows and doors were securely closed. It sucked blood from the victims while they slept. If one was able to catch the "Soucuyant" before it was able to put on its skin, then the human form would die. A potential victim could keep the "Soucuyant" out by placing salt and garlic in the doorway or on the window ledges.

There were a few "Soucuyants" in Goat Hill but none more powerful than Massa. At least this is what everybody said. There were stories of Massa making the trip across the Atlantic to the African West Coast. On one of his trips, Massa collided with a plane. The plane crashed while Massa sustained only minor injuries. Massa's unique skills were not passed on to his children. Their mother ensured that they consumed lots of salt, which caused their bodies to become too heavy and thus were unable to fly. It was the knowledge of the anti-flying effect of the common salt, which the Rastafarians used in their pursuit of flying back to Africa, one day.

Then there were "jumbie" or ghost stories. These creatures moved like balls of air sometimes transforming themselves into animals like dogs, horses or even pigs. Children were told that when they encountered the "jumbie", they had to change their clothes so that it was worn wrong side out and walk backwards.

Finally, there were Bible stories. Often they were told in a way that reflected the understanding of the grandmother who listened to the priests. To scare the people, the priests always told stories based on the Book of Revelation. That was to prepare the congregation for life beyond this earth. Story telling was usually a grandmother's thing. In many homes, grandfathers were absent. In any case, where grandfathers were present, they were never at home early and even if they were, grandchildren to them were often considered nuisances.

Typically, sundown signalled the beginning of an exciting night. Bunah told her stories to the children by light from a pitch oil lamp. The children listened attentively until overtaken by sleep. Henry yawned indicating it was time for bed. Bunah was surprised that so much time had passed. Perhaps that was the effect of the unpleasant weather outside. As the oil in the lamp was already low and the Home-Sweet-Home lampshade was already partly opaque from the build-up of soot, Bunah made haste to prepare the children for bed. They had no special nightclothes. She got one of her old dresses for Henry. It did not matter whether the grandchild was a boy or a girl, he or she got a piece of the grandmother's clothing in which to sleep. There was no grandfather in this house, hence there were no men clothing available.

Henry in his grandmother's old dress looked like a diminutive priest with an oversized cassock. He was the first to climb the four-poster bed. Although the bed was only about three and a half feet high, most of the grandchildren had some difficulty climbing it. The younger ones were helped by older ones or by Bunah herself. Henry took his position to the back of the bed where it jammed against the wooden partition. Bunah slept at the front of the bed. She provided protection for the children from rolling off the bed. Once all seven grandchildren were in bed, Bunah took her position. Then, she lit her clay pipe and began to smoke the black tobacco she had grown at the back of the small shack that she used as the kitchen.

The 'Soucuyant", "Lajablesse" and "jumbie" stories were naturally scary for children but some Bible stories also had negative impacts. At first, Henry, Magnus and their cousins were scared by the stories and had difficulty falling asleep. Sometimes they would get nightmares. Henry remembered the time that he saw the end of the world with the skies opening and his grandmother and cousins floating away through the heavens and leaving him behind. It was scary. He cried and shook violently in his bed and ended up wetting it that night. It was the only time that he wet his bed. Later he thought of becoming a priest, such was the effect of the story of the end of the world.

Magnus recalled the story of the first time he slept in his grandmother's bed. It happened during the rainy season and the yard was cold and damp. Bunah and all her grandchildren went in early. The rain poured down, bucket a drop, the thunder rolled with one overlapping into the next. The lightning lit up the living room through the three glass windows on the northern and eastern sides of the old house. Magnus must have slept for a couple hours before he was awakened by a strange sound. He was not sure whether it was the dogs barking in the neighbourhood or a "Souyunant" trying to enter the house. He tried to keep his eyes closed with limited success. At the corner of a half opened eye, Magnus saw a tall woman leaning against the partition. He shook his grandmother who was enjoying her sleep as she dreamt about her children who had migrated and left their children in her care. Bunah assured her grandson that all was well and encouraged him to get back to sleep.

Next morning, Magnus looked in the direction of where he had seen the strange creature. There was only his grandmother's church dress hanging on a nail on the partition. Above the dress was the church hat. There were no clothes cupboards or wardrobes and the 'going out' and church clothes were all hung up on nails or on a cord connected to two nails affixed to the partitions. During the night, the shadows created by the streaks of light from the kerosene lamp and those that radiated from the moonlight coming through the cracks in the wooden building produced images of funny looking creatures. They reminded him of the characters described during story telling time. The "lajablesse" that Magnus saw during the night was transformed when his grannie was all dressed up in her blue dress draped with multi-coloured glass beads and the Victorian church hat, mismatched with the dress and the white shoes. He was unaware that the clothes his grandmother was wearing was what he had seen during the night. As Bunah and Magnus began the walk to church that morning, it never dawned on the young Magnus that he was holding the hand of the "lagablesse" he had seen during the night. As he grew older, the stories seemed more farfetched and he believed in them less and less. His sleep became uninterrupted.

Henry, unlike most of his friends, had his paternal grandmother living a stone's throw away from Bunah. He was able to commute each mealtime between his mother's house and those of his grandmothers. That was particularly an exciting exercise on weekends and school holidays. He started with his meal at his own home then, he took a three-minute walk to his first grandmother's house. There he might get a bake, a piece of coo-coo or some coo-coo "puaw". If the meal was not ready, she always had something else to give him. That was typical of grandmothers; they would always anticipate a visit from the grandchildren and would sacrifice from their own meagre supplies to make the children happy. For example, a grandmother would keep a piece of roasted bake, sugar cake or roasted corn in her apron pocket to give to the children when they visited.

Once the situation was evaluated and he realised that he had received all that were available, Henry turned his attention elsewhere. Henry headed out to his second grandmother. This only required a one-and-a-half-minute trot. There he might receive a piece of cassava bread or a corn dumpling on a stick. The piece of stick broken from the nearest available tree, was used to prevent the hot dumpling from burning Henry's lips since it was taken from the pot before the meal was finished cooking.

Many children figured out early in life how to play their parents, particularly their mothers, against their grandmothers. Henry's mother complained that his grandmother spoilt him. When the mother said no the grandmother said yes. His mother knew that a spanking to Henry in the presence of Bunah never ended well. Once he escaped the grip of his mother's right hand and the cut-skin from the whip in her left hand, he would run to his grandmother for protection. Seldom did his grandmother consider him wrong or disobedient.

Instead, she would reprimand her daughter with a series of short phrases and questions, thus:

"You mad or what?

You want to kill the child?

That is enough!

Why you taking out your rage on the poor child?

You forget all the stupidness you do for me?"

Henry soon learnt that notwithstanding the protection that he would have received from his mother's hands, that his grandmother was nonetheless a benevolent disciplinarian. She was different to his mother and never scolded in vexation. She was always measured in her actions. She allowed things to settle down, and then she would call him and say:

"Henry today you very rude to your mother. You fret up when she speak to you. You ain't tell the truth. Wasn't you who break the dish?"

He responded, "Yes grandma"

Grandma: "So why did you lie?"

"I don't know grandma?"

"Well I go punish you. Tomorrow after school, you not playing with you friends. You must come home immediately. There is a fowl laying in the bush. You would go and look for the eggs"

She knew that this was good punishment, since he loved playing with his friends and did not like searching the bushes for fowl nests.

There were many lighter sides to the relationship between grannies and their grandchildren. Sometimes, what grannies did seemed to have meaning only to them. The younger grandchildren seemed to enjoy one exercise and Bunah was always grateful for that. Before the introduction of the iron comb, women, particularly grandmothers made many attempts to hide their true age. Perhaps this was a feature of women worldwide. Grandmothers, who were often in their mid-forties, hated the appearance of grey hair. As there were virtually no hairdressing facilities available, these older women utilised different approaches to remove traces of grey hair. It was in these cases that grandchildren came in handy. With the iron comb and dye, grandmothers began to straighten and dye their hair.

One method was by removing the grey hairs. While granny sat on a stone in the yard or a bench under the tamarind tree, many small hands would be searching for hairs that had turned grey during the week and pull them out one by one with their small fingers. Eventually, grannies would begin a process of self-balding. Continuous removal of these grey hairs gave them the appearance of *"sen-sen"* fowls.

A second method of appearing younger was for the grannies to dye their hair. The older granddaughters had that task. However, when granddaughters were not available grandsons would take the role of the homemade hairdresser. They mixed black dye with water in a dish then pasted it on the hair. The dye was left in the hair for a short while before it was rinsed out.

It was during one of the hair dressing episodes that Bunah chose to engage her grandson, Henry on the topic of marriage. Once his grandmother had found out about the pending departure of her grandson, she decided that it was time for her to give him a lecture on marriage. Growing up in Goat hill, both young men and women could have experienced one or more episodes of advice about the type of partner that was acceptable. Although Henry knew that the time would come when it would be his turn, he was not prepared when it came. He thought only of his girlfriend from another village, a good five miles from Goat Hill. Moreover, he never imagined that the advice would come through grandmother Bunah.

She was more restrictive than most of the other matriarchs on the subject of the selection of lifetime partners. There was no particular explanation except that she was the village counsellor on relationships. The situations that were encouraged were limited. For Bunah, marrying up, that is, marrying into a family that was financially better off was a criterion at the top of the list. For example, although St. H was in love with one of her daughters and was a steady young man, she pretended that she was not in approval. Nonetheless, he would be encouraged to carry out many of the tasks around her house which were usually assigned to a soon to be bridegroom. She would often reinforce his interest by saying, *"Work hard for the girl, St H. Boy, work hard for your girl."* However, later he realised that notwithstanding all his efforts and the encouragement that he received, he was never considered suitable because in the final exchange between him and his intended mother-in-law she said to him in a mocking manner, *"Wah you ain't go an meet the woman you have them children with."*

Just before Henry left, he had a one-on-one with his grandmother Bunah who initiated the conversation. It came out of the blues.

Bunah: *"Henry oi, so you going to travel one day so you have to promise me something."*

Henry: *"What is it Nah?"* and Henry waited with great anticipation to hear what he was to promise.

Bunah: *I aint want no pickie hair picnee, you hear me?" Ah see you going around Congo man daughter. You better know that you can't bring she in this family."*

Henry: *"Why Nah? But Nah she is a pretty girl."*

Henry teased his grandmother because he had his eyes fixed on a brown-skinned girl. Bunah did not know. If she had known, she would not have had this conversation. A girlfriend whose European ancestry was obvious would have met Bunah's skin colour and hair texture criteria but approval may not have been guaranteed since Goat Hill people considered below-side women, that is, women from the southern side of the island, fierce and controlling.

Bunah: *"She too black"*

Henry: *"But Nah, my sisters blacker than her."*

Bunah: *"Never mind, comb go break in she hair. Plus, Congo man people and them is a set a crazy people."*

Henry: *"But, I ain't know nobody belonging to Congo man family who crazy."*

Bunah: *"You don't know but she grandmother was crazy as a bat and she grand uncle kill himself. I ain't want no crazy people in this family, you hear me?"*

Henry: *"But ah hear that me uncle who went to Cuba to work was crazy too."*

Bunah: *"Never mind what you hear them covetous people around here saying. Is people who do him because he was very bright. He could'a become anything he wanted to be. Was the brightness that spoiled him".*

Henry became quiet as he internalised what his grandmother was saying.

Bunah: *"And you have to be careful with those girls who are Seven Day Adventist, they not good Christians. Remember that we is Anglican. Them Roman Catholics not too bad but people does have trouble marrying in them church if you not Roman Catholic. And as for them Baptists that does ring the bell and tie their heads with all kind of pretty colour cloth, is only Obeah them studying. But not all Baptist bad, you know. But you see that one, Mercy, next door to your Auntie by the coconut tree, be careful with she and she daughters. She hand well dirty. You see how them, she first two girls' husbands turn ting in the place?"*

Henry, being unprepared for this, was naturally restless but he had no choice but to listen.

Bunah: *"I see ah Grenadian boy eyeing you auntie. When she come I have to tell she I aint want no Grenadian in this family. Them is the worst kind a people. Me grandaunt and Diahee get married to Grenadian man and they catch their nen nen. Grenada man does make Goat Hill woman eat the bread the devil knead.*

Is ok if ah Goat Hill man married a Grenadian woman and brings her up here. So boy, if you get a Grenadian girl she better have good hair that won't break comb and you must not live in Grenada with she. Bring she up here. *We could keep an eye on her. You know them Grenadian woman eyes too long, so you have to be careful."*

Henry: *"So Nah what's about the men from St Vincent?"*

Bunah: *"I don't know between the Vincey and Grenadian who better. Vincey man does kill their wife. Them is ah set ah hangmen."*

The conversation ended abruptly as it had started. Bunah's assessments were not always right as Henry later learnt, but she gave them repeatedly with great conviction. She hoped that Henry would take her advice seriously. Soon his journey would begin.

Following the death of Bunah and the migration of Henry, a younger set of grandchildren enjoyed the love and protection of Madevine. It was the turn of George and Nicholas to sleep with her, as she was now the only adult occupant of the house. The boys had a routine. Just before sundown, they had their dinner at their mother's house and headed for central Goat Hill. Madevine who they fondly called I. A., always left their second dinner for them. That was one of the advantages of having grandmothers around. Children could have a double of every meal, particularly on weekends and school holidays.

Madevine was sometimes crude in the way she spoke to the boys but they understood that she meant no harm. Often she would annoy Nicholas in the manner in which she offered him dinner.

She would say, *"Come boy! Yaa! You ole gorilla"* and then handed the bowl or plate of food to Nicholas.

He would respond, *"Me is no dog. I ain't want u food"*

He would refuse to take the food. When Nicholas was hungry, he would make the same fuss but eventually he would take the food from where Madevine had placed it on the right hand side of the small wooden table in the living room. For George, it did not matter how Madevine offered his food to him. He ate it, always. In fact, he was excited when Nicholas refused because it meant that he got a second serving by default. He always found room in his belly for anything extra.

Once dinner was over and the boys had washed their feet, it was time to lie on the floor at the side of Madevine's bed to listen to her stories. Madevine had a way of telling stories, most of which were based on activities of her peers in the village. She told the boys about those delinquent and lazy boys who grew up to be 'nothing'. Sometimes she shared with the boys some of her inner thoughts on everyday issues or challenges that she had experienced during the day. For example, one night, 'out of the blue', she called out to Nicholas without really intending to do so and said, *"Nicholas oh! You know, I just realise wha I should'a say to Iris".*

Nicholas was unsure what his grandmother was talking about, except that for the past week she had complained about not receiving her money from Iris.

With some curiosity in his voice, he asked, *"I.A, wha u should'a say to Iris?"*

I.A. responded, *"I should'a say to she, Iris oh! All that cock you take you couldn't even lay a small egg but you complaining me eggs too small".*

Iris had used the excuse that the eggs she had purchased from Madevine were too small, and she was unwilling to pay for them.

Madevine's sojourn with grandchildren was a long one. Grandchildren out-grew their grandparent's house at about age fourteen. After Nicholas and George came a new group, Albert, his brothers and cousins. The interaction between grandmother and grandchildren was organic in nature and changed slightly with every new group. Madevine had always been busy taking care of most of her needs by herself, but as she got older, she depended more on her grandchildren. To the grands, she was becoming more 'miserable' as she required more help from them in running errands or doing things around the house. Albert was the favourite. He would comply most times with Madevine's requests. Occasionally, Albert would conveniently forget to go to JB's shop to 'trust' two 'Phensic' tablets for his grandmother. This would get her into a rage but she would soon quiet down. Unbeknown to her, Albert even at a young age, disliked going to the village shops to 'trust' items or to go to the neighbour to borrow a coconut. He was somewhat naïve and ignorant of the economic reality of many homes in the village that were living 'hand to mouth'.

Generally, the boys had learnt to invent excuses for avoiding the tasks assigned by their grandmother. These excuses, however, disappeared when there were adequate inducements of food, a small change or 'sweet-talk' (commendations). To minimise the amount of assignments that they must respond to, Albert's group arrived just after dark except on Saturdays. The complaint of headache by Albert, all week, to avoid going to his grandmother's house to sleep vanished on Saturday. The thought of smelling and eating freshly baked bread and buns was a great 'pain-killer'. Saturday was the baking day and to benefit properly the boys arrived early when the sun was still out and just as the first set of bread came out of the oven. They would be present when the buns went in the oven. The boys never understood why she did not put everything in together as there was always enough space. Later on in life Albert and his mates understood more about heat transfer and that bread and buns behaved differently in the dirt oven.

Like the boys before them, Albert and his group were mischievous. They would play pranks on Madevine. During a humid night, which was not infrequent, Madevine would fan herself with pieces of cardboard or 'celotex'. The 'celotex' was also used for spanking the misbehaving boys. When she wanted to sleep and the boys were still monkeying around on the floor where they slept, she would shout at them and sometimes in a rage would throw the piece of 'celotex' at them in the dark. Most times, she missed her targets and the boys would confiscate it and hide it under their pillows. One night, Albert caught the piece of celotex and hid it under his pillow. When she went looking for it, Albert directed her to one of the other boys. She was suspicious, and searched under his pillow and found it. After giving him a few smacks, she said to him, "You secret murderer". This was how Albert got one of his nicknames, which lasted for a few months.

Although it appeared that grandmothers paid greater attention to their grandsons, close bonds also existed between grandmothers and granddaughters. Henry's youngest sister was particularly close to her grandmother. On one occasion, the grandmother got a 'draught' from changing her clothes with the window opened after a hard day's work in the garden. The cold or the flu that she caught resulted in her being bed stricken for a few days. The granddaughter, Linda, who was only about five years old at the time, knew of the circumstance that led to her grandmother's illness. This was the first time that she had seen her grandmother sick. She was saddened. To show empathy with her grandmother, Linda, one afternoon after school opened the window so that the breeze could enter, removed her clothes and remained in the breeze for a few minutes. By bedtime, she too was coming down with a cold or flu and next day she was unable to go to school. She remained at home and cuddled up close to her grandmother. That continued for two days. Linda had not been happier in her life. She got sick to be close to her grandmother.

Some children came to their grandmothers on holidays from other islands. Peter, who was born in Goat Hill, went to Trinidad as an infant. He visited his grandmother on three occasions before he was ten. His mother placed him on one of the wooden boats that sailed the choppy seas during August. Although Peter was seasick on all the occasions that he travelled, he was never perturbed about the trips because spending time with his grandmother and his cousins was more fun than he would experience if he remained in Point Fortin, Trinidad. As a grandchild not domiciled in Goat Hill, Peter got special treatment. His grandmother did not neglect the other grandchildren, but she reminded them that they had her all year round. Peter got the biggest mangoes, the ripest plums and when at nights he was sure to have a spot on the bed closest to his grandmother. On his last trip to Goat Hill before her passing, Peter used his pocket change to purchase a cheap silver bracelet for her. This bond between them was unbreakable and exemplified the power of a grandmother on the psyche of her grandchildren.

While most grandmothers had a positive effect on their grandchildren, some grandchildren resented their grandparents. Some grandchildren were treated like slaves, working from sunrise to sundown. They carried out chores best suited to others twice their ages. They were flogged as much as children who worked on the slave plantations many decades earlier. Often the unexplained behaviour shown towards children by their grandmothers may have been manifestations of their own suffering during childhood. In few cases, where there was no intervention when that happened in families, the cycle continued for generations. However, in other cases, the excessive pampering observed was due to a deliberate effort by grandmothers who had suffered, to break the sorry cycle. Generally, grandmothers tried to overcome their own guilt for being inadequate mothers to their own children. Whatever the explanation, in Goat Hill, grandmothers were some of the most important people in the lives of children.

5

Festival times and Goat Hill's children

CHILDREN CONTRIBUTED TO the family by doing their fair share of work. Seldom was a child abused resulting from excessive work or deprived of attending school. Despite all the routine chores, there were festive times and they looked forward to them. These included Christmas, carnival, Easter, Big Pond Maroon, Regatta and sometimes the occasional stone feast. For elders, time went quickly, but for the children of Goat Hill, Christmas and the other festivals took too long to arrive.

5.1 Christmas

Christmas was a good time for everybody in Goat Hill. When it was around the corner, it was easy to know. The evenings became cooler as the northeast winds cooled by the early winter air from North America penetrated the nights. The days were shorter as the sun moved furthest away from the islands. All the corn, harvested by this time, had been dried in the sun on the rooftops. This was to avoid being feasted on by the chickens in the yard. The 'bukusu' (seim or hyacinth) beans and pigeon peas had begun to blossom and those who planted early were able to have rice and peas for Sunday lunch. Every pasture changed its colour from green to yellow as the grass reached a mature state with its flowers turning to seeds providing unlimited food for the birds. Grass was plentiful. The children left the cattle tethered to one spot for a day, thereby reducing the amount of effort required in caring for their animals. Notwithstanding the reduced attendance by owners, the skeleton frames of all the animals: sheep, goats, cattle and donkeys, whether loose or tethered, were covered by muscle and fat. Milk production increased since the cows ate to their full contentment. There was no need to purchase imported food for the pigs as the villagers who were unable to consume all the okras and pumpkins, produced in large quantities, used the excess to feed them.

The chickens in the yard supplemented their daily ration of cracked corn from their owners with un-harvested corn in the fields, butterflies' larvae, and the multitude of flowers and seeds from other plants. They laid eggs in spots they considered convenient and safe. Popular locations were underneath the house, in grass lines and fence lines, and under boulders that provided protection. Sometimes they would use a dark corner on the inside of the house or the kitchen. Once the children found nests before egg-sucking dogs and manicou did, they could have a feast for breakfast. The children also collected eggs and secured them for the Christmas cakes, which were mainly, sponge and fruitcakes.

Christmas time was the best time to sell the animals reared during the year. As grass was plentiful during the months before Christmas, the animals reached maximum weight, and could fetch the highest possible price. The money collected from any sale could pay for some of the things that parents needed.

At this time, berries, a plant known by names such as Jujube (Chinese) and downs, dunks or dungs in other parts of the Caribbean produced a wonderful fruit. Unlike its flowers, which produced a faeces-like smell during the pre-dawn hours, the berries were delicious. It was also good for making a wine that smelt like 'peardrax'. It was a plant introduced to the Caribbean region. In the village, there was a tree by Lizie's Copper. It produced the sweetest fruits. There were two other trees. These produced smaller fruits that were slightly acidic in taste. As the legend goes, a Bajan called Mr Rocke brought the first Jujube plant to Goat Hill. He visited the village not intending to stay for long but eventually settled there.

The days leading up to Christmas in the year that George turned ten were happy days. Food was in abundance. Corn porridge, plain coo-coo, coo-coo and peas (coo coo-pau) coo-coo with pumpkin, coo-coo and okras, peas-soup, fried eggs, sour milk and homemade butter were all available. Coo-coo is a dish from corn flour, which has its origins in West Africa. Only two lazy families who hated working the lands were without plenty from their gardens. However, they bartered the fish the husbands caught for produce from the neighbours' gardens.

For the older villagers, Christmas came too quickly. Della would say, *"You ain't turn around good yet and Christmas is back already. It shows how fast we are getting old"*. When George was about five, like other children his age, for them, Christmas took a long time to return. George and his young friends planned all year for the coming of Christmas and would ask their parents almost every month, "When is Christmas coming?" At ten George remembered the happy times from the previous years. He longed for Christmas, but this year would not be the same. He would have more chores to do than before. His cousin Henry had migrated during the year and, since in his grandmother's home he was the oldest boy now, he was to be the 'man-in-the-house'.

George's tasks started immediately at the beginning of the two weeks of the Christmas holidays. During the first week, his tasks were predictable. He went to check on his grandmother's cow and the dozen sheep and goats. He then had breakfast. He looked forward to breakfast since he would have two bowls of corn porridge with plenty of milk or fried coo-coo with two fried eggs and a cup of cocoa tea.

After breakfast, he and some of the other village boys, accompanied by three of the mothers, climbed the hills above the village to collect firewood. Collecting firewood during this period was more difficult than during the dry season, since the overgrowths in the forest hid the dry wood. The lush green trees with entangled vines, some of which caused itching when they made contact with the bare skin, were a deterrent to the boys so that they did not venture too deep into the bushes. They scouted by walking along the tracks, sometimes having to use their cutlasses to make easier passages. That first week of the holidays, George and his friends took about four to five hours each day to collect sufficient dry wood to make a bundle that was acceptable to their mothers. George had an added responsibility. In addition to securing wood for his home, he was required to collect an extra bundle to give to the elderly couple, Eva and her one-legged husband. Although he hated this additional work, he comforted himself with the thought of the fifty cents compensation at Christmas. That would initiate his savings for the upcoming carnival.

On his return from the hills, George listened to the chickens' cackle. He tracked the location of the cackling emanating from the surrounding garden, and scouted the immediate area for a nest. He had been doing this for the past ten days. He did not have sufficient time to use the alternative technique for locating the laying hideout of the chickens. Other children in the village, who had more time on their hands, located the laying sites for the chickens by following them around. Finding the nests was usually a game of 'hide and seek' between the chickens and the children. When the egg became too hot for the hen to keep, it was forced to dash for its hiding place. George found the nesting places of two hens. According to his grandmother, these belonged to him. George took his ownership seriously and felt that he had the authority to determine the use of the eggs. However, he knew better than to voice such an opinion.

The number of eggs in the nest varied from two to about twelve. Sometimes more than one hen used a particular nest. George took eggs from each nest, hid the four largest before taking the rest to his grandmother. George was so innocent looking at the time when he handed over the eggs, that his grandmother did not suspect that they were only part of George's collection. Those that he hid, he would boil when the opportunity arose and that was when his grandmother and his grandaunt left the house.

Nearly every child in the village owned one or two hens identified as his. That was only in name as no child could determine what to do with the eggs that their chickens laid or if a chicken should be slaughtered for the Sunday meal. Yet it was natural for children to lay claim and to take great pride in giving their chickens extra food at any opportunity. Unlike George, they understood this virtual ownership and when they collected eggs from the nest they took all to their mothers or grandmothers. In removing eggs from a nest, there was one thing that George had to keep in mind. Eight or nine eggs must remain for the chicken to sit on. In that way, a child's ownership of chickens increased during the months that followed Christmas.

At the end of the first week of the holidays, George and his sisters had collected enough wood that would last until after Christmas. The bulk of the wood would be used for the Christmas and New Year's baking and for boiling imported ham on Christmas Eve. George and his sisters then focused on filling all the drums and barrels with water from the communal cistern. That year, it was not as difficult as previous years since the rain had fallen almost every night during the first week of the holidays. As a result, most of the drums and barrels were filled or contained substantial amounts of water. For the rest of the days up to Christmas Eve, George and his sisters were required to make only one trip per day to the communal cisterns, when there was no rain or the rain was minimal.

Generally, at nights, during the Christmas holiday, George and the other children slept soundly. They were usually too tired from the increased daily chores. Consequently, for most nights, George missed the serenading bands, which visited his home as they moved from house to house in the village. These singing bands were often an ad hoc group of villagers. Serenading bands or Hosanna bands, as they were called, sang Christmas carols accompanied by musical instruments. They expected a small token for their efforts. Few band members had any voice training while the musicians were all self-trained. Since there was minimal practice beforehand, in most cases, the renditions of the two most popular songs "Silent night" and "We wish you a merry Christmas" were generally out of tune. Moreover, in many cases, some members demonstrated lack of knowledge of the carols and they misplaced and mispronounced words and phrases. Elfick led the best band. His band had mainly mature persons. Some were from the church choir and included men who played musical instruments including guitars, banjos, mouthorgans, shak-shak and Quatro. Elfick played the violin. Sullivan's was a one-man band. He was good at playing the Quattro and harmonica simultaneously and perfected his skills by performing at every opportunity: Christmas, carnival, weddings, launchings, birthday parties and at home when there was no formal function.

That Christmas was remembered for many things, but in particular the very cold nights. The cold nights was one of the reasons why George slept so soundly. Wrapped in his grandmother's old dress, he did not even venture outside to urinate on the edge of the garden as he normally did when outside was warmer. So cold were the nights that when 'serenaders' exhaled they saw 'smoke' as the hot air condensed when it encountered the cold night breeze. Yet, 'serenaders' braved the nights, and endured the shivering or the knocking of teeth to ensure that they visited every home. They experienced temporary relief when over-proofed rum, which was offered at almost every home, was drunk. Before leaving home, however, as a protective measure, the men sometimes wore jackets while the women wore one of the men's shirts over their dresses.

That year, Headley and Shines started a serenading band. They navigated their way one moonless night using an old torchlight in which the Ever Ready batteries were on their last leg. Shines borrowed his uncle's guitar, Headley used an old pitch oil tin as the drum, Augustus played the shak-shak and Patrick played the harmonica. Before getting into the renditions, Shines introduced the band:

> *"Good night to the master and mistress who dwell within this wonderful mansion. We are the magicians from the East. We have travelled over mountains and valleys, through rain and cold to bring glad tidings in this holy season on the birth of the Lord Jesus Christ. Christmas is the time for giving."*

There were many versions of the introduction by the different groups. Often they made up the lines as they went along. With that introduction by Shines, the group started its presentation. They were not good musicians and the little practice that occurred over two sessions was evident when they visited the homes in the village. Both their vocals and their instruments were out of tune. Instead of singing, they appeared to be reciting, making up words and verses as they went along. They performed four numbers then made their departing speech:

> *"To the generous master and mistress of this house, may you be blessed for your generosity. May your children and grandchildren rise up to call you blessed and May your cup runneth over in this seas."*

Like the introduction, the farewell was also a version with common and made up phrases. Notwithstanding the deficiencies of this all-boys group, they were able to collect a total of eight dollars over twelve nights. They used two dollars to replace batteries twice and the rest went to their carnival slush fund.

Four days before Christmas, it was time to repair his grandmother's wattle-and-dab kitchen and the dirt oven. The repairs had to be completed at least three days before Christmas to ensure that it was ready for the first baking. After breakfast, George and the other boys would head to the "white-dirt" pit. The "white dirt' was a chalk-like clay based soil, found at two spots on private property in the village. George had to walk about half a mile to collect his "white dirt". The owners of the estate lived in the USA and Norma who rented a lot from them, on which her house was built, gave permission to her friends to take the white dirt. No one questioned her authority. Since George's grandmother was a good friend, he had easy access. The dirt was excavated using a fork and was carted away in buckets. He would make three or four trips carrying dirt for the day. Then two days before Christmas it was time to repair the oven and give the wattle-and-dab kitchen a makeover.

To do the repairs, cattle dung was an essential resource. During the second week of the vacation, George and his sisters got up early in the morning and went to the different places where all the village cattle were tethered overnight. That ensured that they would be the first since what they were in search of was in greatest demand at this time of the year. They collected fresh cattle dung and took it home. Cattle dung was used to mix with the white dirt and water to create a mortar which, when dried, possessed great binding properties.

Dudley first worked on the repairs to the kitchen. The holes left from the shelling of old mortar due to wear and tear were filled. In areas where the wall appeared weak and were likely to break-off soon, Dudley used an old piece of cutlass to remove all the old mortar and replaced it with fresh mortar. The fresh dirt mortar was slapped onto the wattle frames in a similar manner as when Dudley worked on concrete buildings with cement plaster. The dirt mortar stuck to the wattle frame as concrete does to steel frames in modern buildings. Dudley smoothed the new mortar with his bare hands after sprinkling some water on the area. He then applied a thin layer of mortar on the eastern wall. He repeated the process on the other three walls. When he had finished his work of art, he left a semi-water proof wall that emitted the smell of the cattle dung for a few days. The following day, Dudley mixed white dirt with water creating a white wash, which he applied to the walls of the wattle-and-dab kitchen. The fresh white paint substitute gave the building a new look. A look that was fitting for Christmas.

Every Christmas some attention was given to the dirt oven. The oven, when it was built, took some skill. Only a few men in the village had mastered the art of building ovens. Dudley was one of those masters. He began by digging a shallow rectangular hole about eight feet away from the kitchen. He packed some boulders in the hole to a height of about two and a half feet. Smaller boulders were then placed in the gaps and were kept in place using the white dirt mortar. The base of the oven was then fitted with pieces of red clay bricks, which were obtained from the sites of the old stone and brick houses built during the time of slavery. The red clay bricks, which originated from England, were known to keep heat for a considerable time. The roof of the oven was built of stone and white dirt mortar, with pieces of discarded corrugated metal sheets that once covered the roofs of some of the village houses holding everything together. There were two openings in the oven, one at the front through which wood was put in, and one to the side through which the ash and burnt wood were removed before putting in the bread, buns and cakes.

For that Christmas, the dirt oven only need minor repairs. The amount of work for the oven repair was at a minimum as Dudley had built it just before the previous Christmas. He completed the repairs that time in half a day.

The chores in preparation for Christmas were well distributed among the children. The job of scrubbing the wooden floor in preparation for polishing was assigned to the girls. Although all the floors were scrubbed, only the living room was polished using Mansion Polish. Polishing was left for Christmas Eve, as all the shine would be still visible to visitors on Christmas day. Visitors were not invited into the living room but were allowed to admire the shine through the open door or window. Access to the house was even limited to the occupants of the house, for the first day and a half, and George had to ensure that his feet were properly cleaned before entering his grandmother's living room. When he did, he had to tiptoe to minimise the number of marks that were left on the mahogany coloured floor.

The floors were not the only things polished. In his grandmother's home there were four Morris chairs, a sofa and a basin stand which were made from mahogany wood. The sofa and the basin stand were over eighty years old, and were much darker in colour than the chairs. These were sanded by two of George's cousins, who were day visitors to the house. The cousins meticulously sanded each piece of furniture, then varnished them with a clear vanish mixed with kerosene so that the application was easier. When the clear varnish was dried, the chairs matched the polished floor. The recently changed window curtains together with the polished surroundings provided an enhanced décor, which was one of the hallmarks of Christmas in Bunah's home.

Next door, at George's elderly neighbours, there were no sofa and Morris chairs. The floor was thoroughly scrubbed but not polished. The curtains were washed and were placed at the windows. There were no new curtains that year. They could not afford new ones. To improve the décor on the small wooden house, Eva obtained some old newspaper and in place of wallpaper, pasted them onto the wooden partition using cassava-based homemade starch. When she was finished each article could be clearly read, but that was not important because both husband and wife were illiterate. Eva admired the black and white photos that accompanied the articles. That facelift of the partition would remain in place until the following Christmas.

The Christmas preparation climaxed on Christmas Eve. Ervin slaughtered a small bull; Decca, Maude, Eastin and Clarabelle slaughtered pigs; and nearly all other households slaughtered a sheep or a goat. The pigs were slaughtered almost simultaneously. The squealing noises that came from the different points seemed to have emanated from one location. The noises in the quiet of the wee hours of the morning woke George and he jumped out of bed.

Ervin had informed the villagers since early August about his intention to kill the bull, which he was rearing under the calabash tree, and had prepared a list of customers who had ordered from one pound to eight pounds of beef. He sold about half of the meat. He gave his friends, relatives and the helpers about a half of the remainder, keeping what was left for his own home. Each helper got four pounds of meat plus a portion of the liver and lungs. The head was salted and placed on the kitchen roof for drying, and was later divided between Ervin and his brother. Decca, Eastin and Clarabelle also sold most of their pork and, like Ervin, distributed reasonable portions to friends and relatives. Only small portions of mutton and goat meat were sold and like the pork and beef, a significant quantity was shared with friends and relatives. In most cases, the suppliers of meat for Christmas did not receive payment immediately. Ervin, who had depended on payments in order to make his final Christmas shopping, was disappointed since he had sold sixty pounds of beef and collected only twelve dollars. The other meat suppliers did not fare better.

Maude and a few other wives made their last trip to town. They were late, as all the other homes had done their shopping earlier in the week. It was the last day for shopping. They needed to return before lunchtime to complete the preparation before time ran out on them. They purchased, rice, flour and sugar by the eighty or hundred-pounds sacks; ham imported from North America or England; locally made coconut oil; margarine; raisins, currants, prunes and black wine for the fruit cakes; barley for the mutton soup; solo, juicy and red spot soft drinks, 'cydrax' and 'peardrax'. Although Maude's 'gospo' and lime trees were full of fruits, she could not offer visitors local juice at Christmas time. Her guests would "cry shame on her"; she had to offer drinks that were obtained from the store. In fact, if news went out that she was offering homemade juice the bands of children would by-pass her home on Christmas Day.

Madevine did not buy any soft drinks since she had made ginger beer. She was the best maker of ginger beer in the village and villagers would book one or two bottles from her for the season. Her ginger beer, which began fermenting from the end of November, was very strong. It was not popular among the children but was loved by the older women. The children, on the other hand, enjoyed Queen Anne's ginger beer. It was weak since it was only fermented for a couple of days. There was no sorrel drink that year. The sorrel crop was late in flowering. Madevine had attributed this to excess rain during the months preceding Christmas.

Maude and her friends purchased groceries at four main shops: Jacobs, Daniel, Bata and W. E. Julien. On completion, the wooden jitney circled the town twice picking up bags and boxes with the owner's names written on them in ink. In addition to groceries, Clarabelle purchased half dozen each of enamel plates, cups and spoons, two enamel bowls in which the soup was offered to visitors and five yards of vinyl floor covering. The floor covering with its different colourful patterns was used instead of floor polishing as it was considered more modern. Soon Big Andrew's jitney was full to capacity and headed to Goat Hill. At each gap, Big Andrew stopped and collected his fifteen cents from his passenger while the conductor off-loaded the women's boxes and bags. Maude checked her goods and being satisfied that everything was in order signalled to Big Andrew who pulled out and headed for the next stop. It was important to check the goods carefully because if a mistake was made, the goods would not be retrieved until two days after Christmas and somebody's Christmas would be spoilt. Maude waited for her children to come with the donkeys to carry the heavier items like the sacks of flour. The lighter items were carried on one's head or by hand.

Meanwhile, Bunah, assisted by her daughter and Aunt Madevine began her baking on Christmas Eve, just after midday. Wood was placed in the oven and the fire was lit. After about an hour and a half, a broom, made from small branches of the broom tree and tightly fastened at the end of a long stick, was used to push the ash and charcoal to the side opening. Once the base of the oven was clear, the buns, bread and cakes were placed in the oven using a long wooden pallet shaped like one of Huriel's wooden oars. The oven was then closed using a small square door and sealed with some old pieces of wet cloth around the edges. That allowed the oven to remain hot for longer.

By six o'clock, the first batch of bread and cakes was ready. They were removed making the oven available to Eva and the other neighbours. To improve the heat in the oven for the next set of baking a new fire, smaller than the original was started. At the same time, George's grandmother started the boiling of the salted ham in a pitch oil tin. The ham covered with water to about three quarters of the tin, was boiled for approximately an hour before the pickled water was thrown out and replaced with fresh water. The water was changed three times before the ham was ready, usually about midnight. The final touch was to stick a few heads of cloves in small incisions made by the kitchen knife.

There would be no midnight mass for Bunah. She was too tired from all the cleaning and baking to make the two and a half mile return trip on foot. Other villagers, who had done their baking the day before and advanced their other chores, went to the midnight church services in the Anglican or the Catholic churches. Bunah placed the baked goods on the table in the living room and covered it with a clean white tablecloth, which was not used since the previous Christmas. George and the other children got a piece of hot bread with some salted margarine. It tasted good and, given a chance, the children would have eaten most of the bread that night. They were never satisfied with the hot bread and margarine that they were given. Bunah knew that their appetites opened widely with the smell and taste of fresh hot bread and margarine and warned them that what was on the table must last until the New Year. At New Year, a new round of baking was undertaken.

Finally, Christmas Day came. George, like most other children got up early and carried out his main task for the day taking care of his animals in the pasture. By six-fifteen George was back at home. His grandmother was busy in the kitchen. The breakfast was stewed liver that came with the meat sent by Ervin, bread baked the night before and pasted with homemade butter, a thin slice of ham and a large cup of spiced cocoa tea with added fresh milk. The ham was miserly shared on Christmas morning, as there was other meat. In any case, the ham would be under strict control for a few weeks. It was often offered to visitors to impress them. Further, it must last as long as possible.

As soon as George was finished with his breakfast, he had a quick wash, and put on the clothes that he had received from his aunt a week before. The parcel that brought George's clothes had also brought clothes and shoes for all his cousins. His grandmother got a lovely dress that was oversized and a hat similar to that which the Queen had worn on her trip to Australia. Max had made that observation.

Once dressed, Bunah gave George a cheap harmonica and a balloon with three feathers, yellow blue and green. Toy guns, flutes, whistles and harmonicas were typical gifts for boys; blonde dolls were favourites for the girls while balls and balloons were given to both boys and girls. With his toys in hand, George began his Christmas visits. He started with the old couple from whom he anticipated collecting at least fifty cents. Although he had just eaten breakfast, he did not refuse the cake and solo soft drink offered to him. Everywhere he went that morning the offering was the same: a piece of cake and a glass of soft drink. By the time he got to his friend Allan's house, he was full but the mutton soup, which was being prepared at Allan's house smelt so good that he decided to hang around until food was offered to him. He knew that he had his rice and peas and stewed pork at home, but that could wait for supper. Parents always liked their children to eat their food before that of the neighbours, but on Christmas Day that was not possible. Children ate wherever lunchtime found them.

As lunch was being served at Allan's house, a group of 'serenaders' entered the yard. About fifteen children accompanied the band. Altogether, there were twenty-two persons. Allan's mother realised that if one person asked for soup, she would not have enough to go around for the visitors, George and her family. She took the pot off the fire and closed the kitchen door. She then brought out a bottle of rum, a bottle of 'peardrax' and pieces of stewed pork that were prepared the previous evening. The musicians began drinking the rum, which they chased with Red Spot soft drinks. The band seemed to take a permanent position in the yard, delaying the sharing of the soup to family members. Realising that he would not be getting any soup soon, George hurried back home where he ate the food prepared by his mother and helped himself to a Solo soft drink.

Just as he was finished eating his lunch, a group of his father's friends arrived. It was evident that they had started the celebrations a few hours earlier. His father brought a jimmy john of red rum, a pitcher with water and half a dozen tumblers. Among the visitors was one of his father's sworn enemies. However, at Christmas villagers let bygones be bygones. Both men greeted each other as if they were bosom friends. All the men were rum drinkers. In less than an hour, the jimmy john was empty. The men played a few old calypsos relating to Christmas, then 'we wish you a merry Christmas" as a signal of their departure. Half the number of men were very drunk by that time, yet they moved to the next house.

While the men and children celebrated and partied, the wives and daughters were marooned at home preparing the food, cleaning up after the men ate, and ensuring that any disorderly guest did not enter the house to soil the polished floors. Luckily, that year there was no rain; hence, the verandas on which most of the entertainment took place remained relatively clean during the day. The only mishap at Bunah's house was the spilling of soft drink intended for chasing the rum by her drunk cousin. As was observed in every other home, Bunah did not show any displeasure as she laboured to clean up as the men continued their drinking.

There were no presents shared among villagers on Christmas Day. That was not part of the custom. The only Christmas cards were those received from relatives abroad. They shared meat the day before and that was the best gift. The sharing of food and drinks, and the environment of peace and goodwill that hung over the village made the celebrations memorable for young children.

Christmas Day, now completed, led to Boxing Day and New Year's

Day weddings and village fairs. The next big celebration for the children of Goat Hill would be carnival. George got up late the morning after Christmas and headed straight to the latrine. He needed to expel all that food that he had eaten the day before. His brother was in there, so he found an alternative, the big black stone that was prevented from rolling downhill by the giant tamarind tree. George relieved himself and pulled a few cotton leaves to wipe himself. There was no washing of hands, although this was taught at school. He then visited his Godmother, Violet. She gave him a fifty-cent piece and a shirt that she sewed herself. She asked him to try on the shirt, which fitted perfectly. He then drank his first soft drink for the day, ate a slice of his Godmother's sponge cake and returned home to show off his shirt to his siblings. Later that day, he caught up with some of his friends and together they visited those houses that missed on Christmas day. Some of the boys were visiting some homes for a second time, but that was okay. That was a good Christmas for him. He got toys, a shirt and ate his belly full. George wore his new shirt and headed to the neighbouring village where a wedding was taking place.

Sullivan was playing his Quatro and harmonica and the crowd sang repeatedly:

"Way Ervin dey? Evrin bam-bam we want to sada Way Ervin dey? he bam-bam we want to sada".

Everybody knew that line. It was the easiest to remember during a wedding celebration. That night George went home and counted his money. He was ready for carnival but prayed that Christmas would not take as long the next time to come.

5.2 CARNIVAL

Carnival in Goat Hill developed during the post slavery period in a similar way to the other islands. Its origin was tied to its colonial past, the influence of European and African religions, an expression of defiance to injustice and a celebration of freedom. It provided the opportunity for the freed Africans and their descendants to mimic their former masters, reciprocating their actions which were meant to denigrate owners. Over time, the importance of the traditions in carnival diminished to be transformed to a time of just simple enjoyment. The occasional movement of some of the villagers between Goat Hill and Point Fortin, in Trinidad, provided the medium through which the new features of carnival reached Goat Hill. Consequently, the stick mas, the calypsos, the ideas for pretty mas and the steel pan music gradually made their way to Goat Hill.

While adults were the main stakeholders of carnival, children enjoyed it as much as the elders, when they were allowed to actively participate. They often created their own activities by mimicking the elders. Creative children tried to duplicate the steel pan by using sets of one-pound empty milk cans, margarine cans and biscuit tins. The flat surfaces of these tins were heated and were hammered to produce distinct sounds. Although the boys were unfamiliar with the concept of tuning pans and had no training in music, creating the different notes seemed to come naturally.

Not everyone took part in carnival. Clarence and his family prayed and fasted during the carnival period. They were Seventh Day Adventists. Some other families considered carnival to be vulgar and unholy and to be a creation of the devil. There were also the staunch Catholics and Anglicans who propagated the idea of the satanic origins of carnival. For all these people, it was therefore taboo to sing or whistle calypsos or even listen to calypso music during the period of Lent following the carnival season.

Activities lasted from Sunday with 'camboulay' and ended midnight on Tuesday, bringing in the Lenten season. On Ash Wednesday, the Catholic tradition became alive again shelving carnival until the next year. The parishioners or the churchgoers, headed in the direction of the Catholic Church in Windward and the Anglican Church in

Hillsborough where the priests administered a cross on the forehead using ashes. Henry always wondered about the source of the ashes, as the priests' residence had no wood firesides. Was this a special type of ashes imported from England? Henry had worked out early that the ritual was taken seriously, as they kept the cross of ashes for a whole week thereafter. He pondered on what might have been the true meaning of this ritual to the parishioners since most of them were semi-illiterate.

Camboulay

Carnival Sunday brought the first communal signs as carnival became evident. It was a time when the young men reached a climax in their preparation and truly commenced the festivities. While the preparation for carnival generally started about two or three weeks before the carnival, for many, particularly the children, it started with 'camboulay' night. On 'camboulay' night, the boys cooked and sang or chanted old calypsos. They blew their conch shells for most of the night disturbing the peace. The villagers tolerated the disturbances. Even a little drunkenness by teenaged boys went unpunished by parents and guardians sometimes.

For that night, some boys led by Headley operated the most desired group. There were other informal groups. In each group, there was a core, which was usually homogenous in some fashion. Boys outside the core found groups to fit into since they quickly learnt where they were not wanted. Although there was, in many cases, no formal selection criteria for the groups, boys of similar age within a two-year range or at the same level at school, belonged to the same group. In addition, there were groups based on membership of the cricket team, the football team or the village youth group and all tended to celebrate separately. In rare cases were there mixed gender participation in 'camboulay' night activities. Mixed gender participation occurred, for example, when the village youth group celebrated together. For a few years, 'camboulay' for the village youth group was an opportunity for young couples to consummate their love relationships. The last village 'camboulay' cook resulted in three teenaged pregnancies and two subsequent weddings. Since then, parents were reluctant to give consent for another youth club 'camobulay' cook, except under the watchful eyes of the girls' protectors.

The main activity on 'camboulay' night was the cooking of the 'Camboulay Pot'. Generally, that did not require superior culinary skills. The approach was always pragmatic and simple which meant a single pot in which everything was cooked together. Occasionally, the quality of the food was given high ratings by the older women who were fortunate enough to get a taste. The simplest dish was the fish broth or a seafood cook-up. Seafood was the simplest and preferred choice where boys had access to sea products through their involvement in fishing. Then there was rice and peas with stewed meat (chicken or local wild meat). That required more attention than the fish broth therefore the main cook ought to have demonstrated some ability prior to the occasion. Finally, there could be peas-soup using green pigeon peas or green 'bukusu' beans with salted meat. The ingredients for the cook would be gathered over a number of days prior to Carnival Sunday.

At first, it seemed that the planning for the night may have been trivial, but a deeper look soon established that good project management was required in executing a good 'Camboulay Night'. Headley, who was Henry's good friend, was one of the best project managers for 'Camboulay Night'. He produced the most memorable 'Camboulay Night' dish using his skills to have on site all the right ingredients and selecting the right people for different tasks. Headley's group comprised a mixture of cricket club members and the class seven of the village primary school. Standard Seven was the terminal class for primary education in Goat Hill. Headley and Patrick who had repeated the class twice were nineteen years old but it was not unusual to find a twenty-year-old in Class Seven. Such then were the ages of the leaders cooking for 'camboulay'.

Headley and his management team met under the big berries

tree by the Copper. For a week, Headley with three of his teammates and two of his sisters planned. It was to be the first such 'camboulay' cook, which started as what appeared to be idle talk about putting on this cook about two weeks before the carnival. Other groups of boys planned while sitting by the roadside grazing their animals or on the pavement in the open area of the schoolhouse after an evening of running about on the playground.

Headley and Patrick's planned menu was a green-peas soup. Money was required for some of the ingredients. The boys pooled together their savings and solicited funds from their relatives. Not all relatives gave, hence Headley and Patrick targeted older siblings and the more philanthropic among the others. Some persons did not give money but donated a pound of flour, two coconuts or some black pepper. Every evening leading up to carnival, members reported to Headley and Patrick about their success in their solicitation and the potential for new funds. That year the funds trickled in, at only a few cents at a time. Headley and Patrick however, were confident that their 'camboulay' slush fund would be healthy by Carnival Sunday.

There was also a plan for non-monetary contributions. These came mainly from the boys' homes and generally, they took them without their parents' consent. Sometimes, targeted participants were invited specifically to provide the 'hard to obtain' items for the cook. For example, as Allan's parents peas bore well that year, Headley and Patrick developed a scheme to get Allan to join the group. If successful, this would ensure that the pigeon peas, 'bukusu' beans and perhaps the salted meat would be available in the desired quantities. The sweet potatoes, cassava and pumpkin were to come from Headley's family garden. It was okay to take as many pumpkins as required since that year pumpkins were available in large quantities and ultimately most would be used for feeding the pigs. Headley decided that his younger cousin would be responsible for procuring the cassava and potatoes from the field. The advice was to undertake the task, under the cover of picking cotton. This was not too difficult as Nicholas was used to going to the garden by himself, so there would be no suspicion when he carried out this task. The most difficult part of the job was to camouflage the area where the ground provision was removed. He would have to get at the sweet potatoes and cassava, without dislodging the vines or sticks.

The possible sources for the meat for 'camboulay' varied. There would be home-prepared salted pork, salted mutton and salted beef. These would have been leftovers from the Christmas season. The only home where there was leftover Christmas salted meat was Allan's home. However, he had shown no interest in providing more than the pigeon peas for that year's cook. Unfortunately, there was not enough money in the slush fund to purchase the salted pork or beef from the village shop. As a result, Headley and Patrick decided to go hunting for iguanas and manicous (opossum) as substitutes. They caught two iguanas and one manicou. However, this was not enough for all the people expected at their 'camboulay' celebration. Therefore, they hatched a plan to steal two chickens from Noel's grandmother flock. These would be captured where they rested for the night on the trees close to Noel's home. It was decided that the best time was about eight o'clock on Carnival Sunday night. At that time, the elderly woman who owned the chickens would be fast asleep since she never went to bed later than about seven-thirty and took ten to twenty minutes to fall asleep. Patrick caught the chickens himself. He had to ensure that there was minimum noise from the chickens during the process or he might be caught if the elderly woman was not yet asleep.

On Saturday night, Headley and Patrick counted the money in the slush fund. There was almost two dollars in the slush fund. That was enough to purchase some of the supplies that were not available from the gardens or from food boxes in which the boys' mothers stored their limited supplies. With the money collected, the boys could buy, at least, the flour, cooking oil, sugar, salt and other seasonings. The sugar was for making a lime squash or 'gospo' (sour orange) squash.

Headley had one secret source for meeting unforeseen needs. A few of the girls his age were romantically interested in him. He used this to his advantage. He frequently worked his magic on DJ. DJ lived with her adopted mother who ran one of the village shops from her downstairs. In the past, DJ had pilfered sugar, rice, flour and sometimes rum for Headley's benefit on her own volition. For that 'cambulay', Headley's plan was to use DJ for supplies only for emergencies. However, he needed to get DJ involved because there was an under-subscription from all the participants, except Aleck who had contributed nothing. In the past, Aleck had never contributed materially to any of the boys' activities. Headley took note and hatched a plan with Allan, Aleck's best friend. They hoped that they would teach Aleck a lesson.

Once everything was in place for the cook, the 'saraka pot', which was only used for community cooking, was borrowed from Noel's grandmother. It was placed on the three stones that provided support above the wood fire, started earlier. All the ingredients were placed into the pot at various intervals depending on their estimated cooking time. First, about ten pounds of mixed green peas were placed in the pot half filled with water. The pot was allowed to boil for about an hour before the meat and ground provision (potatoes, cassava and pumpkins) together with salt, coconut milk from two coconuts, some margarine and other seasoning were added. They lowered or increased the heat under the pot by adjusting the amount of firewood. After about an hour, it was time to put in the dumplings. A special dumpling was prepared for Aleck. Headley took the pack of salts (laxative) from his pocket, placed it in the middle of the dough and rolled Aleck's dumpling. A piece of stick like a toothpick was stuck in the special dumpling to identify it.

The cooks tested the contents of the pot periodically for taste and readiness for eating. Patrick was the taster and by the time the food was finally ready he had eaten at least one person's portion. People believed that his good appetite was due to the 'ganga' that he smoked. He must have smoked earlier in the day. He had gotten some 'ganga' seeds and planted them in an old washtub in his mother's flower garden. He told his mother that the plants were flowers and had her watering them regularly. She never questioned him about the absence of flowers. This was a well-kept secret among Patrick's friends, whom he rewarded with a smoke occasionally for their silence.

On that occasion, no one challenged Patrick, since there was a lot of food for the eighteen boys and two girls who were gathered. When the dumplings floated to the top, it was time to share. Aleck got his special dumpling and it did not take long for the salts to take effect. He went under the bushes regularly while his friends looked on with satisfaction. They hoped that he would contribute the next time.

While the pot boiled, Headley and his gang sang old calypsos. An impromptu musical band was started using home-made percussion instruments such as bottles and spoons, old pitch oil tins as drums, 'shak-shaks' made from the calabash or old milk tins which were filled with small stones, and an old truck wheel hub for playing iron and steel. The calabash 'shak-shak' was an interesting instrument that took time to make. A hole was cut at the stem of the green fruit and as much as possible of the 'gut' (inner contents) was tediously removed. Once that was done, it was left to dry before small stones were inserted to replace the contents that had been removed. A wooden handle was fitted in the hole so that it remained firm. After the calabash was dried, the new instrument was played by shaking so that the stones bounced around to make multiple sounds. Every boy found an instrument and the noise that they made was carried though the village by the night wind blowing through the otherwise quiet community.

Two boys tried singing their own compositions but only one impressed the gang. It sounded very professional. Responding to calls of encore, the singer, the Mighty Shines sang his song several times. He was encouraged by his friends to enter the Island's carnival calypso competition the next year. Although he did not take them seriously, then, he worked on his song during the following ten months, and became the Calypso King the following year. That was four years after Goat Hill's Ursula had captured the Carnival Queen. Mighty Shines was not the only performer at this 'camboulay' fete. Bernard, who later became a calypsonian, was the local panman who created his steel pans using empty five-pound milk tins. With his six tins, he was able to replicate three old calypsos. Subsequently, when Goat Hill got its steel pan band, it was not surprising that Bernard became the main player and captain.

While Headley and Patrick were busy under the Jujube tree, other groups were similarly celebrating. Anthony, also called 'Fresh up', and his team were preparing their own dish under the Debedebe tree. That group was more tolerant of having younger boys in their company. They referred to them as being 'mannish' and used them to assist in carrying out many of the chores such as fetching wood or water or running to the village shop for some essential items that were overlooked. Although the younger boys' participation was restricted to performing chores and sharing in the food, they quietly observed their elders consume alcohol or smoke cigarettes and prayed for their time to come. They were good at keeping these secrets since to squeal on their elders meant exclusion from places where their elders gathered.

Anthony's gang decided to change the menu for that year. For the previous three years, they had cooked meat. It was time for a fish meal. That decision was probably motivated by the presence of Anthony's cousin who was visiting from Aruba. He did not eat meat, so to accommodate him the other option was fish. Further, as Anthony and his other friends were depending on the visitor to contribute heavily to the food and drinks for the carnival season, it was important to treat him well. Four members of Anthony's team had gone fishing on Carnival Saturday night. The catch was good. This meant that their pot contained predominantly fish and other seafood including, lobster, lambi or conch, Congo eels, doctor fish and sea eggs. There was more seafood than dumplings and ground provision. That meant that when sharing the food, they had to search for the dumplings or pieces of potatoes. After eating their fill, Anthony and his gang washed down their meal with large cups of lime juice and 'gospo' squash flavoured with rum stolen from home. Then they all went home. The next day was going to be hectic. They must complete all their chores early then head for

Hillsborough in the afternoon where they hoped to see some Fancy Mas. On their way to town, the boys from the different groups would tell stories which were always exaggerated about the great success of the night before.

That same year, there was also the old men's 'camboulay' pot. Ervin and Eastin were the main organisers. Their activities were slightly different to that of the young men. They had slaughtered a goat, which was the main meat. The men did not do the cooking. Their women organised and cooked different dishes. The cooking was a little more professional than that of the boys. There was rice and peas, stewed goat meat and ground provision all cooked separately in three big pots. While their food cooked the men played dominoes. The losers had to pay for the drinks which arrived by the quarter bottle from Lou's downstairs. After the eating had ended, the drinking continued and the real card game started. That was when Ervin would take his leave since he did not gamble. The new game was for money. The men played All Fours until daylight. The drinking continued until Lou refused to give any further credit. At daybreak, all the participants were drunk with most worse off financially. Charlo had left for Jim's place about four O'clock. It would be a good carnival since he had won most of his 'camboulay' night friends' money. It was time for him and Jim to prepare for the Jab Jab. They were ready for J'ouvert.

Monday Jab Jab

The second type of masquerader was the Jab Jab or Jab also called devil mas. Generally, the Jab Jab was performed in pairs signifying the devil and his angel. Garvis did not fancy the Jab Jab. The Jab Jab was left to his younger brother Cassie. For many years, the two main jab characters were Jim and Charlo. Charlo played the devil and Jim was his angel.

In preparation for their portrayal, both characters were painted black with old engine oil. They had to grease themselves with Vaseline before applying the blackened engine oil. For these occasions, all the villagers of Goat Hill, who were of black ancestry, were in a precarious position as they tried to make fun of the former white slave masters. If they painted themselves white, they could be accused of trying to change their colour. On the other hand, in painting themselves black they confirmed the negative past attributed to their ancestors. For Jim and Charlo such intellectual thoughts were farfetched. They just wanted to enjoy themselves and carry on the traditions.

In addition to the blackened skin, Jim wore a pair of cattle horns and had a bag full of straw strapped to his back. He tied a cow's chain around his waist with about a six feet extension, which he pulled along the ground as he walked. The chain made a noise similar to that made by cattle as they walked along the road. The most important accessory to Jim's outfit was a live serpent around his neck. Two weeks before each carnival, Jim scouted the hills above his house. During the day, the serpents coiled up on a tamarind or gummier tree. Jim never took the chance to capture one on the gummier tree as there was a risk that the branch might break because those branches were fragile. He would go for the one from a tree that posed fewer risks. He used a long sturdy stick with a hook created from a severed branch. The serpent was pulled as it uncoiled from its resting place. Once on the ground, it was placed in a crocus bag before it was taken away for safekeeping in a drum until needed. Jim did not feed it because he was not sure what it ate. There were no animal rights then, so no one bothered with what he did.

In addition to the perception of the devil as a black being, the Jab Jab was not complete or authentic without red eyes and red tongue. Jim's lips and tongue became red by sucking the fruit from a native cactus called the 'Mardi Gras'. For this Jab Jab portrayal, he must have sucked the fruit for many hours as the redness of his tongue lasted all day. On the other hand, perhaps he had a few in the bag which he carried and replenished the redness from time to time. No one ever found out the secret.

As Jim and Charlo moved through the village, Charlo would sing, "You see the devil, way the devil, you see the devil, pay the devil." As Charlo got to the line "pay the devil" he would use the piece of wood he carried with him to administer one or two blows to the bag of straw on Jim's back. In the early morning, Charlo would be careful for the blow to fall on the middle of the bag ensuring that Jim did not get hurt. Later in the day, Charlo was not very careful because by that time he would have been half-drunk from the combination of the rum, given as payment to the devil, and the blazing sun that was typical during the carnival period.

One year, it was during the late afternoon when, due to his drunken state, Charlo seemed to have gone bazooka and landed a number of misdirected blows to Jim. At first, Jim, also in a state of drunkenness, did not seem affected at the time. Some said that Charlo had deliberately injured Jim. Maybe Jim himself believed that, as the relationship between them never seemed the same thereafter. That was the last time that Charlo and Jim played Jab Jab. Since then, many have attempted to play Jab Jab like Jim and Charlo.

Some years later, Cassie teamed up with Gifford in an attempt to recreate the era of Charlo. They had observed them for many years. The new team had little success. No one was afraid of them. Children no longer ran or hid under the bed at the sight of the Jab Jab. Jab Jab was never the same in Goat Hill after Charlo and Jim.

5.2.1 Tuesday's stick fighting and old mas

By six-thirty in the morning on Carnival Tuesday, Goat Hill's children had completed their morning chores and headed to the Junction close to the village school where a small crowd had assembled. There, the young men supported by their backers were preparing to perform their stick fighting which had developed from the time of slavery into a unique Shakespearean version. Stick fighting which originated out of Africa was a ritual where men duelled with sticks or "bois" in gazelles or rings. At the junction where the village school was located, the first two fighters were Alwin from the village adjoining Goat Hill and Desmond who represented lower Goat Hill. They were dressed in brightly coloured flowing cloaks and pantaloons. The dress was somewhat reminiscent of English medieval court jesters. Small round mirrors were pinned on the chest area of the clothing. They covered their faces with hand painted facemasks made from a fine-messed wire.

Since Alwin was coming to Desmond's territory, he was the challenger and went first. He recited verses from the works of Shakespeare, stamping his feet and waving his stick. Alwin had the edge because of his ability to recite the verses accurately and clearly. Desmond kept moving around with some uneasiness, as he wanted to use his stick on Alwin's head. He had it in for him from the previous year. His time came but he forgot some of the lines and replaced them with his own creation. That was entertaining but it did not give him points. Desmond scored better in defending himself and although shorter than Alwin, was able to rip off the padded headgear from Alwin's head. His antics seemed to confuse Alwin who was unable to defend himself resulting in him getting a 'burst' head. Alwin wanted to fight but the elders who acted sometimes as backers to the fighters and at other times, peacemakers calmed him. After this first match, there was a quick visit to the nearest rum shop, where both masqueraders and spectators drank strong rum, chased with water.

There were five other matches, followed by the drinking of strong rum and water, before the best three were selected. Desmond, Headley and Shines were the selectees. They then walked to the next crossroads about one and a half miles away where the competition between Goat Hill region and the Belair region took place. Walter Mills was champion from Belair. The final destination was the Town with stops and competitions at Bogles where Vibert was the champion and Beausejour where champions from Mt Pleasant, Top Hill and Mt. Royal converged to ensure representation of their heroes. The final showdown was then between Heroes, comprising Desmond and the other five champions he encountered on the way to Town, and Banroys from the south of the island. The stick mas ended about midday. It was then time for Pretty Mas.

There was a saying *"You can't play mas and fraid powder"*. Pretty Mas was associated with baby powder. Both Monday and Tuesday were designated for Pretty Mas, but the best portrayals were on Tuesday. It was the time when the masqueraders or 'Ole Mas' characters had their fun. These characters were allowed to cover their faces with a mask made from a piece of cardboard, with cut out holes to facilitate seeing, breathing and speaking. The garments were usually worn-out or torn clothing. Men would mostly wear female clothing, while women wore male clothing. 'Ole Mas' characters were less scary for most small children than the Jab Jab characters. Young children would follow the 'Ole Mas' characters through the village, but would run away upon hearing the voice of the Jab Jab in the neighbourhood. Garvis followed the 'Ole Mas' all day long. He could tell who the masquerader was by looking at their bare feet, the shape of their heads and hearing their voices. He was doing this since he was about five. He followed Sharon, who was the first 'Ole Mas' character on the scene, from door to door. He shouted her name once too often, which sent her in a rage. She grabbed a piece of wood and dealt him five good blows. That was the end of the masquerading for her that day. Soon, Garvis went searching for a replacement. He found his second target and Garvis shouted a name. The masquerader was unperturbed because he was wrong. Then Garvis went too far. He attempted to pull the mask from the masquerder's face. It was his older cousin. Garvis got a good 'cut arse'. However, that was not the end. Garvis soon found another character to harass.

5.2.2 Children in town on carnival Tuesday

For the children, carnival meant a visit to town. Children from all the villages headed for the town. Dressed in their best clothes, boys and girls walked for three or four miles, starting out around nine or ten in the morning. Permission to go to Town was dependent on having picked an increased quota of cotton or peas on the days preceding carnival. If they sold the harvested cotton before the carnival, each child would get from twenty-five cents to fifty-cents. The amount received was based on the quantity of cotton that the child had picked. Children from the different parts of the village gathered into groups to travel to the town. Henry, George and Tass led the group from upper Goat Hill, Headley and Shines led the group from central Goat Hill, while Desmond led lower Goat Hill. The groups met at Belvedere Cross Road just before Cherry Hill.

On the way to town, they would stop off at Mr Rocke's shop in Water Road. That was an important point, as it was there that they could buy a bottle of cold water for two cents. It was one of the two times that most of the children would drink cold water for the year, as Mr Rocke was one of the few shops that owned a Kerosene powered refrigerator. Tass bought a bottle of cold water, which he shared with his two brothers and two best friends. Cold water was sold in rum bottles, which were all made of glass. It was already hot; hence, that was a good first treat of the carnival for them. Cold water was a luxury as there was only one kerosene refrigerator in all of Goat Hill. George also wanted to buy a bottle of cold water but he did not care to share. He decided that he would spend his money when he got to town.

Goat Hill's children reached town just before mid-day. They were all sweaty, but not tired. The children visited the different stalls. Middle-aged and older women sold their pastries and homemade confectionary in small wooden trays on some rickety tables. For most of them, selling was just for the fun or to attract attention since the sales were generally meagre and profit eluded many. The most popular stalls carried a wide variety of pastries including salt-fish cakes and bread. That was the best bargain for the children who were very hungry around midday.

George bought two bread and salt-fish cakes plus a soft drink costing twelve cents. He had thirteen cents remaining. He placed the change in his pocket and tied the pocket with a string. This ensured that his money would not be lost. He was prepared to solicit as many goodies as possible from his friends when they purchased. Among the rest of the group, they bought a few bags of popcorn, coconut tarts, buns, drops, 'fontays', groundnut sugar cakes, tamarind balls, and coconut sugar cakes. These they shared among themselves. Allister bought the bakes and fish cakes as did George, but since he had only ten cents he borrowed from his brother to meet his shortfall. For that, he guaranteed a quarter of the cola to his older brother. Allister saved the rest of his money to play in the games of chances. First, he tried the bottle and ring game. For five cents, he had three chances to throw a metal ring around the head of one of the bottles placed within a ten feet diameter circle. Allister lost his five cents. He then moved to a board game, which was a little more expensive. He pushed his way and positioned himself between two men whom he did not know. They tried to chase him away but he refused to budge. He placed his ten cents on his favourite number, five. The board was spun and he lost. He tried his last ten cents and won fifty cents. That was good enough for him. No more games until next year.

The other children looked at the different pretty mas. The men who were dressed in women's clothing threw powder on people and chanted things that the children did not understand. There was a donkey-man mas, which had made its way to Goat Hill from Venezuela via Trinidad. For this donkey-man portrayal, the individual used a wire frame, which was covered with coloured printed cloth so that when he danced, he and his costume gave an illusion of a miniature donkey being ridden by an over-sized man. Then the bands came. There were two Sailor Bands, one in white and the other in khaki. There were wild Indians with feathers and painted faces, a band portraying the Zulu tribe from Africa and a band with multi-coloured clothing, which looked very pretty to the children. Each band was enclosed by a rope, which was held up by young men who did not belong to the band but volunteered their services. A steel band of about fifteen to twenty players accompanied each mas band. Groups of children followed the steel bands and danced to the music. George, Allister, Tass and the other children from upper Goat Hill followed the white sailor mas. They avoided the khaki Sailor Mas band, as three of their teachers were in that band. They did not want their teachers to see them.

By four o'clock, the children were ready for the return trip having spent most of their money. The return trip took almost twice as long since five to six hours of walking around in the hot sun had drained most of their energy. By the time they all reached their destinations, the sun had almost disappeared on the horizon.

5.3   When Easter came: Kite flying

One of the pastimes of children, mainly boys, at Easter was the flying of kites. All boys tried their hands at making kites. The first type of kite was to use a dried leaf as a kite. That kite needed only a short piece of thread and it did not stay airborne for long. The smallest boys made this type of kite. The upgraded model was to use a piece of cardboard from an old box as a kite. That was a good option for boys who could make as many as they wanted, once cardboard was available.

There was also the flex kite, made from the dried ribs of the coconut branch. However, coconut branches were generally hard to come by. That was because, in Goat Hill and the surrounding villages, there were few coconut trees and further, the dried coconut branches were used for firewood. Flex kites were special. There were a few versions of them. There was the two-piece frame, which produced a diamond shaped kite, the three-piece frame, which produced a hexagonal shaped kite and the four-piece frame, which produced the hexagonal kite with a nose. Only kites with a nose sang while flying. The sounds produced and the kind of balance of the kite in the air depended on the depth of the nose and the adjustment to the compass. The flying compass which connected to the thread or cord used for securing the kite was adjustable. As a lover of kites, Samuel would spend all day long adjusting the compass so that his kite would improve its 'mounting', that is, the ability to increase the maximum height that it could reach.

The main type of kites was framed using pieces of wood or bamboo. Kites were covered with sheets of brown wrapping paper, which were sold in the village shops. When this paper was not available, some children would rip a sheet of paper from their copybook. The most accessible glue for sticking the paper unto the kite was the ripe yellow and golden coloured fruits from the clammy cheery tree. A paste made from flour was also used. However, there were challenges associated with the use of the flour-based glue as Henry found out the first time that he tried it. The flour was intended for making the bakes for breakfast. As he was unfamiliar with the process, the amount of flour that he used left only sufficient for only three or four bakes. His mother noted his excessive use of the flour for kite making and as a result, he received a reduced quota of bakes for a few days following his flour-based glue experiment. Stealing glue from the grocery box in the kitchen was not something that mothers tolerated. The second lesson that Henry learnt from his use of flour-based glue, was that the paper and glue provided a good meal for rats if they found the kite. Henry's first flour-based glue kite was eaten by rats. The third lesson in using the flour-based glue was that the kite was heavy and would fall back to earth during light winds and calm periods, and if it rained, the dried flour would soften causing the paper to dislodge from the frame and the kite to return to earth.

Kite flying began about six weeks before Easter and ran as late as a month after Easter. Henry was known for keeping his kite up in the sky for many weeks, until it was downed at the commencement of the rainy season or if someone in the village was so annoyed by the constant night singing that he would cut the thread one night, causing it to land on the trees of High North. Cutting the cord or thread of Henry's kite during the night was a risky task. He knew the disturbance that his kite could make on a windy night and, to avoid someone cutting it, he would secure his kite by tying it on the highest branch of the mango tree in his grandmother's yard.

Kite flying peaked on Easter Sunday, when there would be competitions for all categories of kites. Prizes were given for the smallest category, the largest category, the ugliest category, the prettiest category, the best singing kite and the kite that flew the highest. Usually, the most entertaining category was the biggest kite. There would be a few big kites about eight to ten feet in height. Six or seven boys holding on to the rope controlled those large kites. They did not last long. Typically, on the first return to earth, because of a fading wind or after diving from heavy wind, they were partially destroyed. It was more difficult to relaunch a damaged large kite to the air. If it did, on the second return to earth it was damaged certainly, beyond immediate repair.

5.4 The Saraka and the Maroon

The children of Goat Hill looked forward to any celebration that brought with it food and drinks. The elders who believed in an interconnection with their ancestors took dreams and visions seriously and always had an interpretation of them. In most cases, a dream required a sacrifice to the ancestors. That was a kind of celebration often referred to as a Plate or a 'Saraka', which was intended to bring happiness to unhappy spirits, to appease ancestral spirits for their wrongdoing, or to overcome the misfortunes of their descendants. Therefore, it was no wonder that at any whisper of a significant dream, children pestered their grandparents about what it meant. For the children, a significant dream meant a day of very good food.

There were many dreams for which an interpretation meant that a neighbour was required to make a plate. Diahee was a professional dreamer. She dreamt about ancestors who complained of being hungry and requested food or about ancestors who felt neglected. Many situations in dreams required the making of a Plate. Once Diahee dreamt about Henry who had already migrated to the UK. In the dream, which was told and retold with enhancements along the way until the target was convinced, Diahee saw that Henry who was crying and asking assistance to find a good job. She first reported that dream to Bunah, Henry's grandmother and advised her to have a 'Saraka' in the yard. Diahee knew that Bunah would be able to afford another Plate since she recently received letters from her daughters and Henry.

As the unofficial postwoman, Diahee knew when everybody received money from overseas. She collected all the village mail from the post office and delivered them to their rightful owners. This she did at no charge. If the mail was a letterform there was no money, however when it was an envelope there was money. Diahee would feel the thickness of the envelope to determine whether it contained a postal order or pound notes. Although some people thought she was illiterate, others considered her the village's accountant. Diahee speculated as to how much money Bunah received by assuming that a letter from the daughter whose son lived with her had three pounds, the other daughters sent two pounds and other relatives, including grandchildren, sent one pound.

Bunah and the other villagers had high regard for Diahee's dreams. On two occasions, when the villagers ignored her and refused to hold a Plate, there were reports of mishaps to the relatives of the ancestors who visited Diahee in her dreams. Since then, villagers responded positively to reports of dreams concerning their family.

The Plate put on for the benefit of Henry was not very eventful. Invitations went out that the Plate would be on the last Friday in February, the week before carnival. Bunah's main responsibility was to provide the pork. Perhaps Diahee's timing for the dream ensured that the pig was slaughtered before Easter. There could be no Plates during the Lenten period, and if Bunah's pig remained until Easter, it would be slaughtered for sale. At least that was Bunah's plan since she had postponed the slaughter from Christmas Eve.

On the morning of Bunah's Plate, Jassie and Decca were on time to slaughter the pig. After a brief libation with rum and water, and a drink by the butchers and the two other men, they slaughtered the pig with great efficiency. Winnie stewed the lungs, kidneys and liver for breakfast for the family, the butchers and early volunteers participating in the day's activities.

By eight o'clock, more volunteers and well-wishers arrived. They brought with them small parcels of rice, corn flour, peas, some ground provisions and chickens. Some offered money in lieu of foodstuff. This was the way of Goat Hill. Each contributed according to his or her means thereby reducing the burden on the host family. There was a buzz in the yard. The village women operated in pairs to accomplish their tasks: peeling ground provision, washing the rice, peeling and slicing onions and garlic, and starting the fire. First, they slaughtered the chickens. As they cut the chickens' necks, villagers looked for the sign that the Plate was acceptable to the ancestors. If the headless chicken came to rest on its back so that its legs were in the air, the villagers would clap. This was the sign of acceptance. By nine o'clock, they had washed and cleaned all the meat, including the donated chickens, with lime and big thyme and sugar apple leaves, and had seasoned everything. The seasoning was modest: salt, black pepper, onions and garlic. Soon all pots were on the wood fire in the yard. There were eight fires to accommodate individual pots for coo-coo, stewed peas, rice, chicken and pork. One or two women were assigned to each pot, which was checked periodically to ensure that the fire was not too high or too low and that there was sufficient water in the pot to prevent the food from burning.

The most difficult part of the cooking was the preparation of coo-coo. This required both skill and strength. As Maude fitted both requirements, she often had this responsibility. Every twenty to twenty-five minutes, Maude removed the cover off the coo-coo pot, then using an oar-like paddle she stirred the contents in the pot to ensure consistency in the corn product. The heat from the morning sun directly from the blue sky, combined with that from the wood fire below the pot, caused Maude to sweat profusely. Every once in a while, as Maude bent over, droplets of sweat fell from her forehead into the pot. This was expected because even when using her fingers, she was unable direct all the sweat to the floor.

As the women sat under the tamarind tree while the food cooked they teased each other about their domestic affairs. Sometimes the joking went too far resulting in short bursts of 'cursing off' between the creator of the 'fatigue' and the recipient. In most cases by the end of the day, the antagonists had reconciled.

When the coo-coo and rice were cooked, women sat on benches and stools and rolled the rice. There was no 'Saraka' without rolled rice and rolled coo-coo. For this plate, Sybil and the other women used bowls and calabashes to roll. Using a pot spoon to beat the hot rice or hot coo-coo, which was still in the pot, until it became sticky to the touch. Then they placed one scoop of the hot rice or hot coo-coo in a bowl or calabash and, with both hands, performed a rolling action. This process was performed quickly, as once the food became cool, the beating and rolling of the rice and coo-coo were difficult.

Sybil was good at making rolled rice and Coo-coo. On completion, her balls of rice and coo-coo were almost perfectly spherical. There were two pots of rice to convert to balls. Unfortunately, they could not beat and roll the rice in one of the pots. This was Winnie's pot. Her rice was not properly cooked and could not be "beaten" to release sufficient starch. This was essential for providing the stickiness required for getting the round shape of the rice balls. They returned the pot to the fire, added hot water and allowed the rice to cook a little longer. The other women, in jest, ridiculed her for poor performance. After half an hour recooking, the rice was ready.

With all the food cooked, they used pond water to put out the various fires. One could not use potable water for such a purpose during the dry season. Then it was time to share the food. As was customary, the women took out special portions, to be placed on the table in Bunah's bedroom. Bunah's relatives had the task of taking the food to the bedroom. They formed a line and received a plate or container with one type of food. Then, they entered the house and bedroom in single file in complete silence, and placed their respective plate or container in the space available. On entering the room, nobody looked backwards. They could not look backwards. The reason for this remained unexplained, but the instruction was given before the selected relatives took their places to begin the procession to the bedroom. The food and drinks on the table in the bedroom remained overnight for the ancestral spirits. The room also remained vacant as no one was allowed to sleep in it. The spirits must be undisturbed.

Once the spirits were served, it was time for the children's fun. Portions of food were placed in a wooden tray about three feet wide, four feet long and about four inches deep. The tray with food: rice, coo-coo, meat, and ground provision was placed on a level space in the yard. The children who were ten and under were invited to '*grappe*'. Primo, who was about seven or eight, had just arrived in the village from Aruba where his parents had migrated before his birth. He joined the children as they stooped around the tray. Those who were unable to get a front space jostled from behind to displace someone in front.

Magnus who had mastered the art of '*grappe*' took a position in the back row where he had the advantage of reaching for the meat section. Pieces of meat were the best rewards for the participants. They could exchange a piece of meat for larger portions of the less desirable portions such as ground provision or coo-coo. Coo-coo was always in the greatest supply so there was no difficulty in getting as much as was desired anytime during the evening. Maude gave the signal to begin. Like hungry dogs, the children attacked the tray. In less than a minute, they were all assessing what they were able to grab. Bits of food were all over their faces and clothes. Primo, for whom that was the first experience, came up with a big 'junk' of pork three quarters of which was fat. Everyone around began to laugh at the sight of Primo. His head was plastered with coo-coo and rice as if his head had entered the tray along with his hands. He had discoloured his Aruba 'nice clothes' with gravy from the meat section, but he held on to his 'junk' of pork.

All who were present ate. Alvin observed that those present had eaten all the pork. His keen interest in looking at the villagers eating was important for him since he had killed a pig the week before and most of the meat remained unsold. As Alvin noticed that all his neighbours were eating non-stop he remembered his unsold pork and lashed out:

> *"Ah see al al you who din buy me pork last week eating pork. All you complained that me pork was from a mother pig and mother pig pork does give all you shitting. But ha see all you enjoying the pork from Bunah's sow pig. Yes, is 'cause it free. Free pork don't give shitting? Al you wicked set of people"*

There was little response to Alvin's outburst. Perhaps the villagers felt guilty because they knew that Alvin was speaking the truth. As darkness set in, villagers filled whatever containers that were available to take some of the 'Saraka' food for family members who were unable to attend. At least that was the reason provided for carting away food, but in many cases, the whole family was present and had eaten two or more servings. There was no drumming that night. Those who expected Sugar Adams and his team to show up for the Big Drum were disappointed, as the dream did not ask for a Big Drum dance. They had to wait a little longer for the Big Pond Maroon where the dance was the highlight of that celebration.

During the night, a plot instigated by Patrick and Shines to sneak into the bedroom where the table was laid for the spirits, and steal the meat, was foiled. Had Patrick and Shines succeeded, the Plate would have been prematurely broken. That would not have been good for Patrick and Shines, as they would have brought a curse on themselves. Further, their action could have caused the rejection of Bunah's sacrifice.

The next morning Bunah formally broke the Plate. She distributed the stale food among the children from her household and the immediate neighbourhood. The use of firewood for cooking preserved the food, none of which tasted sour.

A 'Maroon' was an extended 'Saraka' put on by the community. It was a festival to give thanks for the previous year's harvest and to ask the ancestral spirits to intervene in ensuring a bountiful crop in the current year. Goat Hill's 'Maroon' took place by the Big Pond, the biggest rainwater dam on the island. During the year in which Bunah held the 'Saraka' for Henry's well-being, the villagers cleaned or de-silted Big Pond. That happened every five to seven years. For three weeks, particularly on weekends, villagers removed the silt brought down by the water that gushed through the valleys over the intervening years. They used forks, spades and hoes for digging and buckets for carting away the soil.

To begin the cleaning project, Eclais went around the village and collected contributions from every home. He used the money to purchase refreshment for the volunteers. The cleaning culminated with the 'Maroon'. For the 'Maroon', each household or groups of households prepared food like a 'Saraka' and took it to the site. Like was done for the cleaning, the villagers contributed money for purchasing drinks and for defraying the expenses of Sugar Adams and the Big Drum dancers.

By five-thirty, all the villagers headed to Big Pond. Women carried wooden trays covered with white tablecloths. The trays, placed on tables, lined the side of the semi-circular road on the northern and eastern sides of the Pond. Six of the village women selected for the purpose visited each tray. Clarabelle was responsible for the mutton. She used a wash-pan to collect a portion of mutton from all the trays, which contained mutton. Other women did the same for pork, chicken, provision, rice, coo-coo, and stewed peas. The wash-pans were then placed on tables borrowed from the village school. That food was for the visitors from the other villages who were priority at the time. That gesture was to demonstrate the hospitality of the people of Goat Hill. It was a reciprocated practice. Villagers who were invited to other 'Maroons' were always well treated. In any case, most villagers ate at home before walking down the hill to Big Pond. They appreciated tasting the food prepared by other households, but did not make too much of a fuss if there was not sufficient to go around. However, on that night, there was no shortage of trays, which were all packed to capacity. The *'bumper'* cotton and lime crops had ensured that every household was liberal in its contribution.

Like in the case of the household 'Saraka', there was a *'grappe'* for the children. That *grappe* was more entertaining than the one at Bunah's 'Saraka'. First, there were four trays and about ten times more children. Trays of food with only small portions of meat were placed on the ground one at a time. Groups of children were selected based on their sizes, starting with the smallest. Each child was permitted to partake only once from one tray. There were only small portions of meat in 'grappe' trays. The most skilful children collected whole rolls of coo-coo or rice in addition to a piece of meat. Primo had learnt from Bunah's 'Saraka'. He stayed to the back of the group around the tray and dived ahead of his friends. He came up empty handed this time and his head and clothes remained clean. Primo had a second chance. That was seldom done. However, in this case he was given special treatment as he stood out, wearing his shoes and socks among his barefooted friends. The second time Primo was more successful as he was able to grab a chicken foot. Whatever the pleasure the children experienced from the 'grappe', Mr M. Z. Mark, the schoolmaster, did not appreciate. He thought that it was humiliating. Mr Mark was from Grenada, hence the villagers did not expect him to understand.

The food on the school tables was enough to feed villagers and guests. Women using small enamel trays passed through the crowd with four plates of food at a time. Beryl moved around delivering plates of food and taking orders. Allister stopped her to give his order. Beryl quickly replied:

> "You from the village you have to let the strangers eat first. You too damn greedy"

She then moved in search of a stranger. She did not know the tall man who was standing in her way, so she addressed the stranger:

"Mister you get food already? What you want? You want plenty coo-coo or rice? Oh you don't want meat. You want only stew peas and chicken? Mister you think you in a restaurant. You picking and choosing. Ok, ah go bring it when ah come back."

With Sugar Adams' drummers and singers in position, it was time for the Big Drum Dance to start. By seven o'clock, the Big Drum Dance was in full swing. To begin the ceremony, the organisers marshalled the dancers who entered the circular space provided for the dancing in single file. As the drums began to beat someone shouted: "Wet her down." The dancers began swaying from side to side and threw rice, soft drinks, rum and water in the empty space as they formed a circle with the spectators on the outside. Those who had rum threw some to the ground from bottles or cups and took a drink for themselves. As they threw the rum to the ground, they recited some prayers to the ancestors. This was a libation ceremony required at all functions except a church service. The bottle of strong rum was shared among the other men - the spectators - some of whom also performed the libation ritual. Each man poured some rum to the ground for the spirits before swallowing the remainder from his glass or cup followed by a good drink of water to reduce the burning sensation in the mouth and throat. Once there was an indication that all the elders had shared the drinks between themselves and the spirits, it was time to begin the dancing in earnest.

A short chubby woman in her forties, dressed in a colourful traditional West African wear began the singing with the Chantwell:

"Ina aaaa Ina oooh Ina aaa mamma anoo
Sa la maneo
Ina aaa mamma anoo

Sa la maneo
Ina aaa mamma anoo oy oy"

The first man to be in the ring was Tass Senior who was the main male dancer from Goat Hill. One did not have to know how to dance at first. Once in the ring, the rhythm of the drums and the guiding hands of the ancestral spirits ensured that the movements of the feet, hands and the waist were synchronized. Tass Senior grabbed the towel, wheeled on one leg and as if possessed, moved with some falling motions with perfect balance supported by singers and the crowd. The poor lighting around the ring encouraged the most introverted to participate. George, who always got into trouble at school for not participating in the class singing, seemed to know all the words of the songs and was singing in tune with the drumbeats. His favourite was:

"Diama Diama Ebo le' le' Diama
Aye baca faire Ebo,
Diama Diam Ebo le le
Diama Aye Ebo dancer"

Se Fortune, who never missed a 'Maroon', sat on a bench borrowed from the school. It was too low for her but she was grateful to have a seat. Unaided, Se Fortune would have taken a fortnight to get from her house to Big Pond. Although her mental faculties were in perfect shape, old age and arthritis had taken their toll on her physique. She required additional assistance and her cane for mobility support. Suddenly, Se Fortune asked an old man who sat on a stone in front of her to move. "I want to dance", she said. Without the help of her cane or the younger people standing close by, the old woman got up and entered the ring. She received the towel from the dancer who made way for her. In the ring, she moved her feet, waist and shoulders with such ease that everyone present marvelled. She danced as if possessed for about four minutes before collapsing in the ring. That was her last dance. They took her home in Lennox's jitney. At that point, the dancers, drummers and singers called for an intermission. That was the time for them to eat and rest before resuming.

Se Fortune's mishap did not put a damper on the proceedings. The drumming and the dancing went on until the wee hours of the morning. Some young children slept in their mothers' laps unaware of the goings-on. The more introverted children entered the ring at the urging of their peers. Their dancing drew encouraging laughter from the crowds. The villagers always remembered Tass Senior and Se Fortune during the 'Maroons' that followed. They mentioned their names during the libation segment of the Big Pond Maroon. New dancers were discovered who could open the ring in subsequent years, if Tass Senior was unavailable.

5.5 THE STONE FEAST

The Stone Feast was an important feature on the calendar of Goat Hill, although not timetabled like the other festivals. The ad hoc nature in which the celebration was held meant that children were unable to plan for the high expectations. The efforts children made in preparation by undertaking numerous chores never seemed to provide satisfactory compensation in terms of enjoyment in "smoke food".

During the time of Bunah and Madevine, there were many Stone Feasts. In the year before Vallan migrated, his mother and aunts erected the tombstone for Rose who was Bunah's godmother. As Vallan was the oldest great-grandson and, at the time living with his grandmother and great aunt, he had his first experience of a family Stone Feast. Vallan and his other cousins, Prince and Isaac, were given one task after another during a one-month period including the Easter school vacation. First, there was the task of carrying the sand and stones for the concrete. Valla and his cousins with their donkeys carried partly filled bags of wet sand to the site of their great-grandmother's grave at Meldrum Cemetery. Only two trips per day were possible, since both donkeys and boys were exhausted after the second trip. The two-mile journey was mostly up hill. The boys worked out a way to determine how much each donkey should carry. If three boys could lift the contents in the bag, then it was sufficient for the donkey.

Vallan and his cousins, assisted by a few neighbours, had to collect and break enough stones, in addition to collecting half a truck load of boulders. A truck carried the stones and boulders to the nearest point of the cemetery. The children then carried them on their heads to the graveside. The children did this chore every other day during the last weeks of school before the Easter vacation. Vallan got help to collect firewood for the Stone Feast. That was the least challenging because it was the dry season and firewood was easy to come by. Finally, they had to take the water to fill three drums by the graveside. The water, which they carried on their heads from the well in Windward, required about forty-five minutes per trip. They toted the water over two early mornings, taking advantage of the moonlight. Vallan and his cousins were also lucky, as there were a few volunteers, mostly girls, who assisted in carrying the water. This was the only part that Vallan really enjoyed as he had the opportunity to walk and chat with one of the village girls with whom he was in love.

During the evening preceding the erection of the tombstone, the headstone, which had remained in the wooden crate for two months since its arrival from England, was removed from the crate. They placed it on the small wooden bed in the bedroom that Rose had occupied during her time on earth. The headstone remained on the coconut-fibre mattress covered with a lily white, ironed bedsheet borrowed from a neighbour. Next day, villagers gathered early in the yard. Like in the other celebrations, such as the Plate, villagers contributed in kind and in cash according to their means or based on the closeness of the blood ties to Vallan's family. When all had gathered, the libation took place in the yard.

Following that, the strongman of the village, Dudley, carried the headstone. He volunteered for the job although Diahee was sceptical about one man carrying the headstone. She recalled and shared the story about one man who attempted that feat a few years earlier and died a few days later. Diahee believed that the man's death was linked to him carrying the headstone. That claim was unsubstantiated, although Diahee was convinced. Dudley was unperturbed by the story and marched to the cemetery with the precious cargo on his head, still fully wrapped in the white bed sheet. A small procession consisting mainly of Rose's descendants followed him.

The small procession got to the graveside about seven-thirty in the morning after a twenty-minute walk. At the graveside, Dudley carefully placed the headstone on a dry grassy patch close to the grave of Rose's father. It was positioned in such a way that the foot of the headstone pointed to the east. Another libation ceremony took place before any serious work began. As there was high unemployment during that time of the year, there were more volunteers than were necessary for the digging and the carpentry work before the mixing and pouring of concrete. The older men sat on stones under the tamarind and glory cedar trees, which provided good shade. The younger men used a fork, two shovels, and a pickaxe to excavate some shallow trenches for the foundation, which was completed by nine o'clock.

Lenford, one of Vallan's older cousins, found that the work was progressing too quickly and called for a time out. He had not lent a hand and his mind was more on the rum and the breakfast, which was late. Almost immediately after Lenford's intervention, Diahee and her cousin Christiana could be heard singing as they descended the narrow track. They were carrying the breakfast, which was packed on wooden trays. The trays were so well balanced on the women's heads that nothing had spilled from the open pail that contained the morning's beverage. The breakfast consisted of stewed liver, lungs and kidneys from the pig slaughtered the evening before. For the two Seventh Day Adventists who did not consume pork, there were a few steamed doctor fish. There were also roast bakes and cocoa tea with fresh cow's milk. A thin film of fat floated on top of the pail with the cocoa tea. Diahee and Christiana shared the breakfast. There were no favourites; hence, there was no need for any of the men to grumble because of unequal treatment. The extra food, which was mostly the cocoa tea and a few bakes, was placed on a nearby tombstone, for the men to have later, at their leisure.

Having completed their tasks, Diahee and Christiana left the cemetery. The men resumed the job. Lenford and Decca were the main carpenters and soon the wooden frame was in place. They used recycled board and nails to erect the framework. The frame was not perfectly square or plumb, as it was difficult for Lenford and Decca to work the material. That did not prevent a barrage of insults aimed at the men who had just completed the framing. One old man shouted:

> "Lenford and Decca, you are dry season carpenters. Look the thing is not square. Lenford, all these years you working you still can't read the ruler well. And as for you Decca, you can't see that the board on the south ain't level. Don't make excuses, a bad workman always blames his tools and the materials."

The comments brought laughter among the bystanders and some swear words from Lenford and Decca. This instigated further comments aimed at Lenford and Decca.

> "Fellas have no respect for the dead. You fellas ent 'fraid that one of this dead get up and slap all you. And Lenford, this is you grandmother Stone Feast. You have no shame?"

Work continued. The men placed some boulders in the foundation using size and numbers to minimise the amount of concrete needed. At that stage, motivated by the impending arrival of lunch, the progression of the work seemed to improve. By the time the mixing of the concrete started, lunchtime was not too far away. The men placed the concrete within the boxed structure and properly firmed the mixture. As the sun passed overhead, stinging sunrays replaced the morning shade beneath the tamarind and glory cedar trees. The men who had occupied the shaded positions all morning shifted to the other shaded areas in eager anticipation of the arrival of the lunch brigade. They left the concrete to harden a bit before fitting the marble headstone in place.

Marble headstones were not common as they were installed mainly for the privileged. However, Rose had insisted before her passing that she wanted marble on her tombstone. She had left strict instructions to her children. Before her death, Rose had given her three cows to three villagers for shared rearing and had instructed that for her Stone Feast, they sell the offspring from her cows and use the proceeds for purchasing the headstone. When the family decided to erect Rose's headstone, there were four mature offspring, which were sufficient to provide a good Stone Feast. That was how Rose became the first member of her family to have a marble headstone. She did not wish to have one constructed from concrete with the epitaph carved out with a trowel by one of the teachers in the village. Although the concrete tombstone could have been enhanced by painting the background of the inscription and using a pane of glass to cover the area on which the epitaph was written, Rose had insisted on imported marble.

Before installing the marble headstone, there was another round of libation and rum drinking. The men passed around the rum and each man had only one drink. Then they broke for Lunch. The men expected an abundance of food at the house holding the Stone Feast, so they ate in moderation. During the lunch break, Lenford and Decca prepared to place the headstone in its final position. They placed the headstone in the concrete at a one o'clock angle and at the same cardinal position as when it was brought to the cemetery earlier in the morning. Everyone present admired the new tombstone. It was in great contrast to the other tombstones, which had concrete headstones or headstones from the local yellowish soil that was plentiful on Madevine's land.

The amount of rum in the Jimmy John was running low and Lenford boasted that there was much more at the yard where the cooking was in progress. Vallan looked around and saw that about half of all the material brought to the cemetery was unused. He felt it would be to his benefit if one of his elder relatives died soon. Then in a few years, if the material were still in place, it could be used, thereby reducing the efforts of those who had the tasks of toting water, sand or stone. However, this was not going to benefit Vallan as none of his relatives was ailing and, in any case, he was hoping to migrate to Trinidad at the first opportunity.

Once the work on the new tombstone was completed, each man took whatever tools belonged to him and departed. Some went straight to tend their animals or to their homes. Those who were not satisfied with the amount of rum that they drank at the cemetery headed to the yard that was once Rose's.

As the Stone Feast was on a working day, the children of the village congregated in Rose's yard after the school day had ended. They were fed with typical "smoke food." The calabashes and enamel plates with rolled rice, rolled coo-coo, stewed peas and small portions of meat were passed to the first children in sight. Each child was given a pan-cup of lime juice to wash down the food. When they were finished, the dishes were washed and a second set of children were fed. There was always enough food to feed the children. There was no 'grappe' at this Stone Feast. Rose had left strict instructions that at her Stone Feast, the children should be well treated and there was to be no 'grappe'.

That night there was no Big Drum dancing. However, there was a little prayer meeting where hymns were sung and more rum consumed. By midnight, it was all over. The Stone Feast had been successful and there were no mishaps. Lenford felt good, as he had managed the rum drinking well. Vallan continued to wonder why he had made four trips for sand instead of two.

5.6 Regatta on Breeze Hill

An island regatta took place annually around the last weekend in July or the first weekend in August. It lasted for three days with an opening on the Friday night and closed with a prize giving and dinner for the participants on the Monday evening. There had not always been a regatta. It began when boat captains started competing annually, racing their fishing boats around the island for a few cases of beer and a few bottles of rum. The prize was not kept by the winner, but instead was consumed by all the participants. The regatta was transformed or took a more formal and structured format when a white Jamaican arrived on the island as an entrepreneur and got involved in the local culture.

During this regatta season, all roads led to the town. Men, women and children walked for up to four miles to get to town. Those who could have afforded the ten or fifteen cents took the wooden buses: the Brook and Lennox bus from the northern side and the Andrews buses from central and east. There were many activities in the town. There were donkey races, gambling games, local food and plenty drinks. A good time on each of these days was measured by how drunk one was at the end of the day. There were occasional clashes and fights between young men who, in most cases, had consumed too much alcohol.

For Goat Hill boys, regatta meant something else. That was a good time to congregate on a neighbouring hill, Breeze Hill, which was about one hundred and fifty metres lower than High North. At that location, there was an almost panoramic view. Most of the villages to the south and to the east and northeast were in sight.

Peep, Robbie and the boys from Goat Hill would journey to Breeze Hill where they would join up with Charles, Tony and Brigo from Belvedere, Samuel and his crew from Limlair and groups of boys from Belair, Cherry Hill and Bogles. Seldom would the crowd include girls except where the parents were confident that the older brothers would provide adequate protection for their sisters.

The boys would carry with them whatever they could scrounge from their parents' limited food supplies. With good luck, they might have some flour for dumplings, some cooking oil or margarine, pieces of salted meat: pigtails or salted beef, which were mostly imported, salt, white potatoes and onions. Some years they carried some corned pork, corned mutton or corned beef and other local products that gave a much better flavour to the anticipated meal. The supplies were generally basic, but the boys would cook a meal, the taste of which they would recall in their adult years.

Depending on how early the rains came that year, green corn would be available so that each boy would have three or four ears of corn for roasting. Sometimes, they had a chicken, stolen from one of the boys' homes. They stole the chicken the night before, then killed and cleaned it in the wee hours of the morning. In the process, they took measures to ensure that no adult was around. The boys were always confident of being undetected. However, this was not always so, as sometimes they were unaware that an adult had seen them. Usually the adult turned a blind eye.

The regatta consisted of three main races for working sloops and a number of races for smaller fishing boats. The first main race was on Sunday after lunch. On Monday, there were two races. The first race started at about nine in the morning while the second race began at about two in the afternoon. The starting times were not important to the boys as their immediate concern was the cooking on both days. With firewood gathered from the surrounding bushes, they would start a fire. Cooking was not complicated. The instructions for the order in which ingredients were to be thrown in the pot would come from the boisterous boys who each considered himself the best cook. While the meal, a kind of soup with chicken or salted meat base, dumplings and ground provision bubbled over the wood fire, they stripped ears of corn and placed them on the fire below the pot. In this way, roasted corn was available for consumption before the main meal.

To protect themselves from the stinging midday sun, the boys would find a good shaded tree, and where possible, reinforce the canopy with branches from the evergreen trees that surrounded the campsite. While some of the lazier boys, like Brigo, rested in the shade, others would begin a game of cricket on a makeshift pitch. Playing cricket on these makeshift pitches was not easy but was great fun for the boys who participated. It required running downhill to retrieve the ball then running uphill to the assigned position. When a batsman's stroke resulted in a lost ball, he got six runs and the game was likely to end prematurely. The batsman who was responsible may have enabled his team to win the match but would suffer ridicule from all his playmates for ending the fun.

Some boys would pretend to be following the races. It was uncertain whether those who did so were able to differentiate the boats; for being so far away, all the boats looked alike. On a good clear day, however, as the boats made their last tack to the finish line, the boys who had very good eyesight, almost eagle-like, were able to identify the positions of the boats and relay this to the others. By four o'clock, they would gather all the empty containers, which they had brought and head back home. They then needed to do their usual duties such as taking care of the livestock or perhaps collecting water from the communal cistern. Then, they waited until the next year for another regatta.

6

THE GAMES THAT CHILDREN PLAYED

6.1 BOYS AND THE VEHICULAR TOYS

In those days, children had their fair share of chores, but they enjoyed many games. Children built their own toys: box trucks and buses; spinning tops; a variety of toys from bottle tops; and, model boats from gummier trees, coconut shells, clammy cherry leaves and unused pages torn from the centre of their copy books. Samuel was not good at cricket, which was played during the dry season. However, he was good with his hands and could create almost all the homemade toys that were used by children to play and pass the time.

The simplest vehicular toy was the one-wheel roller. A round cover from a biscuit tin or a Klim tin was nailed to a piece of wood or a stick. The tin cover became the wheel while the nail was the axle. By pushing on the end of the stick, the wheel would roll and force the driver to walk or run behind the toy vehicle. As this was simple and required little resources, many of the small boys made one or inherited one. A higher model of the toy vehicle was the two-wheeler push car.

The two-wheeler push car, so called because of the lack of an equivalent at the time, was a homemade toy vehicle that boys pushed on evenings and weekends on the roadway. The push car was made by nailing two tin covers as wheels to the ends of a piece of wood that acted as the axle. The most popular covers were usually from imported powdered milk containers. The axle was about twelve inches long. A piece of wood about four feet long was nailed to the centre of the axle The steering was controlled by using strings attached to nails fastened on the axle about one and a half inches away from the tin wheels. These were connected by a steering piece, which, in the simplest form, was a piece of wood nailed close to the extended stick so that it can rotate on the connecting nail. By moving the control piece, the wheels pushed inwards or pushed outwards so that there was a circular motion to allow the push car to take a corner. A higher version of the steering contraption was to use the cover from the biscuit tin fastened to an empty wooden thread reel, which allowed a smooth rotation. By wrapping the cord around the reel, it was possible to control the wheels by turning the makeshift steering wheel.

A more sophisticated toy compared to the two-wheeler push car was a box truck. Samuel had made one that looked like the Windward jitney. The Windward jitney made regular trips during the day, mainly carrying workers and students to and from work and school respectively. The workers were mostly store clerks and civil servants stationed in the post office. There was a midday trip to carry the workers lunches and for villagers who wished to do afternoon shopping. In those days, there were no restaurants or food places in Hillsborough and since there were only one or two kerosene-powered refrigerators, they cooked fresh food every day in order that the workers had hot lunches. The lunch carriers were delivered within the hour of the food leaving the fire. Samuel had studied the jitney on its morning runs. His replication of the jitney was almost perfect.

Samuel's truck had a hood shaped out of a piece of silvery metal sheet cut out from a biscuit tin. The steering wheel was attached to a pole nailed to the back of the model bus, so that a string wrapped around the thread reel and attached to the front axle allowed for easy control. Other boys had model trucks similar in style to Samuel's but they lacked the quality finish that was the trademark of his creations. During box truck time, usually Easter and August holidays, the boys would gather on the main road and draw lanes wide enough for the model trucks. They created sharp corners in the chalk marked roadways. Hairpin type corners provided the most challenging test for the box truck drivers. Samuel, although a good artisan in the production of box trucks, comparatively was not so good at driving, and he often ran off the road at the hairpin corners. His friend, Tass, was better at driving and was usually declared the winning driver in most competitions. Samuel and his friends would drive the box trucks for many hours stopping only when called to do some unscheduled home chore, when the wooden wheels fell off the truck or when the cord that controlled the steering broke.

Box trucks provided great fun for the boys who were able to build them and in addition created a sense of achievement among those boys. Those who did not own a truck were able to solicit a short-term loan by convincing with promises of future favours. They enjoyed the driving. There were also the bystanders who, feeling disenfranchised, instigated fights often. A fight would start from accidents between two drivers on the chalked roads or because of an unflattering comment about the design and build of the truck or the poor skills of a driver. However, the fight and enmity from those fights lasted only as long as a snow cone in the hot midday sun.

At any time during box truck season, one-wheelers, two-wheeler push cars and box trucks would be moving up and down on the roads; that could for many hours, not see a motor vehicle pass. Designers and builders of these toys often turned out to be the best carpenters and joiners. That was an important benefit to boys making their own box trucks.

6.2 Scooters

In addition to the push type toys, boys constructed different types of scooters. The boys drove the two-wheeled scooters on the roadway downhill or pushed them on the concrete floors of the open sections of the schoolhouse. The two-wheeled scooter resembled modern day factory manufactured scooters that are made of steel and aluminium. Those made by the boys then were wooden. They connected the wood by six-inch nails and used old iron truck bearings as wheels. They configured the braking system by nailing an old leather shoe bottom so that it cantilevered over the back wheel. To reduce the speed of the scooter when riding downhill, the driver must press on the piece of leather so that the friction between the leather and metal provided the braking effort.

The two-wheeled scooter was made for one person. The driver, however, had creative ways for carrying a passenger. Repairs to the two-wheeler were frequent after the first breakdown. The main breakdown was the dislodging of the old bearing wheels as the weight and friction forces were often too much for the flimsy axles. The second major replacement required was the shoe bottom brake. For example, one day when Samuel sped down Madelyn Hill and applied the brake midway, all that the onlookers saw was a trail of smoke as the leather had overheated and began to burn. As boys drove their two-wheelers barefooted, the sole of Samuel's left foot provided enough warning to others against speeding downhill.

Then there was the box scooter, made from a wooden box, like a go-cart. They used the box scooter on the hilly areas when the grass in the pasture was already dry. The dried grass reduced the friction between the ground and the bottom of the cart and provided greater speed. A box scooter would hold the driver who steered and two or more passengers. The driver used his outstretched legs such that his feet resting on the front axle could push heavily on one side thereby allowing the scooter to take corners. If the driver took corners with too much speed, the cart would overturn with its passengers, sometimes causing major injuries.

6.3 THE BEST PASTIME: CRICKET

During the dry season, and particularly during the Easter holidays, cricket was the dominant game in the village. The children played cricket with softballs and hardball, leather balls and compo, wood knot balls (that is balls shaped round from a hardwood, like guava wood), balls made from crushing juice pans and milk pans, balls made from molten plastics, and grugru balls. Grugru is a small fruit from a type of palm. It is the size of a golf ball and is washed down the Orinoco River and carried to the shores of Carriacou by the currents of the Caribbean Sea. The pain from a blow with the grugru to any part of the body lasts for many days. When in season, green 'gospo' also became cricket balls. Generally, they did not last more than an over; hence, they needed to be in large supply otherwise a game would be short-lived.

Then there were all different types of bats. There were imported bats owned by the cricket club or the school. No individual owned an imported cricket bat. These bats, imported from England, were treated with linseed oil rubbed in on the surface when they were not in use. There were bats made from dried coconut branches and shaped like the imported bats. These bats lacked flexibility. There were bats made from the wood of the clammy cherry or juniper trees. There were also bats made from half rotten or discarded pitch pine or white pine wood. In his day, Henry was good at making any type of bat except the imported ones. There would be competitions for making bats, where the only compensation was acknowledgement by the village boys to have made the best bat.

The boys made the wickets from anything straight and sharp enough to penetrate the hard dry ground. To facilitate penetration, they poured some pond water or some dirty soap water from the house closest slowly on the ground to enable maximum infiltration.

Once they had poured enough water on the spot, they hammered the wooden stumps into position using a stone. One person would hold onto the stump in its upright position, while another, using the stone, would drive it into the ground as a pile driver does. Seldom were the stumps at the same height, but that did not take away from the enjoyment of the game.

Cricket was not a democratic game except when played at school or in inter-village competitions. Other than these, the owner and makers of bats would bat for as long as they wanted. Similarly, the owner of the ball would bowl as long as he wanted because he could end a game by just walking away with his ball.

Cricket was played everywhere, once there was a bat and ball, a surface, a bowler and a batsman. The game would start with only two players and the number of players would grow with time. There would be an interchange between bowler and batsman with the batsman becoming the bowler and the bowler the batsman. Henry and his friends had excavated a strip of land in the pasture as a cricket pitch, using a fork and shovel. That was okay during the dry season, but as it was planted with corn and peas in the rainy season, it was lost until the following year when renovations were carried out to improve the surface.

Playing cricket, using homemade bats and balls without pads or helmets, was a dangerous activity. However, it led to the development of great eye and hand coordination and swiftness of feet. When the fast bowlers delivered to Samuel as an early teenager, to get out of the way of a fast swinging wood knot or pan cup ball he would jump and skip or slide sideways so that the ball passed a whisker from his face or his leg. When the bowlers directed the ball to the bottom of the stumps in 'Yorker' fashion, Samuel would protect his bare feet by jumping vertically or sideways. If his timing was off, he was sure to receive a nasty blow. One wood knot ball on the shinbone would result in a swollen leg or worst yet if it hit the forehead that cut would require many stitches.

Tass was not good at making balls or bats but he could play cricket well. Consequently, they treated him as well as Henry the bat maker. The younger boys or those who were clumsy had their chores during the cricket game. Their jobs included finding the ball when it was hit into the bushes or collecting it when it crossed the boundary mark. The boundary mark was always imaginary but everyone seemed to know exactly where it was. The unmarked boundary only became a problem when there was only a small difference between the runs on both sides. A lost ball caused the game to stop temporarily. All eyes would be on the boundary. Fingers would be pointing to an area of green with no special feature where the lost ball might be found. There would be no need for an umpire to determine the number of runs for the shot. It would be six runs for a lost ball.

Every game had two official umpires and many more unofficial umpires as there were spectators. Every spectator was also a commentator. There were shouts of various instructions, "Catch! The man out!" When the ball missed the bat and stumps, and was way outside the pitch, there was a shout: *"Umpire! How's that? He out."* Then there would be quarrelling among different sections of the spectator-umpires.

Picking two teams for a game was a ritual. First, the boys would agree on the two captains. Each captain would pick a member of his side, alternating until all the available boys had a side. If the total number of players was odd, the extra became the Jack-on-both-sides. He was never as neutral as he was supposed to be and he was always accused of batting better for one side than the other. This did not matter much as the Jack-on-both-sides was always the least-abled player.

Some cricket matches between selected teams lasted two days or three days. They began after school and continued until the sun disappeared behind the hills. Tass liked to be batting late in the afternoon as that allowed him to start the batting the next day. Sometimes, Tass had to retire to avoid a strike by the fielding team. The fielding team would refuse to continue if Tass did not give up.

The greatest cricket excitement for children was when there was a match on the school grounds. There were matches between Goat Hill and the other villages, matches between Goat Hill and other islanders who travelled by sail boats from Petite Martinique, Union Island, Canouan or Mayreau. For the villagers, a cricket match was a mini festival. The visitors had to be entertained fully. The villagers slaughtered one or two goats for the occasion. Village women and girls, sometimes accompanied by one or two men cooked in the big three-legged iron pots under the trees that surrounded the school grounds. Strong rum and lime juice would be in abundance. There would be coconut buns and lime juice for the children. And when the match was finished the party continued until it was time for the visitors to return to their villages or, in the case of the overseas' guests, to endure one or two hour sailing in the wee hours of the night.

In those days, many talented cricketers never reached their fullest potential. In today's world, one or two would have made the national or West Indies teams. However, those were the days. There were no cricket scouts to identify cricketing skills, although one or two, after migrating, played county cricket in England. For example, Roy, the teacher, was a fast bowler. Roy had left with a reputation of being a cricketer with potential, which only materialised when he went to England.

6.4   Pitching marbles

Every sport had its season. Like cricket, pitching marbles was a popular pastime among boys between ages six to fourteen. Marbles was a great game because it was played anywhere. Marbles, the size of grapes, were multi-coloured glass balls. During marbles season, one could tell who the best marble players were. When they walked the road, the marbles made a sound like a 'shak-shak' as the many marbles bounced against each other in the swinging pants pocket. Those boys who were poor marble pitchers, but could afford to buy one or two dozen marbles at a time, went around with a full pocket of marbles, pretending to be good marble pitchers. Then there were those who had learnt to save their marbles over a number of years. They too were often poor marble pitchers who walked around with a pocket full of marbles.

Besides the glass marbles, there was the gab, a brown or white coloured ball made from real natural marble. The gab was larger than the glass marble and the larger diameter improved the chance of hitting a glass marble placed in the competition ring. Small iron discarded ball bearings also made good marbles. As they were unbreakable, they were preferable for the pitcher. The 'Tarr' was the name given to the marble that the player controlled. The player placed the 'Tarr' between the thumb and the first finger and directed his shot from a distance to the ring of play. In his marble days, Henry was the king of marbles. On a good day, Henry would win up to three or four dozen marbles.

The game took place around the ring of play, a small nine-inch circle, marked using a stick to carve the ring in the dried grassless soil. On other surfaces such as the main road or a concrete driveway, the boys used a piece of chalk or a stone to place the marking for the circle. A baseline, which formed the base from which the pitching took place, was drawn about two to three feet away from the circle. Each player placed the agreed number of marbles (a wager of sorts) in the ring. The object of the game was to remove marbles from the ring with the pitching marble. The player, from a bending or stooping position, placed his playing hand on the ground directly behind the line from which the pitching marble was cannoned into the ring with marbles, one chance per player, unless the player removed a marble. That player continued until he failed to remove a marble, then a next player would get a turn. Henry would settle his iron marble between his left thumb and first finger and using the appropriate muscles in the left hand direct his iron pitcher to the ring. Any marble that he removed belonged to Henry. Sometimes his iron pitcher would break the glass marble. That would be a loss to Henry. He must ensure that he removed the glass marble intact.

Henry would continue in his bending position and using his pitcher or 'Tarr' would knock out marbles one after another until the ring was empty or almost empty. Only then would another player get the chance. Henry was not that greedy. He would return marbles to former owners, even if the game was for keeps – that is the player could keep the marbles he removed. In fact, if Henry did not do so, the game would be over, unless it was just a friendly game. Henry gave back marbles to continue the game, which he liked doing and at the same time enjoyed being owed a favour by some other 'Lowlings'. Sometimes the game ended in confusion and one had to learn to grab from the ring to get his marbles. The game always ended after a grab.

6.5   A GAME OF STONES

Children loved the game of Stones. It was a cheap game as the only resource was a few small stones no bigger than the marbles. There was no need for storing or saving, except for a 'Tarr' – the stone that the player must catch after tossing the stones in the air. Over time, a player understood the aerodynamics and so could judge the varying speed of the 'Tarr' as it went up and down, and how it behaved in a light or heavy breeze, which punctuated the game. Goat Hill was always a breezy place.

Stones was mainly a girls' game, played individually or in teams of two or three. Each player would have six stones. The player starting the game would have all the stones of the players in the palm of her hand. The other players must then agree on the number of stones one had to pick up at a time, after the spin. To 'spin', the player must raise the hand a little and then turn it over so that stones fall to the ground in no particular pattern but the player must ensure that at least one remained on the back of her hand. That remaining stone she had to 'catch' by raising her hand again and turning it over so that the stone fell inside her palm. If the player failed to catch the stone, that player was 'out' and another must start the game again. When successful in 'catching', whatever the player caught she put aside. She then chose a special stone, which she sent up in the air and must grab the specific number of stones agreed on at the beginning and still catch the stone she sent up in the air. The player repeated the process until she had picked up all the stones. It could be one at a time, two at a time or more, which raised the difficulty of the game.

A player could get 'out' in many ways. If any of the stones fell off her hand in the process, she was out. If she failed to catch the stone she had thrown up, that was also out. When she picked up less than she should or left less on the ground than the number agreed to, that was also out. If her hand touched any of the stones while she was picking up the stipulated number, she was also 'out'. Touching the other stones was referred to as 'shakes'. The player could pick up more than the stipulated number of stones or leave more on the ground. The player had to pick up all the stones successfully to win or end the game. The loser had to get some 'bains'. 'Bains' was a kind of punishment. The winner administered 'bains' by clapping on the loser's out-stretched hand or slapping the loser's hand, which must be placed on the ground. The winner sent up a stone slapped the loser's hand and still caught the stone as it descended. Receiving 'bains' was not a pleasant part of the game and often it ended in fights. Confusion would start when the loser pulled her had away causing the winner to slap the wall on which the loser's hand was resting.

The players changed the complexity of the game by increasing the number of stones to be collected from the surface or using multiple stones in the air. Most times the right hand was used and the 'lefties' were expected to use their right hand. However, when the left hand was used the challenge was greater, but not for the 'lefties'. In a way, it was a type of juggling game. Often the best stone players were the ones perceived as poor at arithmetic, but who were able to count stones taken up or left on the playing platform in a nanosecond. Playing Stones helped to improve children's ability to count and reason and they learnt to master the skills of eye-hand coordination.

6.6 Spinning tops

Top spinning had its season too, although at times it occurred simultaneously with cricket or marble playing. The boys, who were excellent spinners, made most of the tops. Lucile, Samuel's first cousin, was one of the few girls who was a good top spinner. The local tops were made from guava wood. This wood was hard and could resist splitting. Lucile's top was made from pitch pine wood. She always depended on her brother to make her top. He shaped the top from a piece of two by four pitch pine wood that he found lying under the house. It was a piece of wood that her father had left there, intending to use it for making the legs of a wooden stool. The stool would have complemented the two mahogany chairs that the family owned.

Lucille's brother used a cutlass to carve out the top from about six inches of wood. By the time a good top was finished, the maker had destroyed about two and a half feet of wood. The wooden part of the top was conical in shape, rounded at the top and pointed at the base. At the base, a three-inch nail was driven into the top to a depth of about three-quarter of an inch. Then the head of the nail was cut off using an old cutlass or a cold chisel. Once the nail head was removed, the end was sharpened by rubbing it on the grinding stone that was used for sharpening cutlasses and hoes. Lucile's brother then smoothed the top using a piece of broken bottle, until there was sand paper smoothness. Finally, he painted a circle on the flattened part of the top with his red ink pen. He found a piece of twine that was used to stich the flour bag and was ready for top spinning.

Some tops danced well. The art that some children developed allowed them to get the tops to spin in one position for what looked like eternity to children – perhaps no more than a minute or two. They would be very excited at that and referred to it as 'sleeping.' They loved it when their top was sleeping. That meant that the top was well crafted. Some tops 'sang' producing a whizzing or humming sound that brought a smile to the spinner. Some tops were not well designed and danced around in an erratic fashion before jumping into a nearby ditch or bush. Others, too heavy, would land awkwardly on their sides or on the flat surface with the pointed nail in the air. These were the dangerous ones. They might take aim at a bystander and administer a puncture to some part of the body, bringing blood to the surface. Such a top was banned and the owner was left to enjoy his top by himself.

Some children got enough satisfaction and happiness in spinning the top by themselves. However, greater fun seemed to be derived from a competition of splitting tops. In that version of the game, instead of spinning the top on the roadway or on the school's concrete floors, a challenger would place his top on the floor and the other competitor would drive and guide his spinner, attempting to let it spin on the motionless top. A skilled competitor would be able get his top to land on that motionless top and spin on it. In the spinning process and given the force from landing, a motionless top made from a soft wood would split open. If the wood were too hard then the nail of the challenger's top would lose alignment. In extreme cases, the nail was forced further into the competitor's top causing it to split open.

Generally, the first attempt caused no damage. Sometimes the boys played 'jig'. A competitor's top would be spinning and a challenger, using excessive force, would try to land his top on the spinning top with the sole purpose of splitting it or making it useless. The game continued by rotating between challenger and competitor and could last for some time. At the end, there could be a draw if both players' tops remained intact otherwise the loser was the one with the damaged top.

Lucile's top had the record for splitting the most tops. The pitch-pine wood, from which the top was made, came from a mature Canadian pine tree. This type of wood produced the best wood chips for lighting an early morning fire on a wet September morning. Lucile was lucky that her top's prowess never landed her in a fight. Perhaps it was only because she was a girl. Adults did not condone fights between girls and boys, and they monitored most of the children's games from a discreet vantage point.

6.7 Sailing toy boats and the making of the shipwright

Young boys under twelve had an affinity for toy boats. Each boy would make his own boat. Ervin was one of the best toy boat makers among the boys. It was not surprising that he became a master shipwright later in life. There were various types of sailing boats. When Ervin was only five, he made his first boat. It was a paper boat made from folding a sheet of paper from his copybook. That was something that boys of his age tried. It was not easy to get the sequence right every time. However, Ervin on his first try was successful. He tried the boat in a small drain that flowed for about two hours after heavy rain. He placed the paper boat in the drain, which looked like a river in the eyes of the six-year-old boys. It moved along with the flow as if propelled by a motor. At least the boys thought so. It was only later in life that they would understand that the water was flowing by gravity and the paper boat was floating on the surface and being carried along, not moving on its own volition. With his newly found skill, Ervin was soon folding paper for his friends who compensated him by sharing whatever they had or singing his praises for the lovely creations.

Soon Ervin tried his hand at creating a non-paper boat. That was the simplest in a series of toy boats at varying levels of sophistication. Ervin made his second version from a small piece of board, no larger than twelve centimetres by five centimetres and one-half to one centimetre thick. He shaped the wood using a kitchen knife. Then, with a piece of broken bottle as a substitute for a wood plane, he smoothed his creation. Finally, the piece of wood that Ervin started with had a V-shaped bow and a square-shaped stern rounded at the corners with the same instrument that shaped the bow. Ervin then drilled a hole on the deck about one-third the length from the bow, using an old rusty nail and a stone as hammer. Once the hole was large enough, Ervin used a piece of green stick ten to fifteen centimetres long, taken from a tree, for the mast. He had removed the bark from the stick so that it was smooth and resembled the Canadian pine poles carried by the sloops in the harbour. After a few attempts, he fitted the piece of stick in position to form the mast.

Ervin then needed to find the sail for his boat. Sails for such a creation as Ervin had just produced would be a mature clammier cherry leaf or a piece of cardboard salvaged from some old cartoon box. Ervin held the leaf-sail in place by passing the head of the mast through two holes. The holes were one quarter of the way from the bottom to the top of the leaf and as close as possible to the centre line. With his boat now completed, Ervin led a posse of his classmates to the nearby pond where he tried the boat. It was an immediate success. The wind caught in the clammier cherry leaf, pushed the toy boat across the pond in a short time. Ervin did not have to retrieve it from the other side of the pond as many of the boys who wanted to maintain friendship with him, volunteered to retrieve it.

Other boys made a cruder boat using a dried mango seed as the hull and a piece of stick and a leaf as mast and sail respectively. Ervin did not bother to try his hand at this. He thought that it was too basic. After seeing his new creation, all the boys with their mango seed boats lost interest in them, discarding them in the nearest bushes. It was time for them to try their hands at Ervin's latest invention.

The following year Ervin upped his creations. His third creation was the most sophisticated boat made by boys three or four years his senior. He made his boat from gummier wood worked into shape with whatever tools were available to him. First, he had to find the appropriate branch from the gummier tree. Green gummier was preferable as it was easier to work into shape. Like the mango seed boat, the gummier boat had a mast. He cut the sail to suit from old bed sheets or old shirts. The tools he had were a cutlass, a piece of broken glass bottle, a stone as hammer, and rusty nails. Although limited, the tools were sufficient for the task.

Ervin had observed the shipwrights, in the bay, building and repairing the schooners and sloops. He admired the one built by a man named De Roche who had arrived from the neighbouring island of Bequia. Ervin tried his best to replicate De Roche's sloop called Island Pride. He worked the green gummier wood to perfection. The hull was well balanced and the keel well positioned to provide perfect symmetry so that when he placed the boat on the floor it was able to stay upright without toppling over.

Ervin had overheard the experienced sailors from the village say that yachts were fitted with a block of lead attached to the keel, which made it unsinkable. He had never seen such, as in those days, yachts were not pulled up on the beach for repairs. However, he used his imagination. He had seen older boys dismantling old car batteries to salvage lead but had never seem them use it. He negotiated with the village bus driver who had four discarded batteries at the back of his house. Unaware about the dangers in handling lead, he dismantled two old batteries and reclaimed about half a pound of lead in numerous pieces. Then he needed some sand, which he found on the side of the road left there by personnel from the works department. The works department had recently completed repairs to a culvert that had been broken for two to three years.

Ervin melted the pieces of lead in an old pot then poured the molten lead into a hole, which he had made in the sand. The hole matched the shape of his boat's keel. Before the molten lead could solidify, he placed wooden sticks through the lead making two holes. Ervin then removed the sticks before the lead cooled. He used three-inch nails to fasten the solidified lead to the keel. Ervin was convinced that his boat would be able to weather the heavy winds on St. Hilaire Pond, without capsizing. St. Hilaire Pond was the place for mini toy boats regattas.

By this time, Ervin had spent several hours over a week to get to this stage. He was now almost there. Like the less sophisticated versions, the boat also required a mast. He took greater care to create the mast. A piece of pitch pine flooring board one inch by six inches and about eighteen inches long was ideal. It was not too difficult for him to get the material as there were some school repairs going on at that time. Ervin, a sweet talker, was able to convince the foreman on the job to give him a piece of board that had remained after the repairs to the main door were completed. Although the foreman pretended that it was a big favour to Ervin, it really was not as that piece of board would have eventually made its way to somebody's house as firewood.

With the tools at hand, Ervin worked the piece of pitch pine board into a perfect eighteen-inch cylindrically shaped stick like a bandmaster's baton. He then used his crude tools to get it transformed to a mast and fitted in position about one-third the length of the boat from the bow. The boat was then rigged with a mainsail, a jib and a foresail. Finally, Ervin painted the boat with the paint he had salvaged after the painter had completed his job on the school. The boat was now ready, for all the regattas, those at the ponds and those on the beach. Ervin's boat was the talk of the town. When all the regattas were over and having won all the races, he was ready for the next challenge of becoming a real shipwright. By the time he was eleven, Ervin was working alongside men four times his age. Eventually, he donated his boat called the Clipper to the school. The school displayed the boat in the craft centre for over thirty years. During that time, Ervin's name had gone afar as the master shipwright.

6.8 THE MAKING OF COMPLETE INDIVIDUALS AND THE BENEFITS OF GAMES

The games that children played in Goat Hill were critical to their development. They developed athletic skills of eye and hand coordination when they played with homemade equipment. They learnt time management skills as they balanced their home chores or school assignments with roadside games. The children learnt about teamwork from working in teams to build toys, being part of a cricket team and working together in small units to accomplish many other tasks. They learnt about arithmetic and developed measurement skills by playing marbles, stones and other games. They learnt leadership, organisational and negotiating skills by organising small competitions and using strategies to convince a parent to allow a child who did not complete a given assignment to participate in an activity. The children of Goat Hill's community acquired all these skills, which are formally included in modern day school curricula, informally and experientially.

Nowadays, children in the village have electronic games on the computer and the cell phone. Seldom are they encouraged to make a traditional toy. Yes, they are gaining new and different intellectual skills. However, associated with these electronic toys and games are new and emerging maladies, due to a lack of exercise that is fundamental to their development. The games of yesteryear helped to keep the children fit. Many of today's children in Goat Hill, like many children around the world, are overweight. Recently, one of my civil engineering teaching colleagues pointed out that the impact of the absence of these old children's pastimes was evident in the classroom. Many students have difficulty conceptualizing some basic engineering concepts that come naturally from making your own toys or playing the simple games of yesteryear. The games that children played in days gone by had tremendous benefits. The gestation of many future careers found initiation through these games. Perhaps were not appreciated then, but in retrospect, they were critical to the children's wellbeing and the community as a whole.

7

Socioeconomic activities in Goat Hill

7.1 The economic base

The people of Goat Hill were almost exclusively subsistence peasants. The main economic activities centred on small farm holdings, which provided the main food staples of corn, ground provisions, beans and peas. In addition, there were a few cash crops including limes, cotton and peanuts. The production of sugar had long disappeared with the abolition of slavery leaving its legacy of decaying sugar mills that dotted the island. Some of the old sugar mills were renovated as tourist attractions in the current period. Livestock production, which was part of an integrated agricultural system, provided small cash flows for some Goat Hill households. Cattle were exported to Martinique, and sheep and goats to Trinidad where they were in high demand for Hindu and Muslim festivals. Turkeys and chickens were exported to Grenada, where the plantation class improved their Sunday meals with what was available on the plantations. Dogs were also exported to Grenada, for use by hunters. The payment for most of the produce, delivered in La Baye, Grenada, was in the form of cash and ground provisions or fruits. In Trinidad, they were paid primarily by cash, which they used to purchase pitch oil, biscuits, household wares and clothes. In those early days, the Trinidad currency was convertible in local currency.

Agriculture, although small scale and subsistence in nature, was well organised. Agricultural experts are now advocating the approaches and practices to guarantee food sustainability. Those practices were employed in Goat Hill for many generations. The production systems involved mixed-cropping or inter-cropping where corn was planted with legumes and ground provisions. The legumes, that is, pigeon peas and a variety of 'bukusu' beans, produced nitrates for the corn. Sometimes the inter cropping was with corn, peas and cotton. Cassava was also produced but not in close proximity to pigeon peas. Pigeon peas caused the sweet cassava to 'turn' or to produce bitter cassava. The nitrogen compounds produced by the pigeon peas introduced the chemicals for the production of a cyanide compound in the cassava, which caused it to become poisonous.

The people were well versed in the preparations of meals using appropriate combinations of what was produced on the subsistence farm, resulting in one of the most balanced diets in the world. There were okras and a local spinach for leafy vegetables, which provided the vitamins and minerals. There were peas, beans and sesame for their proteins; there were some ground provisions, sweet potatoes, yams and cassava for carbohydrates; and there was corn as the main staple. Also produced was the pawpaw, which was a wonderful fruit and served as a green vegetable when cooked green, or as a meat tenderiser for the meat from the livestock that was often kept for too long, so that their meat was tough. There were plants that grew during the rainy season that were useful at the dinner table. There were native plants some of which were used as supplement vegetables. For example, a hybrid between a 'coraille' and a cucumber, called wild cucumber, was used as a green vegetable. So too was the local spinach which served as a substitute for the dasheen leaves. Most households had at least one of the following fruit trees: sugar apple, soursop, guava, and yellow plum or red plum. A variety of citrus, mangoes and bananas were found in some valleys where runoff was higher than on the hilly Goat Hill.

The only fertilizer that farmers used was pen manure that was composted from the collection of cattle dung in the pastures; pig manure from the pigs, which were tethered under a large enough tree for shelter; and chicken waste from the occasional chicken coop but more often from under the trees in which the chicken roosted. The chickens identified their own resting place by choosing a tree that they returned to every night. As if with wisdom of their masters, they chose trees that were close enough to their owner's house such that, in the case of attacks by the manicou, their owners could rescue them. They did this by using the flambeau to locate the predator hidden in the trees. Most fields, however, were only fertilised by animals' waste, which was deposited during the dry season as they foraged for food. It was in the dry season that animals were first tethered in the fields after all the harvesting was completed.

There was also a small fishing industry, which provided fish that was consumed two or three times for the week in an average peasant's home. Fishing was of two main types: fish pot fishing and line fishing. Fish-pot fishing was a supplemental activity. A few people used fishing nets for catching jacks and anchovies, which were also used as bait. A meal of anchovies and roast bakes was a wonderful meal.

People of all occupations in the village: teachers and headmaster, carpenters and masons, farmers and persons with no specific skills would fish if the opportunity arose. Yet, most people considered fishing a demeaning career. Children who had learning difficulties or who the adults thought were not making academic progress were often jeered at by prophesying that the best they would become was a fisherman or get work on the roads. Excess fish was salted and dried and was a good addition to the protein content in a meal. The dried fish also provided the source of a small cash flow to the fishers' families. The fishmen sold the fish in La Baye, in Grenada, for cash or bartered for ground provisions (for example, dasheen, tannia, and eddoe), coconuts, bluggoes, plantains, bananas, and mangoes when they were in season. In those days, there was no viable fishing industry in the northern part of Grenada as most of the able-bodied workers were employed on the surrounding estates. In any case, fish, particularly, fresh fish was not a significant element in the diet of these estate owners and workers.

7.2 The Madevine's village shop and the Big Stone

In the early days, commerce was limited. There were three small shops in the village. Ms. Daughter operated one from her living room. She traded only in two items: biscuits that came from Trinidad in some square metal containers that held about eight pounds, and sugar cakes. The biscuits were retailed by counting – eight biscuits for a penny. As she did not own a scale, she learnt how to sell so that when her tin of biscuits was exhausted she had the four dollars to purchase a new tin. She would credit biscuits only to her trustworthy customers. In established shops, particularly those outside the village, serious shopkeepers owned scales and retailed their biscuits by counting or by weighing – two ounces, three ounces and quarter pound. Villagers consumed biscuits only in the absence of bakes, so purchases were seldom more than a quarter pound. The sugar cakes that Ms. Daughter sold were made from grated or chipped coconuts. A favourite pastime of the older boys when they managed to save five cents was to purchase a few biscuits and a sugar cake. They placed the sugar cake between two biscuits to produce a 'sugar cake biscuit sandwich'.

In those days, supper for the family could be one and a half dozen biscuits so that each child received two or three while the adult got about five. There was no worry about checking the quota of daily intake of calories. Calories consumption was always within the healthy eating range.

The second small shop was Ms. Browne's shop. She also operated from the living room of her modest house. Ms. Browne sold rum, purchased from a contraband wholesaler, in quantities of a bottle or half a gallon. That was enough to keep sales for one week. Sometimes, a female customer, like Gilly, would visit Ms Browne to purchase an eighth of rum. She would put the small bottle in a brown paper bag then pushed it under her frock, in her waist or in her bosom. For many years, by doing that Gilly was able to hide her drinking problem. Ms Browne's yard was a gathering spot on a month-end for a mixture of Goat Hill and Belvedere boys. They would sit and enjoy a couple of drinks from the two or three eights that they purchased. They never bought rum in larger quantities than an eighth. Cousin Lou ran the third small shop in her downstairs. Like Ms. Browne, she too sold mostly strong rum in small quantities.

In addition to the two living room shops and Cousin Lou's, there was the village shop. The village shop, also known as the Big Stone Shop or the shop in the house by the Big Stone, got the name because of its proximity to a big white stone shaped like a jitney. The shop was located in the downstairs of Madevine's house, the biggest in Goat Hill and perhaps across the neighbouring villages. Construction of the house started during the decade following the emancipation of slavery. Madevine's grandparents who were freed slaves were able to save enough from their meagre savings on the sugarcane estates to purchase the timber and roof material for the upper part of the house. The completion took place sometime after the devastating cholera epidemic of 1850 to 1856, which left almost 4000 persons dead in Grenada. There were only a few deaths in Goat Hill. Madevine's great granfather was one of them.

The lower level of the house was made from stones and mortar. The stones were cut and shaped in blocks from layers of limestone that were left by nature buried one to two feet below the surface of the earth. The mortar was a combination of sand and white lime made from burning dead coral and conch shells, then mixing it with egg yolks. That was perfect cement as the structure had survived over one hundred years.

Back then, the village shop was in full swing.

There were not many items in the village shop, only what was required for basic village needs. There was sugar in bags weighing 140 pounds, wet sugar in drums and sometimes wooden boxes, molasses in barrels or drums, rice and flour both in bags of 100 pounds. Kerosene or pitch oil, which also came in drums, was kept in a narrow corridor. This corridor ran lengthwise in the downstairs separating the outer longitudinal wall from the section in which most of the merchandise were stored. There was cooking oil, a product of coconut, in five-gallon containers, which were placed below the roughly made counter. Cooking oil was not a big selling item as nearly every household produced its own cooking oil from coconuts purchased in La Baye. The villagers purchased other household items from the five established merchants in Hillsborough.

Madevine sold everything in her shop. When empty, she sold the drums, which contained wet sugar or pitch oil for storing rainwater or garden products like dried corn, peas or beans. She sold the jute or crocus bags in which rice and sugar came for transporting and storing corn during the harvesting season. In addition, these bags were premier sleeping mats. Each child had a bag on which to sleep. These bags would be seen spread on some stones in the yard for airing or drying after being urine soaked during the night by children who were unable to control their bladder. The flour bags were always in high demand. When cleaned of all flour remnants, they were used for making shirts and dresses, or under garments for both men and women. To get a flour bag, villagers must put in an order many weeks ahead. The only insurance against Madevine selling the bag at first opportunity was to make a small deposit. Two pence were sufficient.

Madevine operated the shop as needed. During the rainy season, she spent significant time in her garden and villagers would time her so that they knew when she was at home. That way, they wasted no time visiting a closed shop. In any case, the items available were never required for an emergency and so the purchase could always wait until

Madevine was around. She trusted nobody with her shop. When she locked it to attend to some other matter, the keys were secured in a deep pocket that adorned her apron which was so soiled or permanently stained that its original colour could not be determined.

The village shop and the Big Stone together formed the village centre, where most social activities were planned and sometimes were executed. They came to full life on a Saturday evening. Madevine spent the first part of her Saturdays preparing the dough and firing up her mud oven for baking bread, buns and coconut tarts. The oven, which was always given a facelift at Christmas time, was made from a special white chalky soil mixed with fresh cattle dung to form a mortar.

Madevine's village shop, besides providing basic supplies to the village, also served as the village bakery. At the end of the day when she had completed her baking, one or two of the neighbours would use the residual heat in the oven to bake their own bread. Some households that owned stone or mud ovens made their own bread. However, some households baked only occasionally and Madevine's weekly baking was almost guaranteed, providing for the Sunday morning breakfast.

All the young people of Goat Hill would gather at the Big Stone, which provided the stage space for performances. There they told all the traditional stories. There would be lots of singing. The singing of school songs and hymns provided the opportunity for mass participation of the children. Sometimes visitors, mainly young men, whose hidden intention was securing a future partner, would be welcomed. However, they were monitored to ensure that there was no sneaking off to the side bushes with a village girl. The monitoring was never fool proof and occasionally a village girl would get pregnant, mysteriously, as she would have had little known opportunity to date. The explanation was that it could only have been at the Big Stone on a moonless night. The Big Stone was held responsible for teenage pregnancies and coerced marriages.

Saturday nights saw the best of the Big Stone, especially on a full moon night during the dry season when the chance of rain was small.

On such nights, the village elders joined the young people. However, on such occasions, there were usually two separate conversations taking place. The elders switched between French patios and the local dialect laced with phrases from West Africa. The elders used patios to hide "big people" conversation from the young children. The use of patios allowed conversation of a sexual nature among the adults. Nonetheless, some of the children bright enough, were able to make sense of the conversations, and had to pretend a lack of understanding, since to do otherwise would have resulted in a couple slaps behind the head.

One story that many children repeated without understanding was the one called *'the moon bright as day turn back e day."* That was in fact a warning of sorts given to an approaching lover to indicate that the husband was at home. The wife, looking out in the moonlight and seeing the shadow of her lover, pretended that she was commenting about how clear the night was, suggesting that it was as if the day had returned. Villagers also used the expression to tease men who were unaware of a commonly known or sometimes just rumoured observation that their wives were known to be unfaithful.

Small children played coup on Saturday nights around the Big Stone. The game was more interesting during the rainy season when there were good hiding places provided by the crops in the garden. In the dry season, there were fewer hiding places. All the leaves would have already turned brown and were falling or whatever had survived the hot sunny days, hungry animals that foraged for whatever remained in the field had consumed them.

Long after the running of shops by Madevine, Ms. Daughter and Cousin Lou, a few shops got started. Unfortunately, they were all short-lived. Further, being small operations with poor credit management systems, the shops went bust. In the first few weeks of operation, shops appeared to be doing well as nearly every villager would patronize it. Not every villager was well intended as there were those who saw their opportunities for easy unsecured credits.

Although all the *'bad-pay'* villagers were well known, they were still able to play on the goodwill of the shopkeepers who lived in hope. Bad pay people knew when they reached their credit limit. They hid from the shopkeeper for as long as possible then they pretended that they had forgotten about their financial obligation. In some cases, they were bold-faced with their dishonesty. For example, when reminded about an outstanding bill, Linley said to Mr. P, *"Ay Ay Mr. P, you know how long ago I eat and shit out wha I take from you. You want me to pay. Mr. P you carn run shop if you aint credit people."* That was the end of Mr. P's shop. He consumed the stock himself and never sold another pound of sugar after that speech from Linley. Many years later, he was able to laugh at the episode as he retold the story to his friends.

8

MIGRATION FROM GOAT HILL

MIGRATION MANY DECADES ago and like today provided major socioeconomic benefits to Goat Hill. It dampened the effects of poverty. In the early days, families were large averaging around seven or eight but there were women who had as many as eighteen children. Notwithstanding the high birth rates that were characteristic of the early days in these communities, the population remained stagnant, sometimes experiencing negative growth. That was the impact of migration, which had effects like those of a major natural disaster. The migration stripped the village of most of its able-bodied young men, as they were encouraged to look for employment elsewhere. Sometimes young women too took their chances. Were it not for migration, houses would have been too small to accommodate the growing extended families.

8.1 ESCAPING THE GREAT DROUGHT

The great drought in the 1930s gave birth to the beginning of a series of migrations, which produced unsung heroines like Mable. Everyone called her Tan-Tan. In the years 1930 and 1931, the island experienced a significant drought. During that period, rainfall was less than the average. There was suffering on all the small islands in the Grenadines. The crops all failed and there was no work for the peasant farmers who normally supplemented their meagre harvests with cash earnings by working in the fields of nearby cotton or lime farms. Water was a premium. The owners of small sloops had a two-way traffic to Grenville on the mainland, Grenada, taking seafood, peanuts and livestock on their forward journey and provisions, which were not widely available in Carriacou, on their return trip. It was on these return trips that four or five barrels of potable water were transported to quench the thirst occasioned by that mega drought.

The residents of Goat Hill, like their neighbours, travelled long distances to the coastal hand-dug wells and inland ponds for water. For example, Henry's grandmother and the other village women travelled up to High North where there were two ponds and a spring. High North is the highest peak on the island from which one can get a perfect view of the chain of islands starting from St. Vincent in the north to Grenada in the south and sometimes, one could see Tobago in the distance, on a clear day. Only one trip a day was possible given the long distance that they had to travel. Food was in short supply and often for many households only one good meal was possible during those dire times. Although the ponds up on High North were far from the village, the water was of a better quality than the ponds close by. The nearby ponds had little water, which was highly silted, brownish in colour and sometimes smelly from the decaying vegetative matter that was trapped in the surface flow from earlier rainy days. Notwithstanding the poor quality, both people and animals competed for that water.

It was a difficult time for all the people. Without work and with food and water in short supply, it was not surprising that there was mass migration. All over the world, then and now, people migrate in the hope of a better life. However, it was during that drought that the stronger among the youth migrated to wherever possible. Some went to Tobago to seek work on the cocoa plantations. Some went to Grenville to work in the nutmeg and cocoa fields. To many, the disappointment was great. It was like jumping from the frying pan into the fire. Life was also very difficult in those new destinations. The newcomers were often exploited. They worked for long hours, sometimes from 6 a.m. to 8 p.m. Those long hours did not guarantee timely or full payment.

Like in all adversities, some would survive better than others would and sometimes flourished. It was during this period that Mable, who long afterwards got the name Tan-Tan, left for the mainland and arrived in the town of Grenville. Many years afterwards, Mable told the story of that life-changing trip. The two-bow wooden sloop, which was no longer than twenty-eight feet, was loaded with human and animal cargo. The captain maximized every bit of space as he carried a significant portion of his cargo free of charge (gratis). The villagers from Goat Hill and all the surrounding villages were grateful to whoever might take their half-starved animals, including cattle, donkeys, sheep, goats, pigs and even dogs, for a fair price. A fair price had no serious meaning during this severe drought. The alternative to accepting the price offered was to hold on to the animals for a further week or two hoping for the impossible, a better price. The consequence for those who were foolhardy enough to use that route was the predictable death from starvation of those animals, which meant a total loss to the owner.

When Mable (Tan-Tan) told the story to her grandchildren later, she described how they could smell the stench that came from the boat's hold. Both animals and passengers were seasick for the six-hour journey, passing stress-induced wastes through the mouth and the rear. A mixture of the different animals' faeces, and the seasickness induced vomiting of undigested dry grass and leaves, made even the hardened sailor's stomach upset. It was not strange for one or two of the animals to die during the trip. When that happened, and the weather allowed, they threw the dead animals overboard. This resulted in a loss of income to both the owner of the animal and the owner of the boat, as he had to forfeit his freight.

Once settled in Grenada, Mable did well for her family and herself.

She found work on the Grand Bras and Mirabeau estates. She was lucky, for on her first day at work, one of the female workers, an elderly woman, took to her and invited her to stay at her modest one-bedroom house. Without that invitation, Mable would have had to make it as best as she could in one of the barracks used as living quarters for families.

The barracks, used originally for housing slaves, had seen no improvement for over one hundred and thirty years. They had served the slave owners well, minimising the cost of providing housing for their slaves who provided labour for their agricultural enterprises. Now they served as a place where destitute descendants of the African slaves must seek refuge during droughts in the smaller islands. The living conditions for those free Negroes, who fled from the drought, were no different from those of slavery according to the stories of earlier generations. The conditions for these new migrants from Goat Hill were only slightly better than during the days of slavery in that there was generally more space per dweller and the dwellers had some say in whether they worked on a particular day or not. Nonetheless, getting sick or a decision not to work could mean going hungry for a day or two, unless rescued by a Good Samaritan, who existed in fair numbers.

Mable worked hard and consistently saved a portion of her meagre wages. She noticed that the families who did better in their new environment were those that owned a piece of land. She was determined to get for herself a lot of land. One day, Mable heard that some lands were for sale in the neighbourhood. She approached the estate overseer who acted as real estate agent for the estate owners and made her intention known. She was prepared to purchase a portion. The agent was surprised at that bold young woman. In those days, the only lands owned by women were lands they had inherited. He at first refused to entertain any business discussion with Mable and suggested that she got her husband to come forward to initiate any transaction. Mable was not perturbed and responded that there was no man involved and she was quite capable of negotiating on her own behalf.

Time after time, the overseer ignored Mable who was persistent. That insistence was too overwhelming for him. He began to admire her entrepreneurial spirit. About five months later, he sent a message for Mable. He had decided to sell her two acres. The productivity of that block of land had become too low for the estate owners and it was time to divest of it. Mable seemed to make miracles with her lot, working long hours after her regular fifty-five hours per week on the main estate. On the estate, she earned enough to take care of her husband who had always remained in the background and their three children. With the high production of fruits, cocoa and nutmegs from her plot, Mable made the mandatory down payment and from thereon made the required mortgage payment. Sometimes she paid more than the required amount allowing her to complete the payment ahead of schedule.

That was the story of how that family member from Goat Hill planted its roots in the St Andrews area of Grenada. She never forgot her homeland, sending some of whatever was available on her farm to her parents in Goat Hill. She also returned at least once every two years to visit. The trips on the sailing sloops that first brought her out of the drought, seeking a better life for herself, had changed little over the years. The importance of migration resumes in a later chapter.

8.2   A Goat Hill boy goes to England

Indeed, everyone remembers Henry who was the force-ripe handyman in the family. He had established a reputation for efficiency in milking the cows, grinding corn for lunch or dinner, and was good at making mischief. All the difficult chores that Henry endured, without ever complaining to his parents, grandparents or aunt did not dampen his spirits. He believed that all of this was going to end one day. One day soon, he believed that he would be going to England. Dreams about going to England although not unique to him were somewhat interesting. There was an expectation for that particular dream to be realised. Henry's parents had already tried making a living in Aruba and Trinidad. When he was still young, his parents returned to Goat Hill. Things had not worked out as well as they had planned. Nonetheless, the Aruba experience provided the family with a modern brick house and a small cistern. That was the envy of many in Goat Hill.

Unable to stay put, Henry's father, Uncle Vic, had migrated to England about nine years before, where there was a chronic shortage of labour to rebuild England after the great European War. Once he had settled, and was able to save enough, Uncle Vic sent for his children. It was during that cycle of family reassembling that Henry began his journey of migration like his grand uncle Josiah Abraham, who fifty years earlier had journeyed to New York. There he had enlisted in the US Army during the First World War. Henry remembered the lone framed black and white photograph hanging on the unpainted partition at his grandmother's house. That photograph was one of about five photographs found in Goat Hill. They were all portraits of different young men who had travelled and sent back their first photographs which all of Goat Hill admired. The photograph on the partition at Henry's grandmother had been there so long that it had faded from its original black and white to a pale brown. The villagers told and retold stories of the fortunes of young men who had gone to the Big World. There was very little material evidence to demonstrate the fortunes. Yet the stories, which often were creations of fiction, continued with greater grandeur as time passed. It was therefore not surprising that going to England was a constant dream of many young men in the village.

Henry too dreamt that dream. However, now that the dream had come true he was not so keen on this reality. He was enjoying his young life. He moved regularly between the villages of his father in the south of the island to Goat Hill, his maternal village. That happened nearly every weekend after he had received a new brand bicycle, which was the only one remaining at the time in the showcase of W. E. Julien and Sons. Henry had written to his father in England to ask for the bicycle. The response to his request was not positive as his father lectured him about how hard things were in England at that time. He told his son that he did not pick up money from the streets of London. Henry did not quite understand this and hence he was disappointed.

Not too long after the disappointing response from his father, one of Henry's uncles returned from England on a visit. To Henry's surprise and joy, his father sent him the money for the bicycle. It was after purchasing the bicycle that Henry increased his visits to his grandmother's home. His Raleigh bicycle had been the envy of his peers as only a few working professional adults owned that type of bicycle. His grandmother was proud that he had his bicycle but was always worried that he might get into some accident. Unfortunately, her concern was realised one day. One morning on his way to school in the town, it happened. The report that his grandmother received about the accident on the Cherry Hill road was highly exaggerated. Henry recalled the faces of the frightened Madonna Sisters (Catholic nuns) as his bicycle flew over the hood of the small car, which was driving slowly up the hill towards him. He received only small bruises although his bicycle sustained some damages.

The accident happened not too long after he had started high school. He was one of the first students of Bishop's College. Bishop's College was an initiative of the Anglican Church to bring secondary education to Carriacou and Petite Martinique. It created more opportunities for the academically inclined young people who otherwise would not have been able to attend one of the high schools on mainland Grenada. He was enjoying his new school especially as his bicycle had made him a star at school. Consequently, he was apprehensive on receiving news that he would be going to England soon. He had made new friends at his new school. He would miss them. He had no choice in the matter. His father, Victor, had decided that it was time for his eldest son to leave Goat Hill for a better life in England. Already, Henry's older sisters had joined their father. There was no way for him to prepare for life in England, except that he had gotten a good primary and early secondary school education. No one from Goat Hill had returned to describe the life. Further, correspondence from his sisters was always silent on the level of youthful enjoyment in that far-away place.

The first part of Henry's journey to England began with a slow and painful trip on a locally built sloop from Hillsborough to St. Georges. This was the mail boat, which made two return trips per week with mail and passengers. Although he was very comfortable on the sea, this trip was different. As the boat made its way through the blue waters of the Caribbean Sea in a southward direction, he looked back at the outline of the small islands in the horizon and could barely see the outline of Union Island. His mind was filled with many thoughts. He wondered whether the weather was better in Canouan and Mayreau, which were further away. He thought of his bicycle that he had left behind. He worried about the ability of his younger brother and sister to manage the animals that he had tended for years. He worried about his aunt and cousins he left in Goat Hill. He would miss his aunt's cooking. He was a 'picky' eater. He did not like coo-coo except when it was left overnight and fried. He also hated ochra (called ochroes by the islanders) in all forms. He could not imagine what the food would be like in England.

On this trip, Henry paid little attention to the small islands that he passed on the way. The golden sand on the beach around Sandy Island was void of beach-goers as this was a weekday. The schools of jacks and sprats, which seemed to be circumnavigating the sandbank, could be seen from far in the clear turquoise water. The seagulls flew above following the jacks and every now and then two or three would dive simultaneously only to ascend, sometimes, with their catch securely held in their beaks. In the past, Henry loved to look at such a scene as it helped him to pass the time. This time he showed no interest as he was contemplating life in England.

Taking advantage of the squall, the captained steered the sloop close to the southern side of Jack-a-dam. The boat was so close to the island that the passengers who were still strong and not yet seasick could count the native trees. These trees were no taller than six feet, twisted by the Atlantic gusts and battered by the salt sprayed from the waves that splashed on the black slippery boulders. The boulders lined the shores of the small, uninhabited island. The local family who owned the island, tried a long time before to populate it with goats, but the island was too dry for most of the year to sustain livestock.

Soon Jack-a-dam was behind them and the two small bare rocks, called Two Sisters, appeared in the distance straight ahead, as two small cones. Two small rowboats, with two occupants each, mere feet from steep the rocks of Diamond Rock, were tossed by the waves, bobbing up and down. There was no place to drop and anchor as the sides of the rocks disappeared almost perpendicularly deep down below the surface of the water. That was a good spot to fish for redfish and groupers. Henry had fished at this spot many times. He noticed the men in the boats. During the time that the boats were visible, one man was seen pulling in about a dozen fishes, which was considered a good catch. Henry looked up in the sky and saw the moon. He thought to himself that that was the reason for the man's good catch. He showed interest in the men and their catch while they were in sight, then his mind went back to his trip to England.

Henry was so deep in thought that he was unaware of the excitement around him. The other passengers were transfixed by a pod of dolphins that were moving in circles around the boat. They jumped out of the water in a synchronised formation, as if planned and rehearsed. During one of their displays, passengers screamed. Those dark grey creatures seemed ready to land on the deck. Perhaps if the boat was smaller or if one of the dolphins was more daring it might have hurdled over the boat. However, that was not the day for such a miracle. It had never happened before and was not about to occur on Henry's first lap of his long journey to the Queen's country.

All this passed Henry as his mind had preceded him to Huddersfield where his girlfriend's father resided. Soon she would be going there. Her father, like Victor, had made it a priority of sending for his children from the islands to be with him. Henry daydreamed of walking from London to Huddersfield. London to Huddersfield in England was not like Harvey Vale to Belview in Carriacou. Henry would later learn that the trip was only possible by train, which was unlike his experiences in Carriacou where he could visit every day. Once his girlfriend arrived, visits would only happen, at best, once a year.

Henry was so engrossed that when the boat passed Diamond Rock, where the channel is called Kick-em-Jenny, he did not feel the difference in the ride, which became rougher nor did he see the goats on the rock. Diamond Rock perhaps got its name from its shape, since a view of the rock from above showed a perfect diamond. There were a few goats at the top, which was about five hundred feet above the deep blue water that surrounded the tree-less and shore-less volcanic island. On previous journeys, Henry had wondered on how the goats survived such harsh conditions. These goats must have evolved to be able to survive on little water like the camels of the desert. Whatever water was available was what remained in the small depressions in the rocks from the frequent showers, during the rainy season. Every year, police officers with rifles would sail to the vicinity of Diamond Rock and from their boats shoot any animal that was within range. When they are lucky, the animal would fall to the shoreline from where they retrieved it. Many years later, the island was cleared of goats, as soldiers and the militia used them as target for practice and a free meat supply until the last one was killed. How many fell over cliffs or into crevices, remained unknown.

The wind picked up and the boat began to make good time. Soon it was to the west of a pair of rocks almost identical is shape, height, size and distance apart as Two Sisters. These were Two Brothers. The seagulls and pelicans flew over Two Brothers, which was white from the guano that the birds deposited over the centuries on the rocks' faces. There were few plants. Two cacti at the summit of one rock stood as military guards in green uniforms. Below the cacti, there were a few stunted evergreen trees, which survived the harsh marine environment by sucking the nutrients from the guano-filled crevices. The cacti for many years stood as monarchs of Two Brothers until they were uprooted by a hurricane and found a watery grave not far from where they were deposited on the western side of their place of origin.

The small sloop, which was the mail boat, sailed past the western side of the mainland with a view of its mist covered mountains in the background. The lush green vegetation intermingled with the yellow and pink poui trees was always an attraction to Goat Hill travellers to the mainland as they compared it with the brownish and dry landscape that was left behind. As the boat approached midway sailing along the coast of the mainland, Henry could smell the spices, which were processed and stored at the nutmeg receiving station. Henry reminded himself that he must purchase some of the spices to take to his aunts in England.

Henry arrived in St. Georges just as the sun was disappearing in the horizon leaving behind an orange red glow in what was otherwise a clear evening sky. He spent the night with friends of his family in the countryside. He did not sleep well that night and had counted all the frogs that croaked around the house between midnight and early morning. There was about a dozen, at least, so he thought. He was the first out of bed next morning, packed all his things and readied himself for a ride on the wooden bus back to St Georges where the boat docked once every two months. There he awaited the tender that ferried the tourists, both Europeans and the new ones that joined the ship at each island stop. Henry was now a tourist, although he did not realise it. He must reorient his thoughts as he began his trip to England.

It appeared that there was a special tender for the locals. It could not take the maximum number of passengers as each passenger boarded with a trunk and a grip (other names for suitcases in those days). It was a short trip from the pier to the MV Irpinia. One of the passengers was returning to England, after his second trip at home, where he had recently bought ten acres of cocoa lands. One could tell that he was a special migrant on this trip. He appeared a bit cocky. Further, his baggage included a relatively weather beaten trunk, which seemed to be partly empty as the porters were able to lift it without too much effort. Perhaps he had left most of his English acquired clothes behind as gifts to his poor relatives. In any case, he was happy that this trip was on the MV Irpinia.

He had travelled twice before on the MV Ascania, which floated with a four-degree permanent list causing it to look like it might roll over in bad weather. The MV Ascania and MV Irpinia were two Grimaldi ships, which provided a post-war market for cheap emigrant ships. Initial services were from Italy to Central America. The MV Ascania, built in 1926, was christened on the Florida route. It was retrofitted in 1955 to provide for 183 first class and 932 tourist class passengers on services from Southampton, Vigo and Lisbon to the Caribbean and Venezuela. Both ships carried mainly Spanish and Portuguese migrants on their way to the Caribbean, and West Indians to the United Kingdom on the return voyages. The MV Irpinia was similar in size and build, but was the preferred ship although it was a little more expensive than the MV Ascania.

Indeed, Henry was a tourist on the MV Irpinia. He felt like a tourist although somewhat out of place among all those white Europeans who had visited the Caribbean and Central America as tourists. He was in one of the cheapest cabins all of which were right at the bottom and windowless. Yet he did not mind. The space was cramped, dark and musty but much better than the conditions his ancestors of Goat Hill were required to endure while being transported through the Middle Passage of the Great Triangle. Henry used the cabin only when he was tired, and that meant for a short period during the night. The resulting sleep lasted for no more than three to four hours.

Meal times were special to him. Red wine flowed at the table without limits. As he had tasted wine only at Christmas, he was anxious to have the free wine. This wine was different. It was not sweet. The wine that Henry and the children drank at Christmas time was sweet. There were three choices: cherry brandy, St. Vincent black wine, which was the product of many tropical fruits and the BG (British Guiana) Black wine. Henry observed how the Europeans sipped their wine. He observed also that the West Indian passengers grimaced when they drank the wine. They did not like it. Ordinary West Indians were not used to drinking wines made from grapes. They were not sweet enough. Henry said to himself "if they could, I could also". He looked carefully at the Europeans, and he mimicked the way they drank their wine. Henry was good at mimicking. The wine did not quite appeal to his taste, but soon he was the only West Indian 'tourist' who seemed to be enjoying it. He drank both red and white. There was plenty to drink.

The first few days of the trip across the Atlantic were mostly uneventful. There were only a few spots of rough seas. For the most part, the sea was as flat as a pancake and as smooth as oil. This, however, did not prevent a few passengers, mainly West Indians, from getting seasick. As this was the first time for a few at sea, and without having seasickness tablets, the slightest roll of the ship caused unprocessed food in the stomach to return to its place of entrance. Henry looked at a young woman vomiting one day and thought, "What if she had to travel from Harvey Vale to Grenville on the seven-meter long sloop, loaded with corned fish and corned 'lambi', a few chickens, a pig and sometimes a donkey or a cow?" Henry recalled the times he had travelled on Mispar and Success between Carriacou and Grenada. Those were the good days and great adventures. Such trips began on Friday morning and occasionally, on very calm days, took up to fifteen hours for the twelve-mile journey. Sometimes, the ship-hands used oars to assist the sails. That task required each man on-board to contribute. Henry remembered being able to go to the cinema in Grenville. He smiled and laughed silently to himself hoping that those around him might not think that he was mad.

Now it was a different time. The MV Irpinia was as heaven compared to the sloops Mispar and Success. Henry, the tourist, occupied one of the cheapest cabins far below deck. After the first night of sailing, the ship berthed at Roseau, Dominica, the nature island and the island where Columbus, if he returned, would see little change. In

Dominica, few passengers disembarked. Henry observed the mountainous and lush green landscape. The next stop was Martinique, one day later. Nearly all the English-speaking West Indians disembarked for a few hours. There was not much of interest for unexpected tourists to purchase so with an eyeful of the French-speaking city, they returned to their cramped cabins and to the ship's dinner, which was lavish by their standards.

As the ship headed further north, the weather changed. It was getting colder. After one week on-board, the impact of the reducing temperatures was evident on the passengers. In addition to language and race, telling the difference between the Europeans and the West Indians was easy. The Europeans sat on deck shirtless. The West Indians moved around wearing three and four shirts. Many did not have clothes for the cold air that originated from the cold lands in the north. Henry 'played' man. He mimicked the Europeans. One day when the boat was now in temperate waters, he went on deck shirtless. He was freezing inside, but did not show it. After three days, he did not feel the cold. His West Indian mates marvelled at his ability. That was good for him; perhaps he would love England.

The MV Irpinia's first port of call from the Caribbean was Tenerife, the largest and most populous island of the seven Canary Islands. The Canary Islands belong to Spain. There were similarities between Tenerife and the islands that were the homelands of the low-income tourists from the Caribbean. The lack of adequate shopping money did not deter the West Indians from taking in the new European scene. Perhaps if there was money, Henry may have found himself in trouble. Two small boys were targeting him to do business with a young woman who was waiting in a small room close by. The boys knew little English but as pimps, they made their intentions clear by using the fingers to simulate the action of sex, pointing to where the girls were hiding. He brushed them off and continued his site seeing. He was not prepared to waste his money.

The next stop for the ship was Barcelona on the Spanish mainland.

At that port, a few tourists departed and some new faces replaced them. Henry and some of the other West Indians marvelled at the size of the buildings, the traffic, the trains and trams. For many of these West Indian 'tourists', it was the first time that they were seeing many of these features in real life. The cruise continued on to Genoa, a small port city in Italy. Henry remembered the name Genoa from his history class. He recalled that there was some association with that city and Christopher Columbus.

In Genoa, Henry found himself reflecting on his journey thus far. He had travelled from Grenada, stopped in Dominica then Martinique before crossing the Atlantic to Tenerife. That trip had boosted his knowledge in geography. He wondered if his geography teachers had any real idea of the places they described to their students. All the West Indian migrants turned 'tourists' had disembarked in Genoa to begin their ride through the continent to England. The first stop was in Paris. The great concern now for the migrants was keeping warm. It was early February and the European winter was still in full force. There was little motivation for sightseeing in Paris. The result of the devastation of the war which was less than two decades earlier, was there for everyone to see. However, the migrants were oblivious of these things as they struggled with surviving in that new environment. From Paris, Henry and the other migrants travelled to Calais, the northern ferry port in France, where they crossed the channel to Dover in England. That was not a bad ride as most of the migrants, by then, had become battle ready for the sea. In any case, the ride was short, compared to the past fourteen to twenty-one days that they had spent in the most uncomfortable cabins on the MV Irpinia.

It was Saturday, the sixth day of February. Henry was now in Dover. As he walked on land, he felt the ground moving under his feet. It felt like he was still on the boat in the ocean. It did not take too long for him to overcome this feeling. He looked at the sign on the passengers' terminal that read Dover. Dover was the name of a village that formed part of the Goat Hill district. He wondered what the reception would be like. He was not hungry after he was lavishly fed for the past three weeks. The 'tourist' life had ended abruptly. He then had to travel from Dover to Victoria Station by train. By that time, he had gotten used to the train as the cross continental ride had prepared him for the London trains. Henry's dad, Uncle Vic, had somehow lost track of the date and was expecting him to arrive one day later. There was therefore no one to meet Henry at the Victoria station. Luckily, a boy from Henry's village who had been in England for two years before was at the station to greet his relatives. He knew where Uncle Vic lived and offered to take Henry home after Henry had indicated that he had one pound. A white taxi driver assured the two boys that the one pound was sufficient to pay for the ride to Henry's dad and to take Henry's friend to his home. There was no change from the pound and the taxi driver enjoyed his good fortune of a hefty tip.

They arrived at Stoke Newington, N 16. As Henry climbed the stairs to the door of his father's apartment, the cold that penetrated his short sleeve nylon shirt and his oversized cardigan did not seem to bother him. He was thinking of what he would do if his father were not at home. He was sure that he had the right address. He knocked. Within a minute, someone opened the door. Yet that minute seemed to be forever to the young lad.

His father was surprised. "Is that you Henry?" exclaimed an overjoyed Victor. "I was expecting you tomorrow," he continued. Henry had arrived in a place overflowing with smog from the coal belching chimneys. He entered his father's one-bedroom living quarters, which was sparsely furnished. There was a paraffin heater which was used for cooking and which made inside as smoggy as outside. He saw a small bed, which was eventually shared between father and son, a table and two chairs and not much else. Henry was disappointed. He had enjoyed much better accommodation back home. He then understood what his father meant about not picking up money on the streets. This was a new discovery for Henry. He felt sorry for his father, and realised then, how great the self-sacrifice his father had been making to provide for his family's needs back at home. Henry was now beginning his life as a Londoner.

On his first day in London, it snowed. As Uncle Vic had to go to work, there was little time to bond. Henry got directions to where his elder sisters lived. Uncle Vic gave the following directions: "Take the N0.102 Bus, ask the conductor to let you off at Bethnal Green station, E2 - continue straight on, take the first right. The even numbers are on the right and the odd numbers on the left. Your sisters live in Apartment No. 81". Henry followed the instructions well but became anxious, as the bus seemed to be taking forever to his stop. Twice he asked the conductor, "Are not there yet?" "Take it easy, I'll tell you when we get there," the conductor replied each time. Once off the bus, he found his way to his sisters. It was a good walk as the first house from the bus stop was number three. His sisters, like his father were surprised to see him. That was how Henry started life with his family in England. It was one of his sisters' birthday. It was a birthday without celebration.

It was a new life. That new life was not what Henry had quite expected. The few books that he had read and the magazines he had skimmed through did not prepare him for what he found. There was running water, which was a novelty. Washing in a tub indoors was new. Back at home, in the Caribbean, there was a greater familiarity with washing on the stones in the rivers but in villages such as Goat Hill, or in smaller islands, there were no rivers. While Henry had experienced electricity in Grenville, he had never seen a washing machine. That would have been a luxury at the homes of the few well-to-do. Washing was of a communal type activity and took place around the small earthen pond that was used to harvest rainwater. The villagers also obtained water for washing from the wells. Soon Henry forgot all about life in Goat Hill. He was now a Londoner, an Englishman. He settled for the food that his father cooked. It was rice and pork belly nearly every day. Pork belly was the cheapest meat available. With this menu, as it was winter, when the food was cold the fat from the pork belly congealed and sometimes it was not warmed for long enough before eating. At first, it was difficult for Henry but this menu allowed one to live on six shillings a week. That was part of the sacrifice men made in order to provide for their loved ones back home. Things improved over the years and Henry settled into his two jobs and became a true Englishman. It would be many years before he would return to Goat Hill, perhaps to build a mansion like Uncle Vic did on his return from Aruba.

8.3　Max the lazy migrant

Max was one of the privileged boys of Goat Hill. His mother had migrated to America and had saved enough money to return to Goat Hill. She bought two acres of land and built a lovely wooden house, which stood out for its modernity at the time. As an only child, Max was pampered in his younger days. That must have contributed to his laziness, for he never worked hard. Although forced to take greater responsibility for his life when his mother went blind, he continued to shy away from any hard work such as working in the lands. He did not mind taking care of small livestock but he found dealing with cattle too difficult. Instead, he used his mother's savings to purchase a few cows, which he gave to other villagers, including Dudley, who cared for them. The villagers reared the cows on a shared basis. That shared approach was an equivalent to the sharecropping concept that developed in the USA after the end of slavery. After two years, the cow, which Dudley was rearing, gave birth to a bull. Dudley reared the bull for eighteen months then sold it. Max shared the proceeds equally between Dudley and himself. Max loved this arrangement. After another fourteen months, the cow gave birth to a heifer. Under the arrangement, this calf belonged to Dudley. The next calf if female belonged to Max who always preferred a bull. A heifer for Max would only mean that he must give it to someone else to rear, which increased his waiting time for a return on his investment. Notwithstanding his experience with Dudley, every other year, Max received one calf and some earnings from the sale of a bull so he expanded his total stock of cows. In addition, he got an almost continuous supply of fresh milk. He managed well on this arrangement until villagers refused to take his cows. He sold his cattle and lived off the money until it was finished. That caused severe grief to his mother who died heart-broken not long before Max became bankrupt.

Without work and with his mother's savings exhausted, Max found his first opportunity to migrate. He was selected to travel to Florida to pick fruits. On this contract, Max, not known for hard work, did not make as much money as the other migrants on the same contract. They were paid based on the quantity of fruits picked, and since Max's harvest was always the smallest, his remuneration was the least. He nevertheless was able to find good scheme by which his co-workers would supplement his income. At the end of the first fruit-picking season, Max returned to Goat Hill just before Christmas with five suitcases. He had used most of his earnings to purchase shoes, clothes, and accessories for women. These he had bought from autumn sales at department stores. However, the commodities were of questionable quality. He started a clothing shop in his mother's house. In the first few days, villagers flocked to Max's house and took items on an informal hire purchase basis. Unfortunately, some buyers were never able to save enough to pay Max, while others returned the items some days afterwards, complaining that the items were dry-rotten. The major complaints were that shoe soles dropped off, or the trousers had ripped in the crotch. Soon Max realised that the business was not as successful as he would have liked.

The following year, Max had a second contract for picking fruits in the USA. He had learnt from his earlier experiences to be more selective in the items that he bought for his clothing shop. On his return the second time, Max had four suitcases and two barrels. The barrels were shipped sometime before his departure from the USA and his cousin Lenard had received them. Once Max had settled down on his return home, he reopened the shop. Sales went better this time, as Max did not give credit to many people. This time too, the quality of the goods was much better and people came from surrounding villages to do business. After six months, about half of the items remained. Max gave his cousin the task of selling the remaining items for whatever he could get. This time he had broken even, since most items were sold for about three times the original cost.

Max had a weakness for gadgets. He had brought many things, some of which could not be used because there was no electricity and that was necessary. The most interesting item on his second return was what he called his mobile toilet. As the only sanitary facility used at the time was pit latrines or open defecation in most cases, Max's mobile toilet was a big hit among the villagers. The closest object to his toilet was a potty, used indoors during the night and emptied during the early morning by throwing the night soil in a nearby toilet or into the bushes. Max used his mobile toilet only a few times, as he soon found out that a potty or a pail was easier to clean.

In the third year, Max did not return to pick fruits. He had the opportunity to go to a far off island in the southern Atlantic Ocean. He went to the British territory called Ascension Island. Max did not like the place because of its isolation. There was very little to do except go to work, but the pay was very good. The all-men labour force was engaged in the construction of the BBC Atlantic Relay Station for short-wave broadcasts to Africa and South America. There was no form of entertainment. Max had a substantial savings account at the end of eighteen months. On the return trip from Ascension Island, he stopped off in New York where he once more bought clothes, shoes, hats, caps, and other small items that he believed could be peddled profitably. His most interesting purchases were short wave transistors and a battery powered TV with a small collapsible antenna. The most anyone saw on this TV were white snow-like images.

The neighbourhood children led by Edward gathered to look at the TV. They were creative and imaginative. They described in detail the actions of people and the movements of cars and other objects that they saw. They remembered the silent movies of Charlie Chaplin that they once viewed during a community show put on by the government. They heard voices as the statics from the wireless signals produced noises at different levels. These were only imaginary. Nevertheless, Max was happy for the children and he assured them that next day things would be better. They would be able to see clearer. Perhaps Max believed this himself. He was not aware that he needed access to a TV station to enable reception. Max had been impressed with the black and white movies he saw during his brief stop in New York on his return trip from Ascension Island.

Finally, Max who the village thought would be a bachelor all his life fell in love, or perhaps, someone fell in love with him. He was always well dressed and this attracted many women. However, none had any luck in securing a long-term relationship. It was not that Max was not the marrying type. In fact, he had pursued a village girl for many years, but Marvis' family never approved of the relationship because of his lazy disposition. It was never clear whether Marvis herself was interested in a long-term relationship. Every evening, Max dressed in his Sunday suit, greased and combed his hair so that his Negroid hair looked as straight as that of an Indian. He over applied the cheap Cuscus perfume and whistled and sang Spanish songs, which he had learnt from his contact with natives of Central America, while on his fruit picking contracts. No one understood Spanish; hence, it was never clear whether Max was singing the correct words. What was clear was that he was obsessed with Marvis. Max had two sons, one when he was a teenager and the other when he was in his forties. He was proud of his sons but was never able to take good care of them, as he was often broke.

Max's newly found love was a nurse who had migrated from a neighbouring village to Goat Hill many years earlier. She might have been secretly in love with Max during their youth. It was never clear how this new contact came about. She had been recently divorced and wanting for companionship and love, and offered to marry Max. He could not refuse this offer, as he was under the impression that the woman was well off. He imagined a life without hard work in the USA. They got married and Max followed his wife to the USA. This was the final in the series of migration episodes.

Things did not work out as expected and Max was soon on his own again. However, he was now a permanent resident of the USA and on the way to citizenship. He made a couple of trips afterwards to Goat Hill in order to repair his inherited house to which he added two bedrooms and a water cistern. Max never stayed more than one month on his visits except when he brought items to stock his shop. Then he would remain until he had sold most of the items. America was ideal for his natural laziness. He worked only for short periods. In almost all cases, he had a self-created accident on the job, which provided insurance compensation. He lived his days visiting friends and relatives in New York until his compensation money was used up, then found another job and repeated the cycle. However, he had tried his trick once too often and the authorities caught up with him. They declared him permanently disabled. He ended his days living on a small social security income. Max exploited his migration opportunities but migration exposed the real Max.

8.4 Making It Against All Odds

There was an interesting story told about emigration to England. The story, which was told repeatedly, was about JC. Not all the children of Goat Hill attended the nearby school in Dover. St. H, who later became the ace carpenter and some of his cousins, went to a school in Mt. Pleasant, which was about three to four miles away. It was while attending the school in Mt. Pleasant that St. H met JC, an exceptional boy, who became his good friend. JC was highly motivated and read anything available. Of course, what was available to read was not much as the school library was scantily furnished and the older students had priority to select and to borrow books for a maximum of two weeks.

At age twelve, JC was the most effective reader among those who were under the age of fourteen. Light went off early at JC's home, a practice that was necessary to conserve pitch oil used for the lamps. However, JC had mastered the art of reading in the moonlight. The late rising of the moon did not prevent his night reading.

One day, JC's stepfather, who had just returned from Aruba, noticed him at his favourite reading spot, which was a big black boulder, perhaps two tonnes in weight and half-buried in the shallow chalk-like soil. The stepfather had never seen such a studious boy. He himself was not good at reading and did not think that reading was so important for any young man's future. He shouted at JC, "Are you a queer?" He was not enquiring about his sexuality. Queer was a word used to describe weird behaviours. The stepfather ordered JC to return home. He never forgot this.

He did well at the Eleven Plus examination. Moreover, he had one of the best results for that year. Nonetheless, he was not motivated to go to high school like some of his other pals who became prominent physicians, engineers and lawyers. Back then, he was as good as or better than they were but he showed no interest in attending secondary school. He was haunted by what his parents were likely to say after spending to educate him for five years: "Look how much money we spent on you and look at what you have turned out to be." JC knew that they had low expectations of him. At age twelve, he was not able to overcome the negative labels attached to boys and young men of his time. In retrospect, he appeared to have lost a great opportunity. Notwithstanding, he made a good man of himself later in life.

He spent another four years at Mt. Pleasant before leaving under an unusual circumstance. One day, Teacher Annora, the class teacher, left her class unattended. During her absence, the students became very boisterous. JC, the leader, decided to take control. He stood up and chastised his classmates for their behaviour. He said, "Guys be quiet, this is no way to behave when the teacher is not here." The students respected him and almost instantly, everyone became quiet. Just then, Teacher Annora returned. She heard the noise from her class and knew that the principal would reprimand her. So, Teacher Annora hastened to get back to the classroom. As she entered, the only person who was out of position was JC, as he had not yet taken his seat.

Teacher Annora immediately instructed JC to report to the Principal. He was the scapegoat. He tried to explain why he was out of his seat but Teacher Annora did not want to hear. JC reported to the principal's office. Any such visit meant one thing, punishment. The principal who had seen him coming stood ready with his leather strap in hand. JC attempted to explain what had happened but Mr B would not hear. "Stretch out your hand boy," he said. JC did not comply and continued in his attempt at explaining that he had done nothing that deserved punishment. Mr. B lifted the strap high over his head and delivered one blow. The weal resulting from the strap stretched from JC's shoulder across his back to his lower lumbar area. He was irate. He said to Mr. B, "Don't you 'f—king' do that again." As Mr B attempted to administer a second blow, he grabbed and pulled the strap with so much force that Mr. B almost tumbled over, losing the strap in the process. JC tossed the strap to the floor and walked away. "Don't walk away, come back here young man, take up the strap", said Mr B, seething with anger and foaming at his mouth such that he looked demon-possessed. That was his last day at Mt. Pleasant School. He was unmoved, had no apology and no regrets. He, like boys of this age, was making the transition to manhood. As JC confessed many years later, he was feeling something, then. The community usually described this type of situation using a common saying, "His stones were coming down, getting heavy."

JC went home and explained to his parents what had transpired. They listened carefully to their son. Although they generally subscribed to the accepted position in the community that all benefits of doubt went to the teachers and particularly the principal, this time, they seemed inclined to believe him. They were satisfied that he was speaking the truth. As a result, they did not show resistance to him becoming an apprentice carpenter at that stage. That evening, Mr. B journeyed to JC's home, still in a bad mood. He was convinced that JC would not amount to much. There, they took the decision that JC would not return to the school.

Many years later when JC came back from a successful stint in England, he met Mr. B one more time. Like the previous occasion, that time was also not pleasant. Mr. B, in a tone reminiscent of thirty years earlier, was looking to foam at the mouth once more. JC, however, had moved on. He had forgiven Mr B a long time ago. Mr B would go to his grave still wanting to administer the full punishment to JC - six lashes from the leather strap that had disappeared miraculously, long before the principal's retirement.

8.5   Filling the gaps left by the migrant husbands

Long after the end of slavery on Goat Hill, the priests came preaching that it was a good thing to be married. They made individuals and families feel guilty for having unwedded children. That was not long after the time when the slave master, supported by his priestly countrymen, maximised his human property by giving special privileges to the most prolific, the plantation stud. It was acceptable and encouraged that men could have multiple partners. The slave master himself set the example by having fun with slave women, whether they had a partner or not. Then things changed and the priests wanted the newly freed slaves to change. It was therefore not surprising that in Goat Hill, at the time of mass migration, marriage was not an important status among the people of Goat Hill. Polygamous practices of the earlier periods continued and the nuclear family was not predominant. Hence, the residue of these practices helped to characterise behaviours in the Goat Hill community in the aftermath of mass migration.

Around the time of the second wave of migration from Goat Hill, there were many closet hidden relationship issues of a sexual nature.

There was much gossip. There were many rumours. Many believed that the nature of relationships during and after slavery, and the exodus of most of the fittest men had contributed to the growing trend. Many were the stories about women who provided companionship for one another, in the absence of their husbands. Those husbands had migrated to far-off lands to make things better for their family. Seldom were there verifiable eyewitness reports that could turn the gossip and rumours into undisputed evidence. Hence, it all came down to allegations. However, there was much circumstantial evidence. For example, a wife left behind to take care of the children while the husband had gone to England would have a woman friend move into the matrimonial home. The move would be gradual. First, the visiting female companion would spend evenings providing support to a wife left on her own. The need for such support was real in many cases.

Then the relationship intensified but was often opportunistic over time. For example, the visiting companion would spend a night when approaching bad weather was announced. That was excusable to the villagers. Other opportunities would be utilised and ultimately, the visiting companion would take up semi-permanent residence, replacing the absent husband. She would take the lead role in disciplining the children, and assume control of managing the household finances which was usually based on the monthly allowances sent by the absent husband and father. She would split her belongings between her home and her companion's home or sometimes move in completely, sleeping in the same bed and declaring the bedroom a no-go zone to children, the rightful owners of the house.

While there was a level of tolerance for these relationships, conflicts were possible. In some instances, these conflicts originated from the disapproval of the husband's relatives. Nevertheless, there appeared to have been more understanding for such cases that when a wife who has been left behind developed a sexual relationship with another man in the village, during the absence of her husband. In a few cases, such extra marital relationships led to children, concrete evidence of the liaison.

Occasionally, the extra-marital relationships happened in the presence of a resident husband. That was a more delicate situation and the outcome was debatable. Sometimes there was a break-up of the relationship or acceptance by the husband, who then acquired names, which were not complementary.

8.6 MIGRATION AND ECONOMIC TRANSFORMATION OF GOAT HILL

In the latter part of the nineteenth century, there was migration to work on the estates and plantations in Grenada, Tobago, Trinidad and British Guiana. This explains some of the family connections in the islands even up to today. At that time, the population of Tobago had greater connection to the population of Grenada and Carriacou than to that of Trinidad.

During the first decades of the twentieth century, migration opportunities seemed to have emerged when hope was beginning to be lost in Goat Hill. After the failed attempt of the French to construct a canal linking the Caribbean Sea to the Pacific, the USA took up the challenge. The failure of the French and abandonment of the project in 1880 was due mainly to the deadly endemic diseases of yellow fever and malaria. These diseases left many workers incapacitated and caused at least 20,000 deaths. The construction of the Panama Canal, under the USA, saw the departure of many young men from the Caribbean including some from Goat Hill. To get to Panama, young men of Goat Hill and the surrounding villages first had to find their way by windjammers to Barbados. The journey took between two days to a week, depending on the weather. In 1907, the largest recruitment of contracted workers occurred when nearly 15,000 men travelled to the Isthmus. News got out of the high wages and good living conditions on the Panama Isthmus, which provided a motivation for more men from Goat Hill to try their luck. However, by that time, there were no functioning agents and potential migrants had to make their own way. This was a challenge which caused young men to look elsewhere. The contribution to the development of Goat Hill from its sons working in Panama was not significant. Many who survived malaria or yellow fever, moved to the USA.

During the First World War, a few young men from Goat Hill joined the American Army. For many years, a photograph of a young man, Josiah, hanging on the partition of his deceased grandparents' house reminded villagers of this. Following grandparents' death, Josiah's mother, his aunt Madevine and his sister Bunah occupied the house. Sarah was Madevine's eldest sister, hence visitors to the village shop and Big Stone got a view of the photograph when Sarah was in a boastful mood. It was never clear whether Josiah faced the battlefield as he had cut ties with his family soon after sending the photograph. Nonetheless, every now and then, someone visiting Goat Hill from the Bronx in New York would report sighting Josiah or talking to him on the streets. Apparently, he had not fared too well and was struggling to make ends meet. The village had lost Josiah and Josiah had divorced the village.

Young men also sought their fortunes in the cane fields of Cuba and the Dominican Republic with the expansion of the sugar industry in those countries. Sometimes, some of these men wiped out Goat Hill, the place of their childhood, from their memories. For those who survived the hardships and diseases like malaria and yellow fever, they never saved enough to return to their birthplace. In many cases, they started families in those islands and erased Goat Hill from their minds. However, there was only one man who had returned briefly. He arrived with nothing more than the clothes on his back, two torn pairs of trousers and three shirts stained from sweat and food over an extended period of use. Jonathan had forgotten almost everyone he had left behind on his first departure. The public ridiculed him for returning no better off than he had left which forced him to his second departure. That was the end of Jonathan and his connection with Goat Hill. After he left the second time, no one ever heard about him again.

Later, young men of Goat Hill, like many others in the English speaking Caribbean Islands, went in droves to Aruba, Trinidad and

Curacao, providing skilled and unskilled labour to the emerging oil industry. After the Second World War, new migration opportunities opened up in England. Goat Hill lost its share of young strong residents to this far-off land.

Associated with migration were the remittances that came home to relatives. As the families on Goat Hill were generally close, on average, members who migrated felt a certain obligation to provide for the family members back home. This came in the form of money through postage, as there was none of the modern-day courier services available. The most used means was to place the money in an envelope with the owner's name written on it and give it to someone who was returning home. This was not always a safe method. As in any society past and present, there were always crooks. There were many reports in those olden days of persons who never returned to the land of their birth because somewhere along the way, they had not delivered the promised letter. In some cases, the bearer of the money-filled envelope would have an excuse that was never credible. Some persons claimed robbery on the way home or losing the envelope. The remittances also arrived in parcels, posted from the nearest town to the migrants' residence. These parcels would contain clothes, typically second hand. It did not matter, as the items were American trousers or an Aruban hat or perhaps a long sleeved shirt. Whatever the condition of the clothes, there was always a joy to receive them and to wear them at the celebrations that followed. This was a way of telling everybody that the family member overseas was doing very well. The villagers delighted in wearing their clothing to the Sunday mass, a christening or a funeral.

The remittances from migration were also the main means of improving the housing stock in the village. Every focused young man's principal goal was to construct a house from whatever meagre savings he had accumulated in England, America, Venezuela, Panama, Aruba or Curacao. Migration also brought out the best or worst among the people of Goat Hill, as it did in the examples of Max, JC and Henry.

9

THE GOOD, THE BAD AND THE INDIFFERENT OF GOAT HILL

9.1 THE PERVERT

The story of Madevine's second cousin, the Pervert, who was hardworking, queer and a comedian of sorts was part of Goat Hill's historical tapestry. He seemed unable to control his deviant, sexual urges. Usually, the adults did not take him seriously, but he provided unintended entertainment for children of the village. He was a weird man. Villagers alleged that he was a homosexual, but by his own actions, he showed that he was an exhibitionist and a disturbed individual. He drew a lot of attention to himself and was a source of fun and laughter for the school children and a target for ridicule from adults when his behaviour became extreme.

He never wore any underwear and his pants were often torn at the crotch or at the backside. Some of the holes in his pants may have been from overuse. However, villagers alleged that he deliberately tore his pants to expose his private parts. It was also possible that the holes in the backside of his pants could have been from his constant farting. He was able to produce his farts at will. When walking up the hill to his house with a bucket of water on his head or while weeding in his garden, he farted as fast as he would breathe. He was able to increase the frequency and intensity of his farts when he saw passers-by or when the children were following him up the hilly village track.

One day, the Pervert was at the village cistern to collect water. The authorities had to ration water because of the severe dry season. As he bent to open the tap to fill his bucket, his private parts tumbled out swinging through an opening in the crotch of his pants, with the busted seams trapping and locking them like a guillotine ready to cut them off. Debra, who was the water superintendent and his neighbour, could not believe her eyes. Everyone stood in disbelief, eyes and mouths wide opened. After recovering from the brief shock, Debra shouted at the middle-aged man, *"What is happening to you? Put that thing inside."* He responded, *"Is all you woman who ah to put it inside."*

Had the times been different, the Pervert would have had charges brought against him for a number of modern day offences, including that of being a paedophile. The Goat Hill community also alleged that he treated the submissive victims much better than, the others. He had no interest in girls, although he had a wife. One day, the lone area photographer gave the Pervert a good telling off. As the photographer was on his way to tend his cattle, he noticed that the Pervert sat with his grandchildren around him, feeding two of the grandsons from his calabash of peas-soup and dumplings. The other children, hoping that he would show some favour to them, sat with their eyes glued to the calabash and his hands. Like in the past, there was no luck. The photographer called to the middle-aged man: "Mister, all these and those are yours. Show love to all of them. Why are you treating those two much better than the others?" The photographer had heard of the allegations and rumours before. He was trying to make sense of what he had heard and what he was observing. In his very effeminate way, the Pervert gave a good 'cussing' to the photographer. In the days that followed, he carried on the routine. With eight or ten grandchildren around him, he fed his favourite grandsons. His true intentions became a subject for gossip in the village.

The Pervert, while being accused of victimising his own, was sometimes a victim of children in the village. For example, there were incidents where young children both boys and girls would walk up quietly behind him and poked a stick through the torn section of his pants that provided no privacy to his naked backside. Another prank that the children played on him was that of suddenly appearing in front of him from a hidden position in the bushes and simulated farts from their mouths. These simulated farts were intended to mimic those that he frequently produced. He took no pleasure in those episodes and would complain to the parents, although not directly.

His sexuality became clearer one Thursday evening about six. He had a visitor, an eighteen-year-old who had arranged an appointment with him. At six on the dot, Sandy arrived. The Pervert was pleased. He congratulated Sandy for being a man of his word. He said, "You are a man of your word. You say six and you are here." Sandy then went to the little structure where he cooked, when suddenly the Pervert began caressing Sandy's bottom. *"Ha, Sandrin boy have nice bambam,"* he said. Unfortunately, the Pervert was unaware of the trap set for him. As he became more engrossed in his activities, four young men burst open the flimsy door that was partly ajar. They began raining down blows on the Pervert. Sandy fixed himself and joined in the beating. "Murder! Murder! Ma Maude, help! Help!" shouted the Pervert. There was no help on this occasion nor anytime afterwards.

About twenty years later, the Pervert was lured by two mischievous early teenaged boys through the clammier-cheery hollow, with the promise of anal sex. Excited by the thought of an enjoyable evening, he followed the boys deep into the bushes. With a safe distance from the Pervert, the boys dropped their pants and exposed their backsides to him. With all the excitement in his head, he dropped his pants also and made his move. Each boy grabbed a piece of wood and began beating the Pervert on his private parts. He took the blows without screaming, fearing that someone would hear. The boys laughed at him and ran away, leaving him to nurse his wounds, which were not serious. Without any apprehension, he visited the boys' school, which was not too far away, to lodge a complaint against them.

Mr. B, the headmaster, listened to his complaint and was rather embarrassed on hearing the Pervert's version of the events. He pondered on the logic of the explanations given for the secluded location of the incident. The Pervert did not explain why he was in the bushes or why he had followed the boys. What could have provoked them to be so vicious towards an old man? Mr. B, who was aware of all the rumours, concluded without hearing the boys' version, that it was not a matter to prolong. Closing the matter there and then would spare the school and the community further embarrassment and pain. Without showing any outward emotions, Mr. B was internally pleased that the old man had gotten the 'licking'. He had met his 'breakers'. The rumours continued about the weirdness of that Pervert long after his passing.

9.2 The exploited

Goat Hill was not immune from exploitation of the weak. There were differently abled persons whose limited communication abilities and cognitive disabilities made them vulnerable to abuse in the community. There was one particular mentally retarded soul called Glenis. He was slim, tall and strong. For nearly all of his life of sixty years, many families used him, including his own, working him like a mule. He worked from daybreak to sundown, all day long as the village's deliveryman. He toted over-sized and heavy bags on his head from shop to house, from house to shop, from house to house, from town to Goat Hill and from Goat Hill to Belair. He never once complained. Then when the day was finished, he would be lucky to get as a reward a piece of leftover food. He had little understanding of the value of money. In those days, the smaller coins were of a larger value. If they paid him for his work, it would be with many of the larger coins, such as pennies.

There was also Eustace. Everyone treated him in a similar manner as Glenis, although his communication abilities and cognitive skills were higher. Each of these unfortunate souls had a different clientele. Glenis was more restricted to the area around Goat Hill. Eustace's sojourns were much wider, almost island-wide. He was much more efficient than Glenis. He knew a little more about money and the potential buying power of each notation, so the exploitation appeared to be less. However, he had difficulty equating money to the amount of work that he did and hence he was still a target for exploitation. In the end, Eustace died a tragic death, but not from abuse. A bus loaded with partygoers during a festive period struck Eustace and he died on the spot.

There were other cases where persons with physical disabilities including limited communication skills due to deafness or muteness had their share of exploitation. Often, the relatives were the ones who exploited them. The victims worked as unpaid servants, yard boys or even as farm labourers. The only sin they seemed to have committed was being born with a disability. In those days, the concept of the abuse of the differently abled did not exist in a formal way. Hence, villagers regarded these situations as acceptable and there was little concern about their existence or welfare.

9.3　The making of heroes and legends

During every era, in every society, special people arise who have significant positive impacts on the community. Those persons whom we would refer to as heroes and legends have been responsible for the social and economic developments of their immediate and wider communities. Some receive national awards or gain recognition as saints and martyrs for service to the people. For example, when a firefighter risks his life to save an elderly person in a building engulfed by fire, the community celebrates him as a hero. The two teenagers, who chased an alleged kidnapper on their bikes for fifteen heart-pounding minutes, causing the driver apparently to give up upon realizing that they had followed him, were celebrated as heroes. This was because they had done what was not normally expected. Not often was the teacher who spent forty-five years in the classroom or the headmaster who was teacher, priest, doctor, counsellor, peacemaker and overall advisor considered a hero.

In Goat Hill and in the small islands of the Grenadines, heroes and legends, mostly unrecognised publicly, left many marks of their existence. Heroes came from all 'walks of life'. For example, there was the farmer and livestock keeper, who through observations improved the quality and quantity of the harvests and who shared his harvests with those less successful. Then, there was also the teacher who remained in the classroom for three or four decades, losing or missing-out on the chances to migrate to places where educational and job opportunities were in greater abundance. Heroes also came in the form of shipwrights. They worked for long hours under difficult conditions, yet never received full compensation. The contributions that these heroes made were many times over that of a regular villager.

There were the tailors and seamstresses who designed and made the clothes worn by villagers for paltry monetary rewards. They also operated trade schools, in their modest workshops, training the next generation of clothes fitters free of charge. The hero tradesman who was a carpenter, mason and jack-of-all-trades, acquired most of his skills from trial and error and from raw talent, played his part too. He was different from his other colleagues who performed some skilled tasks without wages, but collected their rewards by sleeping with the poor single mothers.

He never exploited poor women. It may have looked trivial to those who exploited the female neighbours after carrying out a task such as fixing a window. Unfortunately, the women often extended their families with an additional child whom they never wanted. The single mother was not low in morals or promiscuous; she was a victim of poverty. Unlike the roguish tradesmen, the hero carpenter would repair as many houses as possible for gratis. However, when there was a job and the housewives had a little money to pay, he was the first to be contacted. The workshops of the tailors, the seamstresses and the ace tradesmen all operated as the precursors to the modern day technical colleges. For the single mothers, whose children were presenting disciplinary challenges, these trainers in garment manufacturing and carpentry were heroes.

There was the chairperson of wakes and funerals, whose only remuneration was the self-satisfaction of being in charge of the bottle of white rum that lasted all night by limiting the size of the drink and the regularity with which the rum was distributed. In the absence of a priest, he officiated at funerals. He was not afraid of the dead and was responsible for preparing the body by washing and dressing the corpse. His tasks extended to overseeing the after funeral arrangements. Although not highly thought of, his role was essential. He was more than an unpaid undertaker. In his own right, he was a village hero.

Heroes were also found among the village fishermen, who braved the seas using oars and sails rigged on bamboo masts. Among them was the fisherman who knew all the poorer families. These families could not purchase even the cheapest quality fish. That fisherman would distribute most of his catch as widely as possible. The villagers considered him a kind-hearted man, but for most of the poor, he was their hero.

In the earlier days in Goat Hill, the literacy rates were low. However, there was also someone in the village, who wrote and read letters for the less literate villagers. That person had to be trustworthy because he must keep in confidence all the information that passed his eyes. He also functioned as the Truancy Officer - ensuring that delinquent parents sent their children to school. Such a person was also a hero.

9.4 Diahee

There was also the volunteer post-lady. In the old days, there was one post office located in a spare room of one of the more spacious houses. For Goat Hill, the post office was located at the Limlair-Belvedere Junction in the Cox residence. The Cox family had migrated to mainland Grenada for their children to attend high school. There were two letter days: Mondays and Thursdays. These were the first working days immediately following the arrival of the mail boat on Saturdays and Wednesdays. The villagers believed that Diahee could not read. However, this was doubtful. On letter day, one would stand outside of the building, and peep through the pigeonhole that was neatly carpentered into the wooden window and shout the name of the person whose letter one had come to collect. Diahee had to call from the thirty or forty names of the heads of households in the village, as required. She did not call all heads of households each day, only those who had received mail. Most of the mail came from relatives abroad who from time to time would send a 'change', as the villagers referred to the remittances. On a good day, Diahee would collect about twenty letters including notices for registered letters. For those persons who did not go to the post office, she would visit the homes. On her return to the village, she would go from house to house to report: "None today or you have one from your brother". It was this ability in Diahee to memorize all the names on the face of each envelope and not ever giving a letter to the wrong person that debunked the common label of illiteracy attached to her. She was a real heroine. She collected letters twice a week in the rain or in the scorching sun and without any payment. However, some villagers showed little appreciation. Instead, sometimes villagers verbally abused her for knowing so much about the correspondence between family members at home and abroad.

9.5 THE GRANDMOTHERS

As job opportunities in Goat Hill had always been limited, the adult male population in the community was reduced from time to time and sometimes so too was the adult female population. It was common for one grandmother to care for the children of her sons and daughters, in addition to her own at any given time. In these cases, a modest house could be the home of up to twenty children comprising brothers, sisters, cousins, uncles and aunts. Sometimes nieces and nephews were older than aunts and uncles. The grandmothers who invariably were single and were responsible for managing that commune of children, until the return of their parents, who had emigrated and settled in foreign lands, were often superheroines.

These heroines managed impossible situations. It was not unusual for them to have to work in the gardens, growing what they could to supplement the meagre groceries that were purchased from the two pounds sterling that were sent by absentee parents, whenever they were able. Sometimes those grandchildren grew up not knowing their parents and lived with a hybrid mother- grandmother. Less well known were the hybrid father-grandfathers, but they too existed. However, the mother-grandmother's role always overshadowed that of the father-grandfather. Those mother-grandmothers were heroines whose stories were often forgotten. In today's world, these heroines would have been nominated at the national level as 'woman of the year" or perhaps recognised in the annual Queen's Birthday or Independence Day celebrations for their contribution to community development. Some would probably have received the award: Order of the British Empire (OBE).

9.6 NURSE CUMMINGS

During the 1960's a 'Florence Nightingale' in the person of Nurse Cummings arrived in the district to provide service to Goat Hill. Although not originally from Goat Hill, the residents accepted her as one of Goat Hill's own as she integrated completely in the life of Goat

Hill with great ease. Nurse Cummings was a quintessential medical professional, serving the community during the days when there was no doctor assigned to the clinic. She cleaned and dressed all the ulcers on children's legs, occasioned by poor hygienic practices. Her hands were gentle. Seldom would the removal of an old dressing cause pain. Of course, children cried during these episodes, but it was more out of fear than pain.

After her clinical tasks, the nurse would make her rounds in the village to carry out her post-natal responsibilities which were not light, as in those days the birth rate was many times higher than today. As if superhuman, the villagers called out the nurse at nights to attend to presumed emergencies. The messenger usually arrived at break-neck speed to report on the pending arrival of the newest addition to the village's population. Then in pitch darkness, the nurse made her way to the destination by a kerosene lantern or a homemade kerosene torch. The nurse worked day and night, and Mondays to Sundays. Nurse Cummings could not make any firm plans for herself on public holidays, including Easter and Christmas for she never knew when a call would come. The year 1962 was the year when Goat Hill experienced the highest number of births. There were never any stillbirths during her time.

For her efforts, Nurse Cummings received the meagre wage of a district nurse and the benefit of the small living quarters that was in the same building as the medical clinic. The people of Goat Hill showed their appreciation to this heroine by sending her whatever was harvested from the land or the sea.

9.7 THE SCHOOL MASTER

Today some heroes are designated community leaders who are often widely recognised. In the old days in Goat Hill, the headmaster was the community leader. He was one of the brightest in primary school, passing the school leaving examinations at age fifteen. Mr. B started his teaching career at age fifteen in the same year that he passed his School Leaving Examination. He worked his way up by studying for and passing his First Year Teachers' Examination, then the Senior Cambridge and ultimately being successful at his teacher training programme at Mausica Teachers' College in Trinidad.

Unlike the youngsters of his day, he remained at home, teaching the children of the village. He lived in the modest schoolhouse provided by the government until his retirement. Besides this, he settled all major disputes in the village. He was the unofficial Justice of the Peace. He also prepared the last will and testament of the dying. His home was the repository of formally signed agreements between parties in the village. He was the Guidance Counsellor for those in school and those who had left school. He drafted the occasional applications for jobs that required written applications. At one time, he owned one of the two or three wooden boats used for raising the fish pots on the leeward side of the reefs. Those reefs stood prominently as the dividing line between the shores and the horizon in the background and further acted as the barometer of the roughness of the sea. Mr. B was also an unsung hero.

9.8 The sea captains

There was Uncle Moore who had started his career as a seaman on one of the wooden sloops that was typical of the time. He also had a short stint on a larger transatlantic freighter. Saving his small earnings over the period, he returned to Goat Hill and purchased an old one-mast sloop, noted for having the permanent position of last in the annual regatta. Uncle Moore's contribution to the community was in the form of providing a service in contraband mainly from St. Baths. First, he travelled throughout the island and collected from shops and households a list of items (mostly alcohol and tobacco products) which they needed, usually in small quantities. Each client would pay the estimated price of the items in St. Baths. For example, one person might want two bottles of brandy and a cartoon of cigarettes, while another person needed only one. Uncle Moore would then purchase two cases of brandy in St. Baths that he distributed to five people on his return. Finally, having collected the orders, he sailed to his destination. The round trip lasted on average two weeks, but could be longer depending on the weather.

Sometimes there would be a scare, such as the time when he went adrift and ended up in Haiti. That trip lasted nearly three months. On other occasions the boat, which depended entirely on sails, was caught in a sea of calm that saw it moving no more than one mile per day. Notwithstanding the circumstances, on his return, Uncle Moore accounted, to the nearest penny, to his customers and delivered the appropriate orders. Sometimes he would forego the freight for the transportation of the goods as a way of contributing to the well-being of a close relative or someone in financial difficulty at the time. Uncle Moore never became wealthy from providing his service. In fact, he lived from hand to mouth. He was a legend but more than that, he was a hero. One cannot find in today's Goat Hill anyone who would replicate the practices of Uncle Moore.

9.9 Thompkin's Donkey

In Goat Hill not only people were legends and heroes, but animals too. Thompkin's donkey, called Family, was also a hero in its time in Goat Hill. It was true to its name and never left his master unprotected. Whenever Thompkin consumed too much strong rum, he often fell off his donkey. That donkey would stand by Thompkins's side until he had recovered enough to resume his journey. If any passer-by who was unknown to Family stopped and thought of investigating what was wrong, Family would grin, showing its discoloured teeth and get ready to reward the potentially good Samaritan with a bite. When people passed Family standing on the side of the road alongside its master, they would shake their heads and say, "If all families could do like

Family what a wonderful world we could have."

The donkey seemed specially blessed, as it outlived all its contemporaries by more than two decades. When John, Thompkins' son who had migrated and worked in St. Croix, Bermuda and Canada returned on his first trip to Goat Hill after more than ten years, Family recognised him. As John approached Family, tethered under the mango tree, it came towards John as if to kiss a long lost brother. Family was unaware of how it had influenced his master's son in developing a family-centred philosophy in life, which he accredited to his success. However, there were many more heroes than Thompkin's donkey.

Excluding Thompkin's donkey, the question that is relevant today is where have all our heroes gone. Without diminishing the contributions of the modern day heroes, being a hero then required a special spiritual gravitas, not always easily identified. That is why we must remember with reverence the heroes of yesterday. They have paved the way for the heroes of today, so we must celebrate today's heroes and heroines in the context of those that went before.

10

Tragedies in Goat Hill

Tragedies sometimes strike without any warning. Goat Hill had its fair share of tragedies, mostly unexpected loss of lives. Always, individual families were the most affected but many of Goat Hill tragedies cut across individual and extended families and affected the wider community. In a small community like Goat Hill, the sudden loss of a handful of lives was a major tragedy as individuals and the extended families could be seriously dislocated. Whether, the origin of the events was natural like tropical storms and hurricanes, or the collateral damage from war or other manmade disasters, the effect was always the same, intense at first only to fade away with time. When explanations for these events were attributed to a natural phenomenon, villagers looked to the spiritual realm of obeah and witchcraft for answers to relieve their pain and suffering. Since all tragedies were different, for the children of Goat Hill there were a few that stood out. These remained in the memory of the villagers throughout their lives, even as they moved out of their native village for better lives elsewhere.

10.1 A SEA MINE WASHED ASHORE

On the morning of July 6th 1945, a few weeks after the official end of the Second World War, residents of Goat Hill woke up to be greeted by a strange metal object drifting towards the shore. The waves tossed it backwards and forwards some distance from the shoreline. The first to see that strange spherical object were the fishermen on their way to the small fishing boats anchored about fifty feet beyond the floating ball. This strange metal ball was about four feet in diameter. Its contents, although unknown to the discoverers, were up to 700 pounds of explosives.

The huge ball drifted back and forth in the surf for a couple of hours. About midday, four big consecutive waves, characteristic of that time of year, aided by the high tide, pushed it onto the land. The huge ball, deposited on the black sandy beach, soon claimed a spot for itself by using its weight to compact the sand. No one at the time knew that the massive metal contraption, which was intended to sink enemy ships, had escaped from where it was placed. It might have floated around for weeks, unable to find a passing target, and headed straight for the bay at Goat Hill. Luckily, none of the local schooners or sloops had collided with it. There were rumours that the Lady Ladina, the passenger boat that was on its way from Grenada to St. Vincent in 1944 with sixty holidaymakers and crew, may have disappeared because of colliding with one of these mines. However, this speculation was dismissed, as a better explanation for Lady Ladina's disappearance was that the boat had lost buoyancy and sank due to the gas bubbles that floated to the surface after an eruption of Kick-em-Jenny.

Although, the sea mine was resting in no man's land on the shore, Smith the shipwright who was in the process of building the MV Amberjack on a plot adjoining the water's edge laid claim to this new find. No one dared to contradict Smith's claim, as he was the village leader. The hope of sudden enrichment drove Smith's claim. There was a tale that, many years earlier, a strange container had washed ashore and the two people who found it discovered large quantities of silver and gold jewellery in it. Back then, people assumed that they were the lost treasures from the European pirates who crisscrossed the waters around the surrounding islands. No one was able to confirm the story by laying eyes on any actual jewellery, although nearly everyone knew someone who still had a golden necklace or bracelet.

For the first few days, visitors came from the surrounding villages to have a look at the strange ball. No one called it a sea mine then, but that was what it was. Most persons were afraid to get too close. As time passed, there were many passionate discussions among the villagers about what that contraption was and how to deal with it. They were not well read, and they knew little about the goings-on after the just ended war. Many people created possible explanations. Smith suggested that the contents were useful material. Perhaps there was gold within the mine. No one seemed to be thinking of who would fill a container that large, with gold or silver and send it to people unknown to them. Dunstan, who was still quite young, said that it was a bomb from the just ended war. He had read somewhere, from an old newspaper clipping, about those spherical balls called mines. He could not remember where he had read it, but it did not matter now since no one seemed interested. He felt confident that opponents used them to sink ships during the war.

The District Officer notified the authorities. He was on his way from another nearby island when he landed on Goat Hill Bay and observed the washed-up ball lying on the shore. The ball had sunken slightly deeper in the sand from since it was first pushed by the heavy waves. Without a good communication network, it was going to be a while before anyone with military knowledge arrived from the capital. The District Officer had sent a note to the Governor seeking help or instructions. In those days, communication was slow. It would take two days for the District Officer's note to reach the Governor and another three days for a response to arrive. While awaiting a response from the Governor, the District Officer sent many messages to the village warning the men to keep away from the ball and not to tamper with it. The men from Goat Hill led by Smith, while having great regard for the office of the District Officer, were in a quandary and continued to debate all the options on the table.

Ultimately, the villagers ignored the warnings. In the meantime, Smith and his workers drew up a plan of action. They rebuffed all help and suggestions about a way forward. There were no intentions to share the wealth that lay within that strange metal ball. Sankee, Smith's closest friend, watched the ball carefully both day and night, but mostly from some distance. Ronald noticed that there was a lid bolted onto it. That lid looked like the place where they had pushed through the unknown contents. Ronald counted the bolts. There were ten of them and all were in a corroded state, the effects of the long exposure to saltwater. He thought that it would not be too difficult to remove them.

Ronald carried out a more detailed inspection, and tested for a possible exploration. They collected all the available tools in the village and took them to the bay. The owner of each piece of tool kept an eye on it, since if it were used; he would expect to receive some compensation once all that gold and silver were removed. Three of Ronald's friends, who were brave enough, volunteered to assist in removing the lid. Although Ronald was prepared to accept the help, he must first convince his father that Hyacinth was okay. It was not too difficult for Ronald to convince Smith since Smith had always treated Hyacinth as a son. He had loved Hyacinth almost as much as his own two boys he had.

Now it was time to find out what was in the ball. Ronald needed an oversized spanner to fit the head of the bolts. None was available. As a substitute, Hyacinth brought a big rusty wrench. Ronald oiled the wrench and knocked it against the mine to dislodge the rusts that had accumulated from lack of use over the years. As the rusts fell off the wrench began to move. Ronald smiled and told the men and lone woman that were spurring him on to stand clear. He figured that they were too close which would give them an advantage to see the contents in the treasure ball. He tried the wrench on the first bolt. There was no movement. Ronald and his wrench were no match for the bolt. Notwithstanding, Smith urged Sankee to try again. There were three more attempts. On the last trial, the wrench was stuck so firmly around the bolt that even with extra help there was no movement.

Ronald and Hyacinth were now tired and did not observe that the onlookers kept drawing closer, only to retreat upon the shouts from Smith. It was soon realised that the only other option was a sledgehammer. There were four such hammers among the tools brought down to the beach. They selected the heaviest. Ronald's assistant, Hyacinth, was the first to use the sledgehammer on the mine. After a few blows, one of the bolts seemed to move slightly as iron rusts from it and the body of the mine fell to the ground. Seeing the early success, Ronald decided to take charge. After the second blow, a hissing sound from the metal ball grew louder in little time. Then it happened. There was a big explosion. The time was 4 O'clock in the afternoon.

The mine exploded. People heard the noise up to four miles away. Such was the fury of the explosion that it shattered the glass windows from nearby houses. Wind took the smoke from the explosion to the highest point above Goat Hill. Residents at the furthest point on the island claimed to have seen that strange smoke hanging like a cloud over the hills for two hours before slowly dissipating. This may not have been true. Perhaps it was just a figment of the imagination, born long after the incident. Perhaps it was one way for the people who were far away from the scene to connect with it.

The mine drilled itself into the soft and wet sand on the shore. The explosion threw the body parts of Ronald and his second in command many yards away. Within the tragedy was a miracle. The lid of the mine faced the sea. Most of the explosives had headed out to sea; otherwise, there would have been carnage onshore.

When the smoke cleared, the mine was no longer there. It had disintegrated but left a gaping big hole in the sand. Days later, when villagers mustered the courage to inspect the hole, there were some pieces of metal about four feet below ground. They soon disappeared as the waves at high tide brought in enough sand to fill the small crater. Some interpreted the explosion as the sign that preceded the end of the world. Some of the religious villagers who saw the explosion went searching their bibles for answers. They thought that was the fire and brimstone predicted in the Book of Revelation. One elderly man of God jumped on his horse and rode to one of the far villages to see his brother and family for the last time. For him, that was the last opportunity as the end would be at any time thereafter.

It was a sad day in Goat Hill but it was not the end of time. There was no gold or silver left after the explosion. Instead, nine mutilated and lifeless bodies lay on the surf. They had lost their lives in search of treasure. Subsequently, many had become even more dedicated to their religion. Now only a few who are still alive remember the story. Goat Hill had not been to or participated in the war but the war had come to Goat Hill. Decades afterwards, the government placed a small monument at the site in memory of the lost ones: Smith Martineau, Patrick McLawrence, Hyacinth Patrice, Sankee Patrice, Ronald Patrice, Nicolas Roberts, Johnny Rock, Cicely Martineau and Majorie Martineau.

10.2 Fooled by the lull and the concrete house

It had been many years since Goat Hill had experienced a tropical storm or hurricane. In fact, very few of the residents had had any experience of a hurricane. Before the arrival of the Hurricane Janet, the sea was dead calm and no waves broke unto the reefs. That was the kind of weather one expected in August and, since it was, still early September no one was concerned. It was also a time when the whole village was out in the fields weeding the cotton and peas and harvesting what remained from the year's corn crop. Among them, word was spreading that a storm was approaching.

Without any experience, the villagers did not take the pending storm seriously. In any case, no one was educated in disaster preparedness.

Henry tended his two sheep and observed that the animals seemed agitated. Animals are able to sense pending danger. The fishermen had not gone out that day, as there was no wind to push the fishing boats, which all depended on their sails. It was humid. Madevine could not stand the humidity and left her garden much earlier than the usual four-thirty.

All morning the weather looked strange. About one o'clock there was news, which soon spread like wild fire. The doctor who had one of the three radios on the island had heard from the BBC shortwave radio that a storm was going through the Caribbean with a possible direct hit on Barbados. Perhaps it would not come to Goat Hill. Later in the day, it suddenly became very overcast and the wind picked up. By five o'clock, it was obvious that it was not a normal September day. Soon it was dark and the winds began to shake the poorly constructed houses. Most of the houses in the village were small and often incomplete with missing or makeshift windows and doors. Scattered among the small wooden structures were four houses, built much sturdier than the others were. One belonged to Madevine. Although it was old, it was strong. The other two were owned by the brothers, Eastin and Huriel who had saved enough to build a house of concrete and the fourth was owned by Appy Derrick whose house was similarly built to that of Madevine's, but newer.

As the weather worsened, Bulah who had gone to take dinner to her granduncle was caught in no-man's land on her return home. She was scared of the wind and found shelter in a line of four-foot high grass planted by the Department of Agriculture to reduce soil erosion. After a while, she fell asleep and remained all night sleeping in a foetal position. Luckily, the rain was not heavy enough to cause too much discomfort. Next morning, she returned home safely, to the relief of Henry and his mum.

During the storm, at one corner of the village, Lenard escaped from his rented house with his wife and his three infant children. There was a lull in the winds, and he, like most of the other villagers, believed that the worst had passed and the storm was over. It was only the passing of the eye of the storm. Lenard and his family were just approaching the safe house when the winds picked up coming from the south. During the previous three hours, the winds seemed to have come from the north. By the time they reached Monica's house, the winds were once more howling in anger. The flying debris made strange noises as they hurtled through the air for a short while before colliding with each other, thereby adding back-up bass music. The music sounded like that made by violins and guitars. As the family entered Monica's house, a flying wooden plank drilled a hole into the side of the wooden house. This happened only seconds after Lenard and his family were safely inside, and Monica closed the door. It was a near miss. The piece of wood lodged in the side of the house was exactly where Lenard's wife was standing seconds before Monica closed the door. Lenard and Monica's husband spent the rest of the night holding onto the door to prevent it from opening. Next morning when it was clear and Lenard and his neighbours realised how close they had come to death, they hugged each other and cried.

In another part of the village, as roof sheets were peeling off one after another, villagers ran for shelter when the wind had subsided. They selected houses that were still standing which they believed were more secure. Many other villagers, like Lenard, were fooled by the lull during the middle of the storm. Eastin's house was only one-year old. He had constructed it of concrete blocks, in a similar manner to which they built houses in Aruba. It had survived the first half of the storm. As it was still standing, many of the villagers who had already lost their roofs, headed for Eastin's house, which was clearly visible during the flashes of lightening that streaked across the night sky. Eastin's house soon became the hurricane shelter. By nine o'clock, the house was full. Ervin and his family were the last to arrive. They had left their small house although at the time of the lull nothing had happened to it.

As the wind force intensified, there appeared to be no fear by the thirty or so persons seated on the floor of Eastin's drawing room. Why should they be afraid? They were in a well-built house. The wind had not been that strong before the major lull. Suddenly the intensity of the wind increased. The occupants looked up and could see the roof vibrating as if it were trying to dislodge itself from the concrete walls. Without warning, the beltings or ring beams on which the rafters were anchored began to crack. There was a loud noise and the roof on the southern side lifted and disappeared in the night sky. The lamp went out and the house was in complete darkness only to be illuminated by the frequent flashes of lightning, which zipped through the glass windows. There was only a light drizzle. Suddenly, the walls of the building began to crumble and then collapsed. The occupants began a stampede to get out in the open and away from the building. Although there was flying debris, it was still safer to be outside since there was little space in the house to escape the falling blocks. They ran to a nearby house, which was still standing minus its roof.

The night passed slowly. As daylight came, the village began to evaluate the damages. There were four dead in Eastin's house. The collapsed walls had crushed them. Ervin's house was one of the few that was standing in the village. It had not lost a shingle nor a single roof sheet. The inside of the house was dry. The presumed safety of the concrete house had fooled Ervin and his family.

The villagers pulled together whatever resources were available to begin the rebuilding. They could not help but contemplate on the loss. The gardens were all bare as if they had experienced a severe drought. There was not a single leaf on any tree. The storm had destroyed all the standing crops. Only sweet potatoes, which were not quite ready for harvesting, escaped. For many months after, the villagers survived on the charity of other islanders. The villagers referred to the supplies from these charitable sources as other people's labour or OPL. Hurricane Janet had provided Janet houses and OPL but above all the misery, the loss of four lives in a small community like Goat Hill was devastating.

10.3 Lost at sea

About twenty years after the sea mine incident, tragedy once more struck Goat Hill. It was the first tragedy that touched the Francis clan directly. Huriel had gone on his last fishing trip. He was Madevine's only surviving son. She had lost her other son MacGyver tragically sometime before. Huriel, who was the village photographer and grocer, was also a part-time fisherman. His success as a photographer and grocer did not prevent him from going out to sea every other day to raise his fish pots.

The distance to where the fish pots were set was not too far from shore, so Huriel was not always mindful of the weather. There was no weather news available by radio, and fishermen like Huriel, were forced to interpret the overhead clouds for signs of rain or unusual wind. He had his regular crew, one called Brother and the other Eclais. Brother was the youngest and had completed primary school about two years before the incident. Eclais, a family man was a hard working tailor who used the earnings from his fish catch to supplement his meagre earnings as a tailor.

The trio, Huriel, Eclais and Brother went to the beach while most families were still asleep. There was enough light for them to transverse the narrow tracks to the main road and then to the beach without too much difficulty. Huriel wore his aluminium helmet, which was part of his protective gear while he worked at the Lago Oil Company in Aruba. Anytime he took up his helmet, he had good memories of Aruba where he had learnt his photography skills and had earned enough to have one of the best-stocked grocery stores on the island.

Once on the beach, Huriel and Eclais removed their shoes and secured them in the usual spot at the foot of a manchineel tree where they were safe from the rain. The sky was slightly over-cast, which meant that they anticipated rain later in the day. Besides the cloudiness, the sea was its usual calmness. There was only a very light breeze blowing causing some small ripples on the sea's surface. A last quarter moon was just disappearing over High North. Brother, who was bare feet and had nothing to secure, proceeded to retrieve the wooden rollers used for launching the boat. The wooden boat was heavy. There was little time for it to dry, since either Huriel's team or Marquis's team used the boat daily.

Brother placed the rollers in position, one just under the keel of the boat and the other three about twos feet apart. The final one was about six inches away from the point at which the breaking wave died before returning seawards. The rollers made launching easier. Without them Huriel would have needed two additional men for the launching. Brother then removed the props they used to keep the boat upright onshore. The three men began launching the boat, one at the stern pulling while two were pushing at the sides close to the bow. The boat seemed light that day and moved quicker than normal, like if in a greater hurry to get to sea than the three men were.

Soon the boat was launched and was floating. It rolled slightly from side to side in keeping with the motion of the waves that made their way to shore. In the morning light, the boat reminded Eclais of the athletes doing their push-ups during practice sessions. The three men then headed out to sea. Huriel was in deep thought. Perhaps he was thinking about how he would distribute the catch later on.

Three days earlier, four of the fish pots were empty. Perhaps someone had raised them the evening before. The other pots had about a dozen Congo eels. No one paid for Congo eels, however Huriel did not mind too much as his mother Madevine loved Congo eels. With a dozen from Huriel's last outing, she had a feast then. Having cooked some the same day, she salted the remainder, which was placed on the kitchen roof for drying. They would dry within two days once the sun came out.

The morning was almost uneventful. Brother and Eclais were the oarsmen. Huriel was the navigator. Brother and Eclais rowed for about 25 minutes until they were well beyond the reefs and were able to sight Grand Bay point. Then Huriel began to give directions towards the first fish pot. He directed the oarsmen to steer the boat to the north until the tree, where they had secured their belongings, was in line with the middle window of the primary school. Once that line was established, they steered the boat to the west until the northern tip of Petit St. Vincent was in line with the southern tip of Sail Rock. Sail Rock, which was tree-less, was always a good landmark for triangulation by Huriel and his crew. Not many fishermen used it, thus making it more difficult for rogue fishermen, who might be tempted to steal fish or fish pots. Once in position, using these crude navigational skills, it was time to look under the water for the pots.

As the current was not too strong, there was no need to drop the anchor. In any case, while dropping the anchor was easy, Huriel did not enjoy pulling it back on board by himself. Brother used the oars to keep the boat in a steady position. Then Huriel placed the 'diving glass' on the surface of the water and began inspecting the bottom of the ocean for the first pot. The diving glass was a square and wooden homemade lidless box-like equipment with a glass bottom. They made the box waterproof by using tar from the pitch lake in Trinidad. The 'diving glass' was not actually used for diving, but to improve the fishermen's vision of the bottom of the sea where the fish pots rested. It is not clear how it worked but it served its purpose.

Huriel soon located the first fish pot where it was lying in a patch of sea grass, which seemed to be out of place in a field of golden sand. He dropped the metal hook, which fishermen referred to as a drag, and pulled it along the seabed until he hooked the pot. The drag was attached to about thirty feet of rope, as the deepest water in which the pots were set was about twenty-five feet. He caught the pot and pulled it up onto the boat. Both he and Eclais moved around the pot until all the fishes were on the floor of the boat. In that way, from there on, the men pulled in the fish pots one by one. The last fish bank was some way off the sand bank to the west of Palm Island. The pots there were usually very productive and the trio could expect at least two dozen snappers. On their way to that final location, a squall surprised them.

The rain, which was drizzling on and off, began to pour down, bucket a drop. The winds quickly picked up making the boat roll from side to side. Waves began breaking on the bow. Brother was busy at bailing out the water with a calabash kept for that purpose. The squall lasted only about ten minutes.

Two men sitting under a tree in Petite Martinique were looking at Huriel's boat. They were only there because there was a shortage of material to continue repairing the schooner that had pulled up for dry-docking. The squall that hit the boat appeared to be just on a small part of the sea. Everywhere around it was calm. Then it happened. The rogue wave appeared from nowhere. It struck the boat. The boat capsized. One man seemed trapped below the capsized boat. The other two were trying to swim, but it was obvious that only one knew how to swim. Huriel's helmet fell from his head and the current took it. The distance between Huriel and the helmet gradually increased. Then, as it was before the squall, the sea was calm once more. The sun came out in full force. It would have been good weather for a cricket match except that it was the wrong time of the year. Cricket season was during the dry season. The light drizzle resumed. The men in Petite Martinique looked on in horror and could not believe their eyes. The boat, Huriel and his crew were no longer in view. They had vanished.

News from Petite Martinique soon reached Goat Hill. A search party assembled both from Petite Martinique and from Windward. They went to the location and after a couple of hours gave up the search. The news spread as wildfire and soon there were gatherings at Huriel's home and that of his mother Madevine. By that time, the rains had begun to fall again, but this time heavier. That time it became obvious that a tropical storm was in the region. That night there were gatherings at the three homes, but there was no wake as everyone was still hoping for better news the following day. Activities at Huriel's home and his adjacent grocery continued for late hours, since the Delco generator provided good lighting. When Huriel had installed the generator on his return from Aruba, the electric light produced was a great attraction for the surrounding villages, and Huriel's grocery and rum shop became the centre for nightlife in the village. Everyone referred to the generator as the Delco. Delco was the generator's manufacturer.

The following day came and there was no better news. The search had ended. The village must reconcile its fate. It had lost three good men. The villagers attempted to find an explanation. They considered all possibilities. Someone then revealed that only Brother knew how to swim. The other men had no chance. Not prepared to accept the physical explanations, the tragedy was rationalised as obeah. They pointed fingers at George Solomon, the obeah-man. There were two versions of Solomon's intervention. The first was the story about a stolen cow chain. The villagers alleged that someone had stolen Huriel's cattle chain. He then commissioned Solomon to find and punish the culprit. Before Solomon could use his craft, the culprit showed up at Solomon's place and pleaded guilty. Solomon was in a quandary, as he could not then punish the culprit who was a close associate of his wife's brother, neither could he abandon the process that had begun. The only solution then, was to sacrifice Huriel who was not prepared to pay an increased amount for his safety. The second alleged story was that Huriel and his fishing team often raised other people's fish pots and it was these persons, still unknown, who had paid Solomon to punish him.

Like the voodoo men of Haiti, or the witch doctors of West Africa, Solomon was a feared man and was always at the centre of village mishaps. There might have been a rational explanation of that tragedy but it was easier to stick with the folklore. Whether it was the chain or the fish pots, Goat Hill had suffered another tragedy.

About two weeks later, Huriel's helmet washed ashore on one of the bays. Madevine never fully recovered. The photography business did not survive and the grocery lost its prominence. Huriel's unborn son at the time of the tragedy, Albert, is now a reminder to the village elders of that tragedy. No one ever told Albert the story fully; he depended on overhearing occasional chats about the tragedy. Besides these times, only once did he hear his grandmother Madevine talk about his father.

This happened during the time when he and his brothers and cousins went to be night companions to Madevine.

The greatest impact of this tragedy was on Samuel. This was the same Samuel who had damaged the sole of his feet when speeding down Madelyn Hill with his homemade scooter and who had confronted Pupa on his way to look after his animals. Not long after Samuel's father passing, his brother Elias, who was only seventeen, went to England. It was hoped that he would be able to help his family financially. Elias's departure triggered Samuel's transition to a forced-ripe manhood. On his father's passing, Samuel, at eight or nine years of age, soon became the man of the house. This new status was sudden, as his older brother migrated to England soon after their father's death. Samuel had to work in the garden during the crop-time, and see after the cattle and sheep, which were the family's wealth. Without agreeing to it, Samuel accepted his role of sacrificing for the family's survival. He missed school often and was unable to attend secondary school with his close school friend Cosnel. His sacrifice allowed his younger siblings to have opportunities he had missed. He paid the ultimate price. For this one boy, the loss at sea was one of the greatest tragedies of his time.

10.4 The Burning of Maude's Kitchen

Goat Hill had its share of tragedies over time. Early one Thursday afternoon, during the dry season, fire started in Maude's kitchen. Like all other homes in the village, Maude's kitchen was a smaller building separated from the main building or living quarters. In each home, there was a main building divided into a sitting and dining room combined and a bedroom. A second building housed the kitchen, and in some cases, a third structure housed a latrine and sometimes doubled up as a bathroom. Maude's kitchen was one of the biggest kitchens in Goat Hill. It was large enough to house an indoor fireside, and a loft in which dried corn, still in straw, was stored from year to year. Most of the other kitchens in the village were wattle-and-dab. The smoke from the wood fire in Maude's kitchen kept the weevils away from the corn ensuring that good planting material was available for the next planting season.

Maude's kitchen, unlike other village kitchens, which were single compartments, had a second compartment. In one corner of the second compartment, there were four forty-five gallon drums. Two drums contained corn seeds from the last two years, and one drum stored pigeon peas from the most recent harvest. The fourth drum was about one third filled with a mixture of beans from the harvest in the earlier part of the year. She treated the drums with the peas and beans with black pepper to protect them from any possible insect infestation that would make them useless for cooking.

Maude also had a wooden couch without mattress in the second compartment. She used it for resting while her food cooked. On that particular day, Maude had just put the dried pigeon peas to cook and was waiting for them to burst. She was using the typical wood fire that would take about forty-five minutes to an hour to burst the peas. Maude was always good at estimating the time when the peas would be ready, that was when the peas burst. Then, she would add the dumplings and ground provision. It was always obvious when the peas had burst; as the outer coating would split open by which time the water in the pot would turn to a greyish brown colour.

On that fatal day, Maude had dozed off while lying on the couch. She was overwhelmed by the refreshing north eastern sea breeze, which flowed through the open window located to the east of the kitchen. The sweet cool breeze had taken a toll on her as she drifted in and out of a sleep. She was aware that she needed to check the pot from time to time since she did not want the water to be depleted, such that the peas would begin to burn. A soup with burnt or partly burnt peas never tasted right and Maude did not want to upset her husband or her two nieces and nephew. They would know what had happened because a soup from burnt peas did not smell or taste right. Yet, she did not get up from her couch to check the pot as she felt too good lying there.

It was probably the same north eastern sea breeze, which had enabled the fire. At some point, the breeze fanned the fire under the pot of peas causing sparks to lodge in the dried corn straw in the loft above. No one could be quite sure how the corn caught fire, as it was difficult to imagine how a spark could have survived the four or five feet vertical movement without being naturally put out. Nonetheless, strange things do happen.

Garvis first saw the blue smoke curling from above the roof of Maude's kitchen. By this time, the wind was gradually losing its strength, hence the smoke seemed to be hovering, moving first towards the hill to the west then reversing easterly from where it originated. At first, Garvis thought that it might have been a charcoal pit close to Maude's kitchen. He had seen smoke behave similarly, hovering over a charcoal pit in the early mornings. However, he quickly recollected that there was no charcoal pit near to Maude's house. In any case, most charcoal pits were started early in the morning and this was already late in the day. He ran to Maude's house and saw flames through the gaps in the slots of the vertical pieces of board that enclosed the fireside. He then smelt the burning straw and corn. The smell reminded him of the popcorn machine that was in operation during the last bazaar, which he had attended.

Garvis started shouting "fire, fire" at the top of his voice as he jumped around. He was trying to get the attention of anyone. It was only then that Maude got up and realised she was engulfed in smoke. She clambered through the open window to escape. Under normal circumstances, she would not have attempted that. She was not small in stature and was not the athletic type. Nevertheless, she had manoeuvred out without a scratch and stood looking at the fire, shocked and in a daze. She knew not what to do. She wailed and wailed uncontrollably. Her neighbour and cousin, Gulcia came to her side. She too was crying. They tried to comfort each other while the kitchen was burning. All that Maude could think of was, "Why did I fall asleep?"

Her husband had gone to a job about five miles away. There was no telephone; hence, it would take some time for him to get the news. What would she say to him about the corn, the peas, all the groceries and most importantly his dinner? Luckily, as was discovered many days afterwards, the corn and peas in the drums were only slightly affected. One or two layers of seeds in direct contact with the metal were roasted or parched. Those they separated later on.

There was a gathering of villagers, who had brought buckets of water. That was the first time in the village that a building was on fire. The children in the schoolyard also saw the fire and were all shouting in unison "fire, fire". Then a brilliant idea came to one of the teachers. The school principal, Mr Brathwaite, endorsed the idea. Immediately, there was a twenty-five-man bucket brigade of children and teachers with buckets on their heads, moving as fast as possible up the hill. The only fire tender, which was in the town, could only carry about two hundred gallons of water. At most times, however, it was empty as it was the dry season. There had never been a successful attempt to save a building from fire on the island.

The bucket brigade arrived. It took no more than four minutes, which was about half the normal time for getting from the schoolyard to Maude's house. By this time, the fire had almost completely gutted the kitchen. They used the water from the bucket brigade to prevent the fire from spreading to the main building. They poured water on the side of the main building closest to the kitchen. This required an agile person. The best man for that job was Dudley. He was strong and a quick mover. The young and old admired his agility. When he traversed the island on his many errands, or to or from one of his job sites, he walked without seeming to get tired. When he walked around a corner, he would lean his body at an angle of about sixty to seventy degrees to the horizontal, as an expert cyclist on the racetrack. Only when he became old did he use the services of the bus or accepted a ride from the taxi drivers. Once when he was perhaps in best physical condition, he walked from his home in Goat Hill to the Seventh Day

Adventist Church, three and a half miles, in less than thirty minutes. The Goat Hill bus passed him, as he started fully dressed in a three-piece suit, minus shoes. By the time the bus had collected and dropped off all its passengers who were either going to work in town or just to do the weekly shopping, Dudley's bass voice could be heard by the bus driver and his conductor on their second trip to Goat Hill. They had spent less than three minutes off loading the passengers before returning to Goat Hill. Tass, the bus driver, estimated that Dudley must have taken only a couple minutes longer than the bus to make the journey of three and a half miles.

As if directed by some unknown force, Dudley appeared out of the blue. He grabbed a bucket and ran towards the area attempting to get about halfway between the kitchen and the main building. He got to within six feet of the position, which he had in mind. This was the closest he could get. In this position, it was possible to withstand, momentarily, the heat from the fire.

Dudley splashed the water towards the roof of the main building. He directed the water to the closest point between the two buildings that was at the point where the eaves of the roofs of the two buildings were about four feet from each other. It was at that point that the fire was attempting to cross over. He moved in and out with great speed. Walking on the asphalt road at 2:00 pm when the ambient temperature was 35 degrees Celsius must have been the preparation for this occasion. As he emptied one bucket, another was filled with such precision that it was difficult to believe that it was not planned. Those buckets appeared to come from nowhere.

As it was the dry season, getting to Maude's house was unhindered by planted gardens. Even the big stones in the narrow tracks could not slow the progress of the water carriers. They came from all directions. Some containers and buckets were full, some half full or contained as much as the person could have carried. In some cases, the contents were insignificant, as much of the water had leaked out through the numerous holes, which had caused it to be previously condemned.

There were all kinds of buckets: square ones, round ones, dented ones and rusty ones. Even some of the night pails in the village were converted to water buckets. At the peak of activities, Maude's neighbours were empting their water drums and cisterns to refill buckets in order that the appetite of the fire could be controlled.

The bucket brigade that left from the school soon completed a second trip as the flowing adrenalin ensured that no one got tired. Soon the flames subsided. The fire had consumed the kitchen. It was a miracle that they saved the main building. Now everyone was tired. The charred marks on the main building, where the fire had begun to cross over, remained on the house until about thirty years later when they repaired and repainted the house. They rebuilt the kitchen subsequently in concrete and a gas stove replaced the fireside cooking. Any fire would have a harder time destroying the new kitchen.

That was Goat Hill's first tragedy by fire. It was a miracle. The fire had destroyed only the kitchen. Luckily, there were no fatalities. The fire was an incident that brought the best out of the neighbours. The post-mortem on the fire and the people's responses carried on for many days. There had never been a clear answer as to what really had happened.

10.5 IGNORING THE ANCESTRAL SPIRITS

Another tragedy in Goat Hill was the premature death of Henry's grandmother. Henry's grandmother, Bunah, descended from the Francis bloodline, one of the first families in Goat Hill. Sometime after the abolition of the slave trade, Bunah's grandparents, who were the parents of Madevine, had settled in Goat Hill and built a two story three-bedroom house. This was the house by the Big Stone. It was the envy of the village. The wooden upper floor provided the living quarters and the lower floor, constructed from local stone blocks held together by cement made from burnt coral, was the village shop. Madevine operated the shop, and before her, her mother did. They never fully stocked the shop. After many years, and the passing of several generations, the family decided to demolish the house, salvage whatever re-useable material they could, and build a smaller building. Financial resources for this new building were expected to come from the fourth generation's children who had migrated to the UK.

The demolition was to take place during the dry season. All preparations were well on the way when someone in the village had a dream. Clarabelle dreamt that an ancestor came to her and told her that the old house should remain and that the ancestors were unhappy about the planned event. The elders interpreted the dream or vision and came to different understandings. Some believed that the long gone ancestors needed a sacrifice of some form. Perhaps a plate like that undertaken in a 'Saraka' or maroon would suffice. This was not to be, although they considered the dream and the possible negative consequences. Bunah and Madevine ignored the demand of Clarabelle's dream and vision. Instead of having the plate before any activity started in relation to the demolition, Bunah and Madevine wanted to minimise expenditure by combining the two plates.

On the eve of the demolition, Jassie and Cleave who were Bunah's second cousins from a neighbouring village, teamed up with Bee and Decca of Goat Hill to begin the preparation. About four o'clock, Jassie and Cleave had completed their day's work on a construction site not too far away. They came to advance the following days' work. They helped to remove the galvanised sheets on the roof that evening so that the major demolition could begin early the next day. The roof was over one hundred years old and had survived four hurricanes but was still in perfect condition. The last time the house had any repairs was about thirty years earlier when they replaced two panes of glass.

Jassie was in charge. He and two other men climbed the roof using a wooden ladder. Once on the roof, they used their pig-foot to remove nails that secured the sheets to the latticed rafters. He removed the first sheet and passed it down to Decca who was responsible for securing it for later use. While removing the fourth sheet, Jassie was startled as the sheet on which he was standing began to slide. There was no time to take evasive action or to protect himself. As if directed by the ancestral spirits, the sheet slid off the roof. Like a sea surfer, the sheet below Jassie's legs was airborne for a period that may have only been one or two seconds, but for the onlookers it looked like eternity. The sheet landed on a flat area between two big boulders as if guided by an invisible pilot. Jassie and all who witnessed that were shaken.

Everyone was now looking for an explanation. It was a miracle that Jassie had not sustained physical damage. Finally, they agreed that this was a sign. The ancestors were not happy with what was going on. They had given a warning to the elders who were gathered and they had ignored the warning. How should they interpret the sign after that near mishap? There were some agitated discussions. Some said to abandon the whole project and leave the old house alone. Others thought that since the activities had started in the wrong way there was an urgent need to make things right. That meant communicating with the ancestral spirts immediately. Decca and Bee were the propagators of the second viewpoint, and as the proponents, they were happy to take the leading role.

As there was no strong opposition to Decca and Bee's proposal, the process of appeasement began. To appease the spirits, Decca and Bee called for the rum and water. At first, they brought out a rum bottle with some of its contents missing. Decca rejected that. He shouted, "You want to make the ancestors angrier". Soon they replaced the partially filled bottle with a full one. With rum in the bottle and a large cup filled with water, Decca and Bee, followed by the other men and women, some of whom were scared, began a ceremony of libation. They moved from one corner of the house to another and poured some rum on the ground. Following that, they poured water on the same spots. Then Cleave who was observing how much rum they had poured at the first two corners, shouted that they had not poured enough and that this could cause greater vexation among the spirits. Clarabelle called out to Decca and accused him of being too stingy with the rum. She continued, *"You 'fraid it won't have sufficient remaining for you to get drunk?"* Decca ignored the 'piccong' coming his way from Clarabelle. He was engrossed with beseeching the forbearers for forgiveness of the descendants for any wrongdoing. He also asked for their protection and protection of their guests. They passed the rum bottle around and everybody who had a glass or a cup took a drink of rum followed by water.

Once the impromptu libation ceremony was completed, it was time to decide on the way forward. There were some discussions among the elders but they reached no consensus. The men who were originally on the roof were now reluctant to resume. Therefore, they postponed the work on the roof to the following day. It was now time to prepare for the cooking part of the next day's activities.

Jassie again took charge of the proceedings. There was to be the slaughtering of a pig, which Bunah had reared for this purpose. There were also two goats and two sheep for the occasion. The sheep were from Bunah's daughter and the goats were contributions from neighbours. The first animals they slaughtered were the sheep. That was the easiest part, as the sheep provided no resistance. Then it was time for the goats. There was some excitement as one of the goats almost escaped its captors. After slicing the neck of each goat, Patrick as directed by Jassie, carried the goats' carcasses to the clammier cherry tree, tying them by their rear legs to a low branch that cantilevered almost horizontally from the clammier cherry tree. The clammier cherry tree was one of the few trees that retained green leaves at that time of the year. They removed the animals' skins, followed by the internal organs. They washed the liver, heart and kidneys and seasoned them before stewing. The butchers and their assistants had the first call on these organs once they were stewed.

Then, it was time for the pig. The pig, sensing what was about to take place was uneasy and began squealing and snorting. It tried its best to escape its captors but without much success. Soon it became quiet after Cleave had used the old worn-out cutlass, converted to a butcher knife, to end the poor animal's life. The men put the pig in position, and without any ceremony butchered it. They collected the blood and cooked it with minimum seasoning. This the men consumed. The only men who did not consume it were those who followed the Seventh Day Adventist and the Jehovah witness faiths. They cleaned the pig on a makeshift butcher's table assembled on the boundary between Bunah and her neighbour's properties.

The bottom half of a metal drum, which they had converted into a pot, was already on three big stones. The fire below the makeshift pot was devouring the dried wood fitted between the stones, providing enough heat to boil ten gallons of water in record time. They covered the carcass of the pig with some jute bags and poured the boiling water over them. Once they had removed the bags, Bee and Cleave, using sharpened knives, began a process of shaving the carcass. After a while, they were having difficulty in getting a clean shave. It was at that time that they used the bags again to cover the carcass and poured more boiling water over them. That process was repeated until the pig was completely and neatly shaven. Then they did the final shaving using Ervin's barber razor.

It was now about 6.45pm when the cleaned pig's carcass was ready. Like the sheep before, the men strung the pig on the extended branch of the clammier cherry tree. Cleave cut opened the carcass on the stomach side and removed the internal organs. Unlike those from the sheep, these belonged to Bunah and her family. She would use them for breakfast for all the volunteers on the following day. By that time, the sun had long disappeared over High North and it was getting dark. It was about time to light the kerosene lamps, as the light at the doctor's house two miles away on Belair Hill was already aglow. The villagers of Goat Hill used that light, as did the surrounding villages, to signal the lighting of their lamps on evenings.

To improve the visibility of the area under the clammier cherry tree where the butchering was proceeding, Bunah prepared a 'masantoe'. The masantoe is a glass bottle filled with pitch oil (kerosene) and a wick made from bits of jute bag. With her masantoe ready, Bunah, from time to time, turned the bottle upside down so that the wick received a fresh flow of kerosene, causing the lighting to improve. It was on one of those occasions when flipping over the bottle to refresh the wick with fuel that some kerosene flowed through the wick and landed on Bunah's long cotton dress. In panic, Bunah's hand with the masantoe struck against one of the big stones in the yard. The bottle broke. More kerosene splashed on Bunah's frock, but that time the wick fell off and immediately she was on fire. There was complete confusion. As the fire spread on Bunah's clothing, she began running in all directions like a blind person, tumbling over stones, falling, getting up and continuing her panic run. She made not a single sound although the pain must have been excruciating.

It was the first occurrence of something like this. For a short moment, no one moved to help the traumatised woman. Perhaps nobody knew what to do. Finally, she collapsed. Then Bee said "Quick! Get a bag and wet it". That seemed to be taking forever. Jassie got a crocus bag and pushed it in a nearby drum filled with water. He tried to beat back the flames with the wet bag but his effort was feeble, as he seemed scared that he too might be set alight. All of Bunah's grandchildren who were present began to cry. Henry, the oldest grandchild at the time in Goat Hill was not around. Perhaps if he were present he may have known what to do. He was a very intelligent boy, the 'brains' in the family.

Once they had put out the fire, the men realised that Bunah was unconscious. A car came and took her to the hospital. Lloyd, Bunah's cousin from Grenada, was the medical doctor on the island. When he saw the condition of his elder cousin, he was moved to tears. Bunah had suffered one hundred percent burns to her body. At the hospital, the nurses placed her on a hospital bed and covered her with a white sheet. They placed the sheet over the extended bed heads to avoid it getting into contact with her body. She went in and out of consciousness. Perhaps she was better in that state since she did not feel the pain.

Not once did she cry out in anguish.

Next day, the workers demolished the house. Although the volunteers consumed the pork, goat and mutton, there was no libation ceremony that day. Perhaps the living was angry with the ancestors. There was no food placed on the table overnight for the spirits. The boys who had planned to steal from the plate would be disappointed, but they will await another plate at another time. Everyone was sad, and as the sadness overflowed, there was no sweetness in the mouth for the food. Everyone prayed for Bunah's recovery, which would not have been possible even with technology half a century later. She never recovered and died a few days later.

Her two daughters who were still in Goat Hill were devastated. The news went to England to her other two daughters, Leah and Anne, the twins. Her sons-in-law and Henry's older siblings who had already migrated also received notification. Unfortunately, they could not return to Goat Hill for the funeral. Bunah's extended family on her father's side was there to support her children and grandchildren who were still in Goat Hill.

It was Jassie and Bee who directed the building of the coffin. They occupied a shaded area on the side of the road. First, they built a temporary workbench then they began work on the coffin. They were good at that, as they had built many coffins before. All the carpentry required for fabricating the coffin, they did by hand. The men built the coffin from white pine board, which being a soft wood was easy with which to work. Once the carpentry was completed, they covered the coffin with mauve coloured cotton cloth. Mauve was the favourite colour for coffins in those days. Henry and the other grandchildren observed the activities, as this was the first death in the family. Some of them who were too scared to get close to previous funerals in the village showed courage on this occasion in getting close to their grandmother's coffin.

Bunah's body remained on ice overnight at one of her daughter's house in Goat Hill. Placing ice in the box with the dead was the only means of preserving it at that time. That night there was a small wake.

The family served Cocoa tea and Crix biscuits with some corned beef. The men drank white rum lavishly. Those who got drunk found a place under the house or any convenient spot to sleep out the alcohol.

On the day of the funeral, the undertakers washed the body in the traditional fashion. It was not an easy task for the matriarch in the village, as there was no skin on most parts of the body. They threw the dead water in an area where no one was expected to pass, as it was taboo to walk on 'dead water'. The body was dressed and placed in the coffin. Once viewing was completed, the men covered and secured the coffin by nailing it along the top edges.

It was a three o'clock funeral. The relatives placed the coffin on Edmond's truck, which was an all-purpose transport. It led the procession to Tebeau. Bunah's grandchildren began the short period of weeping and wailing before the truck left. The very young grandchildren were not quite aware of what was happening. Two or three of them tried hiding underneath the small wooden house. The older grandchildren, led by Henry, wept uncontrollably. All relatives, including the grandchildren, had pinned on them a ribbon made from the leftovers of the mauve cloth. By five-thirty, they interred Bunah's body in the Francis family cemetery and the mourners then went their separate ways. She was only sixty-three and had anticipated happy days in her twilight years with her grandchildren. That was not to be.

Things changed at the house by the Big Stone. Magnus went to live with his aunt and Henry in Harvey Vale. Henry's weekend visits became fewer and fewer. Henry reminded all that even if there was only one loss of life, the gruesome death had touched everyone. Perhaps, many have forgotten this tragedy. Although Henry was not present on the day of the tragedy, thirty years later the incident was clear to him as on the first day. His other cousins, some of whom were not yet teenagers, also remembered the day. It remained one of the major tragedies in Henry's family history. The suffering of one individual, witnessed by many, was the real tragedy.

11

DEVELOPMENT AND CURSES

ECONOMIC SURVIVAL FOR the small community, Goat Hill, depended on a combination of hard work by the villagers, a spirit of community and good fortune, which fostered a culture of innovation and entrepreneurship. There were very little natural resources left for exploitation. The shallow but rich soils on the hilly terrain, which provided evidence of former volcanoes, had suffered serious degradation. The first peoples who settled in the village had over-exploited the limited available land through decades of intensive agriculture. The limited land space provided no opportunity for expansion. Only the sea and the resources therein remained underexploited until recently, since they did not see it as an economic resource.

The optimists did not consider the economic future that gloomy. The landscapes, including beaches, pleasant climate and unique cultural heritage that incorporated the characteristics of the different peoples from different eras were there for harnessing. The strong family ties that linked the diaspora community to the homeland might continue to be crucial to the sustainability of the community, but the importance may decline. The modern Goat Hill continues to enjoy relatively friendly, caring and relaxed neighbourhoods. It is witnessing a growing community of foreigners that provide a potential niche market for heritage tourism. Goat Hill's current leaders and policy makers are relying on the natural attributes to propel it in the future.

Getting there may not be that simple. Goat Hill must first overcome two curses that were central in its past. These curses or social phenomena that, at times, provided for the community's survival and well-being created a false sense of prosperity and affluence. In so doing, they also created negative impacts that bedevil the social structure, which people have glossed over. These curses are analogous to the oil curse or "Dutch Disease", the paradox of plenty. In the case of the oil curse, a country comes into unexpected wealth and the government and citizens waste it as manifested in 'white elephant' buildings and infrastructure, and unsustainable consumption patterns. In Goat Hill, these curses have led to an unexpected abundance of consumer goods leading to wasteful consumption.

11.1 THE CONTRABAND CURSE

The trade in contraband morphed over the years into the first curse, the "Contraband Curse". For Madevine, her small scale vending in Balgobin white rum from British Guiana (now the Republic of Guyana) or Ibis Brandy from the French West Indies was a way of life. She knew that it was not legal since the colonial administration would confiscate the items when the traders were lax in their transactions. For her protection from the colonial law, she kept small portions of rum in a bottle under the counter in her shop. The remainder she kept in the 'Jimmy-John' under her bed. The Jimmy-John was a glass container protected by woven sisal rope. It held up to three to five gallons of liquid. It had a dual purpose. In addition to being the hiding place for contraband rum, villagers used it at Christmas time for brewing ginger beer.

Everyone in the village recognised contraband for what it was: an illicit practice. Although there was no concrete evidence of people getting into trouble with the law for so doing, there were many made up stories of the customs officer raiding premises and charging people. In one case, though, on a neighbouring island, a story was told of the islanders digging a grave on the beach and daring the custom officer to leave the safety of his hired boat to make a landing. The story was that the officer and boat made an about turn and headed for the bay from which they first left. Many years later, the body of a government official from Grenada was found floating in a harbour in Harvey Vale. It was alleged that he was the victim of a clash between tax collectors and contraband operators. Notwithstanding, the cases of the grave on the beach or the floating body, the boatmen, the shopkeeper and the rum drinker were all aware that they were breaking the law and were extremely careful with their activities.

In the early days of the contraband trade, the range of goods was limited mainly to sin goods: tobacco and alcohol products. In many cases, the contraband trade was opportunistic, in that boatmen, who plied the Eastern Caribbean Sea in their locally built sloops and schooners, would also engage in contraband. They smuggled whatever was available using the meagre earnings from their legitimate occupation. Typically, the contraband supplemented their sailors' wages. There was no motivation for profiteering and in many instances, the contraband goods were handed over to the consignee at cost price. Later on, due to heavy excise taxes on alcohol and tobacco, helped to transform contraband into a highly lucrative business in these two items. For a while, the villagers referred to them as Goat Hill's cocoa and nutmeg. That was to convey the idea, that while people on the mainland produced cocoa and nutmegs for a living, Goat Hill villagers depended on rum and cigarettes. At first, the trade served many well. Some families depended on that to send their children to school, particularly when students who made it to secondary school had no choice but to attend one of the secondary schools in St Georges on the mainland Grenada.

There were stories of the students becoming involved in the contraband trade, and using the proceeds for their full upkeep while being away from home. In one case, two friends, one from Goat Hill and the other from a nearby village, pooled their pocket change together and started their business with two bottles of white horse whiskey and one cartoon of Three Fives cigarettes. Before long, they were selling to the school teachers and their friends. The business lasted while they remained at school and allowed them to eat a little better than their other mates at the boarding hostel. In the wider context, some small traders used the trade to start small retail and grocery businesses. Some of these businesses survived to become household names around Goat Hill.

In recent times, the contraband trade has expanded as the line of products widened to include a range of alcoholic drinks, appliances from the most basic to the most sophisticated household appliances, electronics and garments and other products and has become a means of enrichment for a few. The potential high profits in illicit trade in these items motivated persons to become involved. There were opportunities for shopping in duty free zones and the avoidance of paying duties and taxes in Carriacou. The low prices of these consumer goods, in relation to the prices on the larger islands, created the curse. Cheap and easily available alcohol induced excessive drinking. As a result, all the ills, social and health problems associated with excessive drinking, became a phenomenon in Goat Hill.

There were cases where those directly associated with the contraband trade sought no other form of employment. Instead, they organised their financial and social lives around the illicit trading, one trip at a time. When they had exhausted the earnings from one trip, they made another trip, resulting in the development of a cohort of young men and women with low motivation for regular or permanent employment. They were also good candidates for other social problems.

Another consequence of the contraband trade was the negative impacts of under-age drinking. This is also a contemporary social problem facing Goat Hill and the surrounding villages. Although not researched formally, there is anecdotal evidence that the contraband trade facilitated the introduction of a drug trade in Goat Hill.

11.2 THE REMITTANCES CURSE

The second curse is the curse of remittances. Remittances have been the main economic contributor in Goat Hill for over fifty years. Like in many other small isolated communities, it has become an entrenched cultural practice. Since the first wave of migration, the remittances from people in the diaspora have contributed to the well-being of the family members who remained behind. Like religious people who are committed to faithfully paying their tithes to their chosen church, people of Goat Hill in the diaspora have a similar obligation to their extended family. However, while there are historic documented rationales for the payment of tithes, there is no equivalent for remittances. Henry, JC and Max knew that it was their responsibility. They never quivered about it. In some modern day religious denominations where many adhere to the payment of tithes, many of the leaders of these churches use the collected tithes for their own benefit and live extravagant lives. Meanwhile, the contributors to their fortune often live a life where many basic needs are not available. In contrast, the providers of remittances give a false sense of security to those who benefit, as many of those in the diaspora struggle to make ends meet. In essence, remittances are like an unwritten form of tithes, expected from those in the diaspora to their extended families back at home.

11.3 CONSEQUENCES OF THE CURSES

Stable and relatively low prices are crucial to developing the new economy of Goat Hill. Small communities like Goat Hill, in open economies, are generally price takers to the extent that domestic prices are influenced strongly by developments internationally. The prices in Goat Hill seem not to follow economic theory. The high prices observed for some items such as domestic transport or freight on goods from the mainland tend not to have any explanation besides that of the effect of the contraband and remittances curses. These curses have implanted superficially high prices on goods and services, prices that are not to the benefit of the community.

If one goes to any of the vegetable vendors in Goat Hill on a Friday and asks: "Why is the price of dasheen so high?" A typical answer would be, "You don't want it? - then eat the money." To exploit the natural resources to sustainable development, reasonable prices would be important. High prices, which now affect the local population, are not conducive to tourism development. Villagers of Goat Hill are reminded that while the locals have little or no alternatives, the tourists have many options.

It is reasonable to expect that some commodities would be more expensive in Goat Hill than on the mainland. Commodities transported from the mainland or other ports would attract extra costs for transportation and freight. Do the mark-ups only reflect the additional costs for transportation and freight? Are the additional transportation and freight prices reasonable?

Why has Goat Hill become so expensive in the first place? Is it because of the recent influx of 'high-income' or well-resourced people (compared to the local average income) who have returned home that prices are adjusted upward to capture that segment? Is it that the higher prices have not been questioned by the better offs? The cost of three items, all originating locally, provide examples of the unusually high prices. Let us consider meat, fish and labour.

Goat Hill boasts about the capability of being self-sustainable in livestock production. In fact, in most cases the cost of livestock production is nil or negligible as most of the animals are free range on the island. In cases where livestock farmers try to be genuine and honest by securing their animals and by tethering or fencing them in, they are regularly the victims of dog attacks or predial larceny. Notwithstanding, the little effort and minimal cost of livestock production in Goat Hill, the price of meat is twenty-five percent higher than that in Grenada, even when the source of the meat is Goat Hill's livestock in the first place.

Recently, Carriacou and Petite Martinique have become the main centres of fishing in Grenada. Yet, the price of fish there is over ten percent higher than the price on the mainland. Fish is one item where the price remains rigid. When it is plentiful, fishermen from the mainland would come to Goat Hill to sell their fish at reduced prices. Sometimes they sell the fish at half price to the people of Goat Hill. Situations like these seldom affect the price of fish on that day in Goat Hill. On the other side, when fish is plentiful in Goat Hill, prices would not change. Nevertheless, these fishermen have been known to travel to the mainland, expending time and fuel to sell at prices lower than that of Goat Hill's. Is it a case of unconventional economics in practice? In extreme cases, reports indicate that fishermen dump the fish instead of reducing the prices. These are the remittances and contraband curses at work.

These curses also influence the price of labour. Skilled and unskilled labour in construction cost up to twenty-five percent more in Goat Hill than on the mainland. Of course, in Goat Hill labour prices never go down even in the face of a slump in the construction sector. Labourers from elsewhere, in such situations, seeing the opportunity, settle in Goat Hill for a while and offer their services at a lower rate. Why should the villager lower his price? A partial dialogue of a job hunter in Goat Hill may typically be like this:

> "Madam me price is one fifty. And is because it is you I charging this. Is a favour I doing you. Well! Give you work to them Vincey and them Grenadians, when they gone I still here. You know how much for food in the shop? Well I ain't depend on your money. I have enough clothes that me sister send for me. If I broke I just making one call and the money arrives by MoneyGram. In fact, you think I have to work, its only because me fridge stop work and I want to buy a new one".

11.4 Ancestral lands

There is a third and most recent curse and that is inherited ancestral lands. Gone are the days when the extended family members shared in the use of ancestral lands. Many holdings are still in the names of persons who have died over a century ago. Members of extended families work gardens on portions of the ancestral lands. Some build homes on the lands, usually wooden structures that represent only semi-permanence. Permanent structures are discouraged. In the early days, they placed little monetary value on lands.

One of the holdings passed down through generations was under the control of Bunah and Madevine, They and other members of the extended family worked their Goat Hill holdings peacefully for many years. The land was in the name of Bunah's mother Sarah who was Madevine's eldest sister. Sarah's parents had passed down ownership of the holding with the understanding that it was not to be transferred to an individual member. Many younger family members have attempted to transfer portions of the family land but these were thwarted because the earlier generations were true to the ancestral understandings. Eventually, one descendent was able to acquire the property, through legal means with very good intention of distributing to as many as possible. This was partly successful, but it opened the door for queries from distant relatives. How far this will go is anybody's guess.

Land is a finite resource. As the demand for it in Goat Hill has increased, so too has the price. The high cost of living and land speculation and conflicts in undivided ancestral lands are all helping to drive up the price of real estate, thereby putting it out of reach of local fixed income earners. This combination of high prices, together with ownership by "non-belongers" (a term used in many of the northern Caribbean islands), has the potential for future social dislocation and could lead to social unrest. The case of Thomas exemplifies the complexities of the land issue. Thomas is a successful son of Goat Hill who returned to his parents' house, which was in a dilapidated condition.

He repaired it without depending on any financial support from his siblings. The house had sentimental value for Thomas and since he could afford it, the cost of the repairs did not matter much. In fact, it was much more expensive to do the repairs than if he had built a new house. On completion of the repairs, Thomas' brother and sister returned from England and occupied the house. Thomas at first had no objection as he thought that this was going to be a temporary stay. One day the following dialogue ensued.

"What you mean we could only come and stay in the house for a holiday? This is awe parents' house. Nobody tell you to spend money on the house. Because you educated you believe that we stupid. We come back for good. Furthermore, we retired and now we have nowhere to go but here."

Thomas left and never spoke to his siblings again. He died without a reconciliation. This is a result of the curse of ancestral land.

12

FROM AFRICAN SOCIALISM TO TRIBAL POLITICS

12.1 COMMUNAL GOVERNANCE

In the days of Henry's ancestors, Madevine and Bunah, there was great unity among the villagers of Goat Hill and the rest of the island. It was the envy of many people, who encountered them. The togetherness that had distinguished sons and daughters of Goat Hill, a village of peace and harmony went with them by sea and by air to far-away places. Although Henry and JC saw some of this on their return, it appeared to be the remnants as it had almost evaporated. It was evident to Henry and JC but not obvious to first-time visitors. Visitors saw a highly cohesive community. Nevertheless, compared to the time when Henry was growing up, this cohesiveness was highly exaggerated.

When Henry was growing up in Goat Hill, he witnessed only minor intra- or inter-village conflicts. There were regular scuffles and fights among children in class, on the school compound or on the way home. These fights did not last too long. Any adult, including strangers, could intervene and administer some form of punishment to the culprits, after a short trial. It was not easy for the self-appointed judge to get it right as there were as many versions of what had transpired as there were bystanders. If the incident was reported to the parents and the school principal, additional trials could be held and corresponding punishments may be administered. These children 'incidences' often brought the families and villagers closer. The African saying that it takes a village to raise a child was truly befitting of Henry's childhood.

Goat Hill was not perfect, but to Henry in retrospect it was almost. In the family, conflicts were manifested through sibling rivalries to gain parental preference; inter-household rivalries to establish a pecking order in the extended family community; village rivalries during cricket matches at the small community playing field; and, sometimes district rivalries such as' Heroes' and 'Bonroys' or North versus South on Carnival Tuesday when King of the Shakespeare mas was judged. However, these rivalries were short-lived. Many village activities, were communal in nature, such as christenings, weddings, funerals, maroons, boat launching and house-quartering which quickly brought people (individuals and the community) together putting the village on an even keel.

Goat Hill had a communal governance structure based on a patriarchal system. Everyone knew to whom to refer conflict for mediation. The position of mediator was usually held by the schoolmaster. Marquis, who came from another village and married into the Goat Hill Clan, led activities related to the village maroon or a saraka. His leadership did not always go unchallenged. For instance, he might be challenged by a young man who would be told that his time would come one day. Quashie was the leader for the cleaning of the wells or the rainwater ponds. He would call a meeting of the village to decide on the way forward. The village, like the other surrounding ones, was governed by the type of African socialism formalised and practised in Tanzania during the time of Julius Nyerere.

12.2 Colonialism to revolution

When Henry and JC migrated to England during the 1960's, they used a British passport. as At that time, everyone in Goat Hill was a British citizen. Goat Hillians were used to living their simple communal life, unaware and uninterested in the governance under which they lived. They did as was told by the representatives of the crown whose photograph hung in some living rooms. They were reminded of the supremacy of the monarchy when they went to the churches, overseen by white priests. They were prompt in paying their taxes for fear that the crown could confiscate the land and chattel that they owned. The children of Goat Hill, not required to think of such matters of governance, looked forward to the annual school treat on the Monarchy's birthday for which they sang the anthem, "God save the King or God save the Queen".

As time passed, one or two Goat Hillians who were literate or had some property of significance represented the village's interest to the crown. This was due to the introduction of Adult Suffrage. Some of the leaders of this time included Paterson, and a husband and wife Sylvester and Mammie Sylvester. Notwithstanding, Goat Hillians remained almost oblivious to this governance's transformations and continued to roll with the punches.

More changes came, a few years after Henry and JC had settled in England. There was self-government, statehood (1967) and then independence in 1974. The children of Goat Hill looked forward to additional school treats that came with these changes. The food and drinks offered in these treats were not significant in quality or quantity. Nonetheless, for the school children who had few occasions for a party of sorts, these were special.

The political disturbances accompanied by violence of the early 1970s in the capital, St. Georges would have passed unnoticed in Goat Hill, except for occasional shortages in the shops. The shops were regularly overflowing with imports from neighbouring St. Vincent. The disturbances of the early 1970s culminated in the short lived Grenada revolution during the period 1979 to 1983. The residents of Goat Hill welcomed the rhetoric espoused by the revolutionary leaders as it was aligned to their traditional and communal way of life. It was during this revolutionary period that Goat Hill made a big developmental leap. The village's infrastructure benefited from the introduction of electricity and telephone systems. The village also benefited from job opportunities, job progression, and scholarship opportunities based on merit, which had eluded it in the pre-revolutionary period. Henry and JC had missed some of the governance transformation, but they would be there for the next phase.

12.3 Divisive politics

While in England, Henry and JC had observed that at election time people grew animated as they voiced their support for a particular political party, bantering amicably. Sometimes emotions ran high but as a fire from corn stalk at the beginning of the rainy season, they did not last long. Party politics in England from Henry's experience created some rivalry but its influence did not penetrate every fabric of the society. People had their political views but the sense of the broader societal well-being superseded narrow party interests. This was his experience before he left the village, but not so now, to his great displeasure.

Before Henry and JC migrated, political rivalry in the village was limited to backing the Shoe or the Star: the symbols for the parties of Blaize and Gairy, respectively. The *'banter'* and *'old talk'* quickly disappeared after the silly season or campaign period, which was short lived. This lasted for a couple of weeks during the election campaigns. On their return, Henry and JC observed that politics appeared to be divisive, creating inter- and intra-village enmities. In some cases, brother was against brother, mother against daughter, or one family against another. One was either yellow or green; there was no room for neutrality. For the first time, families were fragmented, pierced apart and consumed by tribalism.

Soon, Henry and JC got labels: Henry 'yellow' although he supported neither party, and JC 'green', even if it was well known that he despised most of the advocates of the party to which he was pigeon-holed. For Henry and JC, political tribalism was something that one read about or heard stories about communities in Africa and the Pacific, when men from the West wanted to identify primitiveness and backwardness with the "so called" undeveloped countries.

Henry and JC noticed that the political tribalism identifiable by the coloured t-shirts of the parties, had penetrated the core of the society. There were green or yellow funerals and green or yellow wakes (a wake is a social gathering associated with death, usually held before a funeral and can be for one or many nights). The fifty-year old annual regatta, too, had not escaped the claws of colour politics, declining in quality such that the fiftieth anniversary was almost the last due to the negative influence of colour politics.

Henry and JC observed similar behaviours during Christmas in Goat Hill. Christmas was a time when all differences were forgiven among neighbours who were not on speaking terms during the year. They could feel free and safe to visit one another's homes. They could drink, eat and dance and then all ill feelings would evaporate. Henry noticed that times had changed. In some extreme cases, some yellows would not visit some greens or vice versa and at one time, the beer they drank was based on the colour of the bottle. There is the green beer and there is the yellow beer. JC liked the yellow bottle beer but if he was seen drinking a green beer, he expected some comments lined with *political 'picong'*. He did not take these '*picongs*' at face value; however, a diehard may, sometimes to his detriment.

Diehard supporters of a particular party do not want to be seen socialising with supporters of another party. They seem to be well indoctrinated in one or the other tribal culture and typically boast that the colour of their tribe runs through their veins and claim that their colour will last until death. These are the most dangerous. They are the foot soldiers who would die for the tribe and its leader. However, who can judge them.

Perhaps it is a way of survival, a way to benefit unfairly from limited resources, as the patrimony seemed to be shared among members of the side in power. Tribalism is fuelled by the need to dominate the limited collective resources. The domination is over jobs; scholarships; small and large contracts; invitations to state functions; state lands; grants and loans whether legal or illegal; Christmas hampers and distribution of disaster relief commodities, among others. It has produced a dependency syndrome, which kills productivity.

There are people whose colour may be considered white, as they are "neither here nor there", but this does not stop others from labelling them. There are also the opportunists. They lack any real commitment - are iguana-like. They identify with a colour for convenience, changing as the longshore currents and picking up whatever they can grab as they move along. That is how Henry and JC found the village of their birth. They had missed the period of the Grenada Revolution that was before the birth of the tribes, when peace and harmony flourished.

The flame of division in Goat Hill society is fanned by the hands of sweet-talking, unrealistic promise makers, the politicians, who seek to ensure their fortune, and their family's fortune, from the purse of the treasury. This is a new phenomenon. No festival is spared from the 'scourge' of political tribalism. Tribalism is not of the people, it is not by the people and it is not for the good of the people. Ultimately, the people would rise up and tribalism would be defeated.

13

CACA BAWE FOR CACA BAWE

NOT TOO LONG after Henry returned from England, he found himself in a reflective mood. He had gone around the island and listened to the different stories being told about current affairs. He tried not to get too involved because he was aware that he was a JCB. Perhaps there were some truth to the stories, but he took everything with a grain of salt. He conferred with JC about the views of villagers in his part of the island. It seemed that there were some commonalities. Henry was not a philosopher, but for a layman was a deep thinker. He found himself reflecting on the society that he knew and cherished, Goat Hill. His mind drifted from Goat Hill to England and back. When he was in England he reflected regularly on Goat Hill, and now that he is settled once more in Goat Hill he reflected, albeit less often, on England.

During his years in England, he recognised that there was something special in being from Goat Hill. Why did people from other islands called Goat Hillians clannish? Why? It was the way of life for him and his compatriots seemed to cause others to say "All you from Goat Hill does move as one. All you really a together people." Henry wondered what was it that seemed to make them special.

In England, when there was a wedding involving a Goat Hillian, there was a big party. Every man contributed to ensure that the host was not overburdened with expenditure. Compatriots showed up even when they did not get an invitation, always carrying with them their contributions. An uninvited guest would say "I hear about the wedding and I know that you forget to tell me" And so those with formal invitations were not treated differently to those who arrived uninvited. There was always enough to feed all the guests, as the hosts catered for more than the number on the guest list.

In England, notwithstanding the pressure of long hours of work or the extreme weather conditions, Goat Hillians in England remembered and celebrated their dead as they did in the village. Like a christening or a wedding which was a more joyful occasion, a wake preceding a funeral or prayer meetings on the ninth night (Nine Nights) and the fortieth night (Forty-Nights) that followed the interment, brought the Goat Hillian community in East London together. It mattered not where they found themselves, nothing was lost in the spirit of togetherness.

That was how it was done back home in Goat Hill. In the village there was a saying "Caca Bawe for Caca Bawe". Caca Bawe is the local patios name for the parrot fish.

Henry remembered the first time that he went fishing on the reefs outside Goat Hill. It was the first time he had seen so many caca bawe of all sizes and colours. He could see them through the sparkling clear water as they used their bird-like beaks to scrape up coral, the forest of the sea. They seemed to live in perfect harmony. They never fought with each other. The older and stronger ones seemed to be the protectors of the younger and weaker ones, regardless of colour. Perhaps, their abundance was as a result of their strong communal spirit. No wonder they were important in the life of Goat Hillians who believed that it was good for children. They believed that it gave wisdom to children and ensured that they would not stray from the net that kept the family and the village together. Perhaps that was the origin of the saying

"Caca Bawe for Caca Bawe" which could be translated "one for all and all for one".

As Henry sat on his veranda, with the post card view of the reefs which created a white line between his island and the other Grenadines, he remembered the snow that got trapped along the fences that divided the pastures into lots on the farms in the English countryside, during winter. He was looking forward to all the activities on the village's calendar. His grandson called from London to check on him. He wanted to share the stories with his grandson as he had done with his son. But this was not the time, the fresh sea breeze had him feeling sleepy. As he dozed off he remembered a phrase used regularly while he was growing up; Caca Bawe for Caca Bawe.

> Henry remembered the story from his father,
> The birth of the emigration sousou,
> When the village pooled their meagre savings,
> Enough to send the first man, Hurriel,
> Hardworking, honest and reliable
> To Lago Oil, Aruba,
> All for one and one for all,
> **Long live Caca Bawe for Caca Bawe.**

> Hurriel met men from other villages
> Some pioneers of the new migration destination,
> They helped him settle and find a job,
> Success was expected
> He sacrificed and like a miser he saved enough,
> To accumulate a passage fare and a little more,
> And soon emigration train arrives once more,
> With more men looking for work,
> The result of another sousou hand;
> **Long live Caca Bawe for Caca Bawe.**

The emigration sousou gave birth to a pyramid scheme,
One went, then two, then four, then eight, until
The returned one by one,
To begin a new sousou hand and emigration train
To England, then to Canada, then to USA.
The train travelled to wherever work was available,
Long live Caca Bawe for Caca Bawe.

Henry remembered,
When the outward bound migrant train slowed,
Then the inward migrant trains carried money orders,
Guilders, pounds and dollars,
To build a cistern to catch the rain,
To add and extension on the house,
To purchase a transistor radio that
Broadcasted Auntie K's Sunday afternoon's Kiddies program,
All the way to Trinidad, letters were sent,
To say to those close and far,
We are Caca Bawe for Caca Bawe

Henry remembered,
How the money flowed,
Consistently,
From beneficiaries to sponsors
of the migration train,
In orderly increments,
To bank in the Post Office,
to buy land,
to build a house,
To pay for funeral, stone feast or saraka,
Because **Caca Bawe is for Caca Bawe,**

Henry remembered when,
the barrels flowed into the village,
Like casks of rum thrown overboard,
The boats that arrived during the night,
Dodging the police,
No one saw, no one owned,
The smuggled goods on-board,
Yet it belonged to them all,
Caca Bawe for Caca Bawe.

Henry remembered,
The barrels full of food stuff and clothes,
First for the Christmas,
Or for the Wake and funeral
And then the stone feast that followed one year later,
Each contributed according to his means
Because it was Caca Bawe for Caca Bawe.

Henry remembered,
How the village was transformed,
A mansion built for a grandmother with little time left,
Then bigger and bigger the houses
Spread across the village,
Replacing the Janet houses,
Wood to concrete and glass,
A blessing to all who believed in,
Caca Bawe for Caca Bawe

Henry remembered,
The first outdoor plumbing and hand pumps,
Then Indoor plumbing and electric pump,
No more latrine,
Just like in London and New York

Things improved, unstoppable
For it was Caca Bawe for Caca Bawe.

The sudden rain awoke Henry from his reverie as he was getting wet where he sat. He knew not how long he was in that position. He felt relaxed and wished his dream had continued. Out of the blues he had a visitor. It was JC. The same JC who had done well in London and believed in "Caca Bawe for Caca Bawe. Henry was about to share his dream, but he must listen to JC. JC was the elder, even if by only three years. The elder was always treated with respect, because that was the way of the caca bawe. It was clear that JC wanted to reminisce on the old days. JC began asking questions without awaiting and answer.

Do you remember?
My grandmother,
And all the grandmothers who cared for all the children.
Waiting on a letter with a postal order enclosed,
To purchase flour and salt beef to add
To coocoo and callaloo, peas soup
Sharing with the neighbours in the calabash
And the receiver would say, thank you
Caca Bawe for Caca Bawe

Do you remember?
Before the barrel, the parcels wrapped in brown paper,
Inside, a new shirt or a pair of shoes,
Sometimes too big or too small,
But survived three hand-me-downs,
Never wasted,
Forced to maximise,
The way of Caca Bawe for Caca Bawe.

Do you remember?
When village boys slept,
At the house of Ackie, their leader,
Who spoke seldom but always profound,
The first for a new migrant train to Tortola;
And as the boys retired for the night,
Packed like sardines,
Unaware of the urine odour in the air
Or the bed bugs that feasted while they slept,
On clothes from the parcel,
Made into rags after passing from one owner to the next,
But now with a new use
It made a layer on the crocus bags;
That blocked the wind that otherwise
Sang through the cracks in the floor,
Caca Bawe for Caca Bawe

Do you remember,
The success of Ackie,
The migration train he enlargened,
Sending for all the boys,
Mentoring all,
For success was assured,
Through **Caca Bawe for Caca Bawe**

Do you remember?
The dancing of the cake,
At the cross roads,
Where two families met,
In friendly rivalry
While dancing and singing the song,
Is Henry bambam (backside) we want to solder,

A lesson for the children around, in
Caca Bawe for Caca Bawe

Do you remember,
The rainwater pond, Big Pond,
That was owned by all,
Grateful for the water captured during the rainy season,
From drains flowing through the fields and farms
Depositing all that the water can carry,
Year after year,
Until too much for man or beast to withdraw
In buckets or by mouth,
Then it was time for desilting,
The whole village gathered an early morning,
Men and boys with forks and spades,
Removing the soil, accumulated for five or six years,
To be carried in trays on women's head,
Singing silently as they threw their half wet loads
On mounds on the side of the road
No government gangs, no engineer, no machine
The pond is cleaned and ready for the coming season, because
Caca Bawe for Caca Bawe.
Do you remember,
The maroon by Big Pond,
To thank the ancestors for the previous harvest,
Offering food on trays,
Then ancestors if satisfied,
Bring a bounty harvest next time,
Then all know it's Goat Hill,
And Caca Bawe for Caca Bawe.

Coming out of their self-imposed hypnoses, Henry and JC smiled at each other. They had returned to their childhood to be assured that it was still alive, **Caca Bawe for Caca Bawe**. They could not and did not try to estimate how much of Caca Bawe for Caca Bawe was still alive. It could not die completely. It may have transformed, like the changing climate was impacting on the forest of reefs where the caca bawe established their own villages. Deep down the knew that wealth could not erode; nor politics of green or yellow; nor religion with its many denominations, sometimes cult-like nor separation by oceans for Caca Bawe for Caca Bawe was entrenched in the DNA of Goat Hill.

14

THE NEW GOAT HILL

14.1 THEN AND NOW

On their return to the village, after living in England for many years, Henry and JC found that many things had changed in Goat Hill. Change is constant. The old men they had left behind had died and young men of their time were now old. Young men in the village, sons and grandsons of their contemporaries who had not migrated 'manned' the village during the nights, something that caused Henry and JC to smile to themselves when they reflected on their time before leaving the village.

How things have changed in Goat Hill! The changes continue to amaze Henry and JC. For them the changes are everywhere, some for the better others for the worse. However, despite the changes, the people of Goat Hill are still doing some things done in the past but in different and new ways.

The most obvious change for Henry and JC was the improvement in the standard of living made possible by remittances to the village sent back by those who had done well in the far-off lands. Small two-compartment wooden houses had been replaced by one and two storey houses with all modern conveniences; rainwater barrels were replaced by underground concrete cisterns and overhead PVC tanks making water shortages experienced in earlier times less severe; and, some homes enjoyed indoor plumbing. Globalisation also had its impact. Small supermarkets made it possible now for villagers to be able to purchase items previously available only in the metropole; cable television had replaced storytelling on the Big Stone; and, computer games have overtaken childhood games of top spinning and marble pitching. Henry and JC also found that party politics was debilitating to the fabric of the village. This change became clear to the "Just Come Backs" (JCBs) when they were quickly pigeonholed into a political camp, based on their associates.

Often as Henry sat on his veranda of the house he built from his savings while working in England, he reflected on the changes in Goat Hill. He made mental notes of some of these changes, which were oblivious to the youth. It seemed to him that only his generation and that of his parents had seen the changes. He reasoned that was expected as only they had lived through the decades in the village going and coming.

Henry smiled to himself when he recalled how as a young man it was impossible for African boys to date girls from the neighbouring village where the residents were mostly of Scottish ancestry. Goat Hill was a village of full African ancestry. At that time, the surnames of the villagers were limited to a few African names like Cudjoe and Quashie or a few English names reflecting the names of the plantation owners like Cox and Derrick. Now there are many other surnames in the village, a testament of to the intermarriage of the people from the different villages.

During one of their weekly socialisations at the back of Bill's shop, JC and Henry seemed to be co-chairing a debate, among the returnees or "Just Come Backs (JCBs)" on changes in the village. They recalled the size of the households, which often comprised of three or four generations with as many as ten or more children to one mother. Henry remembered when he was about five or six that he lived at his grandmother's extended family home. At the house, there was his grandmother, Bunah and her aunt Madevine, his twin aunts who had not yet migrated, and cousins ~~form~~ from multi-generations. Children were considered the wealth of the family, as they provided the labour for the fields during the rainy season and the potential for sending back money to help support the extended family when they migrated. Children took care of their parents, and grandparents cared for their grandchildren while their parents migrated or worked at whatever job was available. The men who gathered at Bill's, did not try to explain or evaluate the changes. Instead, they itemized and accepted them.

They noticed that the nuclear family was dominant, old people were sent to homes for the aged where they were often forgotten, and pre-schoolers were sent to kindergartens. The elderly men discussed their end-days and wondered what would become of them. How would they spend their last days?

Modernity is all around. It has transformed a way of life for the people of Goat Hill: young and old. Instead of socialising in the yard under the light of the full moon, young people spend their time looking at cable television, surfing the internet or chatting on their cell phones. Games on the tablets have replaced games of stones and marbles. Games of hide and seek in the garden where crops of corn and peas flourished throughout the rainy season before the annual harvest have given way to computer games.

Young people put on extra weight from lack of physical exercise like what Henry and JC could not avoid in their youth by walking to school, to church or climbing the hills to tend the family livestock. The lack of physical exercise from undertaking household chores and the modern diet were used to explain the growing obesity problem. The villagers ate meat almost every day, mostly imported chicken and turkey parts, unlike Henry and JC, when they were growing up, who had meat only on special occasions. Henry believes that the lifestyle accounted for the apparent early maturity of his teenage cousins in the village.

Notwithstanding the changes, many things have remained the same. For example, young men's dreams are as active as were those of the generations earlier and they continue to dream of making it big in foreign places. Young people still look forward to the assistance of their relatives in the diaspora to migrate to "greener pastures". The rumours and gossip are still there except that they circulate not only in Goat Hill, but also in New York, Toronto, London and Port of Spain. Rumours no longer circulate in days and weeks but instantly using Facebook, Skype, Instagram, Twitter and WhatsApp. The carpenters now work with power tools. Coffins are no longer built in the village; instead, there are funeral agents who provide shiny imported caskets with gold and silver-plated handles, which pallbearers carry, but only for short distances.

Like many years before, attendance at funerals is an important social occasion for the elderly. They seem to overhaul their wardrobes when there is a funeral in the area. The men dress in black suits with matching black hats, while the women in their black or white dresses, sometimes with hats, accompany their men. Funeral is a time for the finest garments to be displayed. Sometimes it seems like there is some silent and subtle competition among the women. How they wished there were more funerals as many of their special collections in their wardrobes would never see the light of day, except for funerals.

Henry remembered how the village dealt with a death when he was growing up. He remembered the death of his own grandmother Bunah. On the night before a funeral, there would be a wake, sometimes called a prayer meeting. Then, Crix biscuits (which are produced in Trinidad) and corned-beef and cocoa tea were served in enamel or tin cups on wooden trays. There was a bottle of rum, which was appreciatively consumed by the drinking men, who sat on the undersized benches and chairs borrowed from the school. The men had sat on these same benches and chairs many years earlier. And when the wake was during the rainy season the gathering was protected from the night showers by a tarpaulin borrowed from a boat man, and rigged up to form a temporary tent for the occasion. At the wakes of better-off families, there were more of the same stuff, and perhaps two or three bottles of rum. At wakes, today, participants are offered a variety of finger foods served in plastic plates, mutton soup, stewed pork and or chicken in addition to bar stocked with a range of drinks including 'top shelf' whiskeys and cognac. Today's wake is a big party and unlike the earlier wakes which were funded by contributions from family and friends, the expenses incurred in modern wakes have become the full responsibility of one or two of the bereaved family members who also have to bear the cost for the use of the funeral agents and caterers. A funeral is now a big party driven by competition for who in the village can have the biggest. Sometimes a loan is taken to fund the occasion. Sadness and grief are soon forgotten.

Today, too often, children show "little respect" for their elders and many young parents are poor examples to children. This lack of respect is explained by the signs of the time, the absence of corporal punishment in the school and the home, and the influence of the television and North American culture, among other things. On the other hand, modern thinkers would say that the young people are more assertive and are more in-tuned with their rights. These explanations however have not convinced Henry and JC that something had not gone awry.

Gone were the days when the villagers depended on fish caught by Huriel in his fish pots or from other fishermen who used sloops to venture far from land. Henry, as a young boy, had noticed that the sails of the sloops disappeared as the shipwrights working on the beach began another day's work. There is no need now for children to look out for these fishing sloops, during the late afternoons, as they sailed between the reefs and Petite Dominque, with their catch of whiting fish, butterfish and rock hind, which were sold at ten cents a pound. The villagers now depend on the by-catches from the numerous locally owned trawlers that roam the high seas for many days in search of tuna and blue marlins. Also gone are the days when Henry and friends could collect conch on the sea grass near the shore. Instead, villagers must purchase conch from fishermen who dive to depths of one hundred metres using oxygen tanks.

In Goat Hill, new celebrations have emerged on the calendar, through the initiatives of the young people. For example, there are the Corn Feast and a Goat Hill Day. The Corn Feast, celebrating all things corn, is in an era when little corn is grown in the village. Henry remembered when the harvest from one season was not utilised over the year and there was no space for storing the new harvest. He recalled when corn was served for breakfast, lunch and dinner. There were corn feasts in every household. Today' corn feast is at the mercy of corn imported from St. Vincent, South America and the USA. When attending the annual Corn Feasts, Henry would shake his head and say to himself "how things have changed". He purchased the roasted corn from the roast-corn vendor at five dollars apiece. In the modern Goat Hill, villagers who want to plant anything in their back yard must fence the area. Over time, the practice of fencing animals in confined areas has been replaced by fencing out animals that are left to roam the whole village all year round. The JCBs when they sit at Bill's, debate approaches to reverse this change. They have difficulty in making any impact, as it seems that only the JCBs are motivated to garden but are discouraged by the perpetuation of the "leggo season".

14.2 THE FUTURE

What would the village look like in the next fifty years? Would limited opportunities for migration lead to over-population and a reversal to material poverty? Would it be part of a growing tourism sector where the youth, particularly women, become a new cadre of servants, waiting on the descendants of those that enslaved their ancestors? The future looks uncertain, but the villagers would not give up hope. Like in the past, they would overcome all challenges and tell the stories of

Goat Hill.

Many religions believe that "What has been will be again, what has been done will be done again; there is nothing new under the sun" as life is cyclic. As such, Goat Hill would live on. It is resilient. How would it cope in an environment of climate change and sea level rise? A recent strategic plan incorporating some of the traditional activities and embracing new concepts is documented in a "Road Map on Building a Green Economy for Sustainable Development in Carriacou and Petite Martinique, Grenada". Goat Hill like many other villages has long respected the environment, where the concept of sustainability was embraced, unknowingly, as a way of life. Nature was harvested to benefit from wind for sailing the fishing boats; the sun to dry the crops; mud, cattle dung and wattle for building the walls of houses and grass to cover their roofs. Inter-cropping and other agricultural practises now promoted as the way forward for food security were ways of life until they were abandoned, temporarily, for changes that mimicked other societies.

In the beginning, it was thought that nothing good would come from Goat Hill. Over the decades, the children of Goat Hill proved many wrong. It has produced sons and daughters who have made their contributions to it, initiating many positive changes. These are the sons and daughters of this and following generations that would secure a bright future for Goat Hill as they adapt to a changing world. They would reject the divisiveness introduced by colour politics, and see the recent ills in the village's aberrations from one or two generations that neglected the true culture of the village. When its history is written decades from now, Goat Hill would still have a prominent place in the world.

CPSIA information can be obtained
at www.ICGtesting.com
Printed in the USA
BVHW082000181021
619125BV00001B/4